# THE ESSAYS OF WARREN BUFFETT: LESSONS FOR CORPORATE AMERICA

# THE ESSAYS OF WARREN BUFFETT: LESSONS FOR CORPORATE AMERICA

ESSAYS BY

## WARREN E. BUFFETT

SELECTED, ARRANGED, AND INTRODUCED BY

## LAWRENCE A. CUNNINGHAM

FIRST REVISED EDITION

**Library of Congress Cataloging-in-Publication Data**

Cunningham, Lawrence A., 1962-
Buffett, Warren E., 1930-
   The Essays of Warren Buffett: Lessons for Corporate America /
selected, arranged, and introduced by Lawrence A. Cunningham—1st
rev. ed.
   256 p. 26 cm.
   Includes previously copyrighted material. Reprinted with permission. Includes bibliographical references and index.

   1.   Corporations–United States–Finance.  2.  Corporate governance–United   States.   3.   Investments–United   States.
4.   Stocks–United States. 5.   Consolidation and merger of corporations–United States.  6.  Accounting–United States.  I.  Buffett,
Warren E.  II.   Cunningham, Lawrence A.  III.   Title.

   HG4061.B8372 2001
   (OCoLC) 38497313

   Library of Congress card catalog number 2001-336907

ISBN 0-9664461-1-9

Copies of this collection are available in larger quantities at special
discounts to use for teaching, training, promotions, premiums or other
purposes. For more information, please contact Lawrence Cunningham, c/o Boston College, 885 Centre Street, Newton, MA 02459 or by
e-mail to Lawrence.Cunningham.1@bc.edu.

*"The speech I love is a simple, natural speech,*

*the same on paper as in the mouth;*

*a speech succulent and sinewy, brief and compressed,*

*not so much dainty and well-combed as vehement and brusque."*

**The Essays of Montaigne**

# TABLE OF CONTENTS

## Lawrence A. Cunningham

Experienced readers of Warren Buffett's letters to the share-holders of Berkshire Hathaway Inc. have gained an enormously valuable informal education. The letters distill in plain words all the basic principles of sound business practices. On selecting managers and investments, valuing businesses, and using financial information profitably, the writings are broad in scope, and long on wisdom.

Yet until now the letters existed in a format that was neither easily accessible nor organized in any thematic way. Consequently, the ideas have not been given the more widespread attention they deserve. The motivation for this compendium and for the symposium featuring it is to correct an inefficiency in the marketplace of ideas by disseminating the essays to a wider audience.

The central theme uniting Buffett's lucid essays is that the principles of fundamental business analysis, first formulated by his teachers Ben Graham and David Dodd, should guide investment practice. Linked to that theme are management principles that define the proper role of corporate managers as the stewards of invested capital, and the proper role of shareholders as the suppliers and owners of capital. Radiating from these main themes are practical and sensible lessons on the entire range of important business issues, from accounting to mergers to valuation.

Many of Buffett's lessons directly contradict what has been taught in business and law schools during the past thirty years, and what has been practiced on Wall Street and throughout corporate America during that time. Much of that teaching and practice eclipsed what Graham and Dodd had to say; Buffett is their prodigal pupil, stalwartly defending their views. The defenses run from an impassioned refutation of modern finance theory, to convincing demonstrations of the deleterious effects of using stock options to compensate managers, to persuasive arguments about the exaggerated benefits of synergistic acquisitions and cash flow analysis.

Buffett has applied the traditional principles as chief executive officer of Berkshire Hathaway, a company with roots in a group of textile operations begun in the early 1800s. Buffett took the helm of Berkshire in 1964, when its book value per share was $19.46 and its intrinsic value per share far lower. Today, its book value per share is around $40,000 and its intrinsic value far higher. The

1

growth rate in book value per share during that period is about 24% compounded annually.

Berkshire is now a holding company engaged in a variety of businesses, not including textiles. Berkshire's most important business is insurance, carried on through various companies including its 100% owned subsidiary, GEICO Corporation, the sixth largest auto insurer in the United States, and General Re Corporation, one of the four largest reinsurers in the world. Berkshire publishes *The Buffalo News* and owns other businesses that manufacture or distribute products ranging from carpeting, bricks, paint, encyclopedias, home furnishings, and cleaning systems, to chocolate candies, ice cream, jewelry, footwear, uniforms, and air compressors, as well as businesses that provide training to operators of aircraft and ships worldwide, fractional ownership interests in general aviation aircraft, and electric and gas power generation. Berkshire also owns substantial equity interests in major corporations, including American Express, Coca-Cola, Gillette, The Washington Post, and Wells Fargo.

Buffett and Berkshire Vice Chairman Charlie Munger have built this $70-plus billion enterprise by investing in businesses with excellent economic characteristics and run by outstanding managers. While they prefer negotiated acquisitions of 100% of such a business at a fair price, they take a "double-barreled approach" of buying on the open market less than 100% of such businesses when they can do so at a pro-rata price well below what it would take to buy 100%.

The double-barreled approach pays off handsomely. The value of marketable securities in Berkshire's portfolio, on a per share basis, increased from $4 in 1965 to nearly $50,000 in 2000, about a 25% annual increase. Per share operating earnings increased in the same period from just over $4 to around $500, an annual increase of about 18%. According to Buffett, these results follow not from any master plan but from focused investing—allocating capital by concentrating on businesses with outstanding economic characteristics and run by first-rate managers.

―――――――――――――

Buffett views Berkshire as a partnership among him, Munger and other shareholders, and virtually all his $20-plus billion net worth is in Berkshire stock. His economic goal is long-term—to maximize Berkshire's per share intrinsic value by owning all or part of a diversified group of businesses that generate cash and above-average returns. In achieving this goal, Buffett foregoes expansion for the sake of expansion and foregoes divestment of businesses so long as they generate some cash and have good management.

Berkshire retains and reinvests earnings when doing so delivers at least proportional increases in per share market value over time. It uses debt sparingly and sells equity only when it receives as much in value as it gives. Buffett penetrates accounting conventions, especially those that obscure real economic earnings.

These owner-related business principles, as Buffett calls them, are the organizing themes of the accompanying essays. As organized, the essays constitute an elegant and instructive manual on management, investment, finance, and accounting. Buffett's basic principles form the framework for a rich range of positions on the wide variety of issues that exist in all aspects of business. They go far beyond mere abstract platitudes. It is true that investors should focus on fundamentals, be patient, and exercise good judgment based on common sense. In Buffett's essays, these advisory tidbits are anchored in the more concrete principles by which Buffett lives and thrives.

Many people speculate on what Berkshire and Buffett are doing or plan to do. Their speculation is sometimes right and sometimes wrong, but always foolish. People would be far better off not attempting to ferret out what specific investments are being made at Berkshire, but thinking about how to make sound investment selections based on Berkshire's teaching. That means they should think about Buffett's writings and learn from them, rather than try to emulate Berkshire's portfolio.

Buffett modestly confesses that most of the ideas expressed in his essays were taught to him by Ben Graham. He considers himself the conduit through which Graham's ideas have proven their value. In allowing me to prepare this material, Buffett said that I could be the popularizer of Graham's ideas and Buffett's application of them. Buffett recognizes the risk of popularizing his business and investment philosophy. But he notes that he benefited enormously from Graham's intellectual generosity and believes it is appropriate that he pass the wisdom on, even if that means creating investment competitors. To that end, my role has been to organize the essays around the themes reflected in this collection. This introduction to the major themes encapsulates the basics and locates them in the context of current thinking. The essays follow.

## Corporate Governance

For Buffett, managers are stewards of shareholder capital. The best managers think like owners in making business decisions. They have shareholder interests at heart. But even first-rate managers will sometimes have interests that conflict with those of shareholders. How to ease those conflicts and to nurture managerial stewardship have been constant objectives of Buffett's forty-year career and a prominent theme of his essays. The essays address some of the most important governance problems.

The first is the importance of forthrightness and candor in communications by managers to shareholders. Buffett tells it like it is, or at least as he sees it, and laments that he is in the minority. Berkshire's annual report is not glossy; Buffett prepares its contents using words and numbers people of average intelligence can understand; and all investors get the same information at the same time. Buffett and Berkshire avoid making predictions, a bad managerial habit that too often leads other managers to make up their financial reports.

Besides the owner-orientation reflected in Buffett's disclosure practice and the owner-related business principles summarized above, the next management lesson is to dispense with formulas of managerial structure. Contrary to textbook rules on organizational behavior, mapping an abstract chain of command onto a particular business situation, according to Buffett, does little good. What matters is selecting people who are able, honest, and hard-working. Having first-rate people on the team is more important than designing hierarchies and clarifying who reports to whom about what and at what times.

Special attention must be paid to selecting a chief executive officer (CEO) because of three major differences Buffett identifies between CEOs and other employees. First, standards for measuring a CEO's performance are inadequate or easy to manipulate, so a CEO's performance is harder to measure than that of most workers. Second, no one is senior to the CEO, so no senior person's performance can be measured either. Third, a board of directors cannot serve that senior role since relations between CEOs and boards are conventionally congenial.

Major reforms are often directed toward aligning management and shareholder interests or enhancing board oversight of CEO performance. Stock options for management were touted as one method; greater emphasis on board processes was another. Separating the identities and functions of the Chairman of the Board and the CEO or appointment of standing audit, nominating and compensation committees were also heralded as promising reforms. None of these innovations has solved governance problems, however, and some have exacerbated them.

The best solution, Buffett instructs, is to take great care in identifying CEOs who will perform capably regardless of weak structural restraints. Outstanding CEOs do not need a lot of coaching from owners, although they can benefit from having a similarly outstanding board. Directors therefore must be chosen for their business savvy, their interest, and their owner-orientation. According to Buffett, one of the greatest problems among boards in corporate America is that members are selected for other reasons, such as adding diversity or prominence to a board.

Most reforms are painted with a broad brush, without noting the major differences among types of board situations that Buffett identifies. For example, director power is weakest in the case where there is a controlling shareholder who is also the manager. When disagreements arise between the directors and management, there is little a director can do other than to object and, in serious circumstances, resign. Director power is strongest at the other extreme, where there is a controlling shareholder who does not participate in management. The directors can take matters directly to the controlling shareholder when disagreement arises.

The most common situation, however, is a corporation without a controlling shareholder. This is where management problems are most acute, Buffett says. It would be helpful if directors could supply necessary discipline, but board congeniality usually prevents that. To maximize board effectiveness in this situation, Buffett believes the board should be small in size and composed mostly of outside directors. The strongest weapon a director can wield in these situations remains his or her threat to resign.

All these situations do share a common characteristic: the terrible manager is a lot easier to confront or remove than the mediocre manager. A chief problem in all governance structures, Buffett emphasizes, is that in corporate America evaluation of chief executive officers is never conducted in regular meetings in the absence of that chief executive. Holding regular meetings without the chief executive to review his or her performance would be a marked improvement in corporate governance.

The CEOs at Berkshire's various operating companies enjoy a unique position in corporate America. They are given a simple set of commands: to run their business as if (1) they are its sole owner,

(2) it is the only asset they hold, and (3) they can never sell or merge it for a hundred years. This enables Berkshire CEOs to manage with a long-term horizon ahead of them, something alien to the CEOs of public companies whose short-term oriented shareholders obsess with meeting the latest quarterly earnings estimate. Short-term results matter, of course, but the Berkshire approach avoids any pressure to achieve them at the expense of strengthening long-term competitive advantages.

If only short-term results mattered, many managerial decisions would be much easier, particularly those relating to businesses whose economic characteristics have eroded. Consider the time horizon trade-off Buffett faced in managing what he considers the worst investment he ever made, buying Berkshire in the first place. The economic characteristics of Berkshire's old textile business had begun to erode by the late 1970s. Buffett had hoped to devise a reversal of its misfortunes, noting how important Berkshire's textile business was to its employees and local communities in New England, and how able and understanding management and labor had been in addressing the economic difficulties. Buffett kept the ailing plant alive through 1985, but a financial reversal could not be achieved and Buffett eventually closed it. This balancing of short-term results with long-term prospects based on community trust is not easy, but it is intelligent. One lesson taught: stay away from businesses without favorable and *durable* economic and competitive characteristics.

Sometimes management interests conflict with shareholder interests in subtle or easily disguised ways. Take corporate philanthropy, for example. At most major corporations, management allocates a portion of corporate profit to charitable concerns. The charities are chosen by management, for reasons often unrelated either to corporate interests or shareholder interests. Most state laws permit management to make these decisions, so long as aggregate annual donations are reasonable in amount, usually not greater than 10% of annual net profits.

Berkshire does things differently. Shareholders designate charities to which the corporation donates. Nearly all shareholders participate in allocating millions of dollars per year to charitable organizations of their choice. This is an imaginative practical response to a tension that is at the core of the management-shareholder relationship. It is surprising that other American corporations do not follow this model of corporate charitable giving. Part of the reason may be the lack of long-term ownership orientation that characterizes the shareholder profiles of many American corporations. If so, this demonstrates a cost of the short-term mentality of America's investment community.

The plan to align management and shareholder interests by awarding executives stock options not only was oversold, but also subtly disguised a deeper division between those interests that the options created. Many corporations pay their managers stock options whose value increases simply by retention of earnings, rather than by superior deployment of capital. As Buffett explains, however, simply by retaining and reinvesting earnings, managers can report annual earnings increases without so much as lifting a finger to improve real returns on capital. Stock options thus often rob shareholders of wealth and allocate the booty to executives. Moreover, once granted, stock options are often irrevocable, unconditional, and benefit managers without regard to individual performance.

It is possible to use stock options to instill a managerial culture that encourages owner-like thinking, Buffett agrees. But the alignment will not be perfect. Shareholders are exposed to the downside risks of sub-optimal capital deployment in a way that an option holder is not. Buffett therefore cautions shareholders who are reading proxy statements about approving option plans to be aware of the asymmetry in this kind of alignment. Many shareholders rationally ignore proxy statements, but the abuse of stock options should be on the front-burner of shareholders, particularly institutional investors that periodically engage in promoting corporate governance improvements.

Buffett emphasizes that performance should be the basis for executive pay decisions. Executive performance should be measured by profitability, after profits are reduced by a charge for the capital employed in the relevant business or earnings retained by it. If stock options are used, they should be related to individual performance, rather than corporate performance, and priced based on business value. Better yet, as at Berkshire, stock options should simply not be part of an executive's compensation. After all, exceptional managers who earn cash bonuses based on the performance of their own business can simply buy stock if they want to; if they do, they "truly walk in the shoes of owners," Buffett says.

## CORPORATE FINANCE AND INVESTING

The most revolutionary investing ideas of the past thirty-five years were those called modern finance theory. This is an elaborate set of ideas that boils down to one simple and misleading practical implication: It is a waste of time to study individual investment opportunities in public securities. According to this view, you will do better by randomly selecting a group of stocks for a portfolio by throwing darts at the stock tables than by thinking about whether individual investment opportunities make sense.

One of modern finance theory's main tenets is modern portfolio theory. It says that you can eliminate the peculiar risk of any security by holding a diversified portfolio—that is, it formalizes the folk slogan "don't put all your eggs in one basket." The risk that is left over is the only risk for which investors will be compensated, the story goes.

This leftover risk can be measured by a simple mathematical term—called beta—that shows how volatile the security is compared to the market. Beta measures this volatility risk well for securities that trade on efficient markets, where information about publicly traded securities is swiftly and accurately incorporated into prices. In the modern finance story, efficient markets rule.

Reverence for these ideas was not limited to ivory tower academics, in colleges, universities, business schools, and law schools, but became standard dogma throughout financial America in the past thirty-five years, from Wall Street to Main Street. Many professionals still believe that stock market prices always accurately reflect fundamental values, that the only risk that matters is the volatility of prices, and that the best way to manage that risk is to invest in a diversified group of stocks.

Being part of a distinguished line of investors stretching back to Graham and Dodd which debunks standard dogma by logic and experience, Buffett thinks most markets are not purely efficient and that equating volatility with risk is a gross distortion. Accordingly, Buffett worried that a whole generation of MBAs and JDs, under the influence of modern finance theory, was at risk of learning the wrong lessons and missing the important ones.

A particularly costly lesson of modern finance theory came from the proliferation of portfolio insurance—a computerized technique for readjusting a portfolio in declining markets. The promiscuous use of portfolio insurance helped precipitate the stock market crash of October 1987, as well as the market break of October 1989. It nevertheless had a silver lining: it shattered the modern finance story being told in business and law schools and faithfully being followed by many on Wall Street.

Ensuing market volatility could not be explained by modern finance theory, nor could mountainous other phenomena relating to the behavior of small capitalization stocks, high dividend-yield stocks, and stocks with low price-earnings ratios. The *piece de resistance* of market inefficiency was the technology and Internet stock bubble that blew up in the late 1990s and early 2000s, marked by stock price gyrations that spasmodically bounced between euphoria and gloom without the remotest nexus to business value. Growing numbers of skeptics emerged to say that beta does not really measure the investment risk that matters, and that capital markets are really not efficient enough to make beta meaningful anyway.

In stirring up the discussion, people started noticing Buffett's record of successful investing and calling for a return to the Graham-Dodd approach to investing and business. After all, for more than forty years Buffett has generated average annual returns of 20% or better, which double the market average. For more than twenty years before that, Ben Graham's Graham-Newman Corp. had done the same thing. As Buffett emphasizes, the stunning performances at Graham-Newman and at Berkshire deserve respect: the sample sizes were significant; they were conducted over an extensive time period, and were not skewed by a few fortunate experiences; no data-mining was involved; and the performances were longitudinal, not selected by hindsight.

Threatened by Buffett's performance, stubborn devotees of modern finance theory resorted to strange explanations for his success. Maybe he is just lucky—the monkey who typed out *Hamlet*—or maybe he has inside access to information that other investors do not. In dismissing Buffett, modern finance enthusiasts still insist that an investor's best strategy is to diversify based on betas or dart throwing, and constantly reconfigure one's portfolio of investments.

Buffett responds with a quip and some advice: the quip is that devotees of his investment philosophy should probably endow chaired professorships at colleges and universities to ensure the perpetual teaching of efficient market dogma; the advice is to ignore modern finance theory and other quasi-sophisticated views of the market and stick to investment knitting. That can best be done for many people through long-term investment in an index fund. Or it can be done by conducting hard-headed analyses of businesses within an investor's competence to evaluate. In that kind of thinking, the risk that matters is not beta or volatility, but the possibility of loss or injury from an investment.

Assessing that kind of investment risk requires thinking about a company's management, products, competitors, and debt levels. The inquiry is whether after-tax returns on an investment are at least equal to the purchasing power of the initial investment plus a fair rate of return. The primary relevant factors are the long-term economic characteristics of a business, the quality and integrity of its management, and future levels of taxation and inflation. Maybe these factors are vague, particularly compared with the seductive precision of beta, but the point is that judgments about such matters cannot be avoided, except to an investor's disadvantage.

Buffett points out the absurdity of beta by observing that "a stock that has dropped very sharply compared to the market . . . becomes 'riskier' at the lower price than it was at the higher price"—that is how beta measures risk. Equally unhelpful, beta cannot distinguish the risk inherent in "a single-product toy company selling pet rocks or hula hoops from another toy company whose sole product is Monopoly or Barbie." But ordinary investors can make those distinctions by thinking about consumer behavior and the way consumer products companies compete, and can also figure out when a huge stock-price drop signals a buying opportunity.

Contrary to modern finance theory, Buffett's investment knitting does not prescribe diversification. It may even call for concentration, if not of one's portfolio, then at least of its owner's mind. As to concentration of the portfolio, Buffett reminds us that Keynes, who was not only a brilliant economist but also an astute investor, believed that an investor should put fairly large sums into two or three businesses he knows something about and whose management is trustworthy. On that view, risk rises when investments and investment thinking are spread too thin. A strategy of financial and mental concentration may reduce risk by raising both the intensity of an investor's thinking about a business and the comfort level he must have with its fundamental characteristics before buying it.

The fashion of beta, according to Buffett, suffers from inattention to "a fundamental principle: It is better to be approximately right than precisely wrong." Long-term investment success depends not on studying betas and maintaining a diversified portfolio, but on recognizing that as an investor, one is the owner of a business. Reconfiguring a portfolio by buying and selling stocks to accommodate the desired beta-risk profile defeats long-term in-vestment success. Such "flitting from flower to flower" imposes huge transaction costs in the forms of spreads, fees and commis-sions, not to mention taxes. Buffett jokes that calling someone who trades actively in the market an investor "is like calling some-one who repeatedly engages in one-night stands a romantic." In-vestment knitting turns modern finance theory's folk wisdom on its head: instead of "don't put all your eggs in one basket," we get Mark Twain's advice from *Pudd'nhead Wilson*: "Put all your eggs in one basket—and watch that basket."

---

Buffett learned the art of investing from Ben Graham as a graduate student at Columbia Business School in the 1950s and later working at Graham-Newman. In a number of classic works, including *The Intelligent Investor*, Graham introduced some of the most profound investment wisdom in history. It rejects a prevalent but mistaken mind-set that equates price with value. On the con-trary, Graham held that price is what you pay and value is what you get. These two things are rarely identical, but most people rarely notice any difference.

One of Graham's most profound contributions is a character who lives on Wall Street, Mr. Market. He is your hypothetical bus-iness partner who is daily willing to buy your interest in a business or sell you his at prevailing market prices. Mr. Market is moody, prone to manic swings from joy to despair. Sometimes he offers prices way higher than value; sometimes he offers prices way lower than value. The more manic-depressive he is, the greater the spread between price and value, and therefore the greater the in-vestment opportunities he offers. Buffett reintroduces Mr. Market, emphasizing how valuable Graham's allegory of the overall market is for disciplined investment knitting—even though Mr. Market would be unrecognizable to modern finance theorists.

Another leading prudential legacy from Graham is his margin-of-safety principle. This principle holds that one should not make an investment in a security unless there is a sufficient basis for be-lieving that the price being paid is substantially lower than the value being delivered. Buffett follows the principle devotedly, not-ing that Graham had said that if forced to distill the secret of sound investment into three words, they would be: margin of safety. Over forty years after first reading that, Buffett still thinks those are the right words. While modern finance theory enthusiasts cite market efficiency to deny there is a difference between price (what you pay) and value (what you get), Buffett and Graham regard it as all the difference in the world.

That difference also shows that the term "value investing" is a redundancy. All true investing must be based on an assessment of the relationship between price and value. Strategies that do not employ this comparison of price and value do not amount to investing at all, but to speculation—the hope that price will rise, rather than the conviction that the price being paid is lower than the value being obtained. Many professionals make another common mistake, Buffett notes, by distinguishing between "growth investing" and "value investing." Growth and value, Buffett says, are not distinct. They are integrally linked since growth must be treated as a component of value.

Nor does the phrase "relational investing" resonate with Buffett. The term became popular in the mid-1990s, describing a style of investing that is designed to reduce the costs of the separation of shareholder ownership from managerial control by emphasizing shareholder involvement and monitoring of management. Many people incorrectly identified Buffett and Berkshire as exemplars of this descriptive label. It is true that Buffett buys big blocks in a few companies and sticks around a long time. He also only invests in businesses run by people he trusts. But that is about as far as the similarity goes. If Buffett were pressed to use an adjective to describe his investment style, it would be something like "focused" or "intelligent" investing. Yet even these words ring redundant; the unadorned term *investor* best describes Buffett.

Other misuses of terms include blurring the difference between speculation and arbitrage as methods of sound cash management; the latter being very important for companies like Berkshire that generate substantial excess cash. Both speculation and arbitrage are ways to use excess cash rather than hold it in short-term cash equivalents such as commercial paper. Speculation describes the use of cash to bet on lots of corporate events based on rumors of unannounced coming transactions. Arbitrage, traditionally understood to mean exploiting different prices for the same thing on two different markets, for Buffett describes the use of cash to take short-term positions in a few opportunities that have been publicly announced. It exploits different prices for the same thing at different times. Deciding whether to employ cash this way requires evaluating four commonsense questions based on information rather than rumor: the probability of the event occurring, the time the funds will be tied up, the opportunity cost, and the downside if the event does not occur.

The circle of competence principle is the third leg of the Graham/Buffett stool of intelligent investing, along with Mr. Market and the margin of safety. This commonsense rule instructs investors to consider investments only concerning businesses they are capable of understanding with a modicum of effort. It is this commitment to stick with what he knows that enables Buffett to avoid the mistakes others repeatedly make, particularly those who feast on the fantasies of fast riches promised by technological fads and new era rhetoric that have recurrently infested speculative markets over the centuries.

In all investment thinking, one must guard against what Buffett calls the "institutional imperative." It is a pervasive force in which institutional dynamics produce resistance to change, absorption of available corporate funds, and reflexive approval of suboptimal CEO strategies by subordinates. Contrary to what is often taught in business and law schools, this powerful force often interferes with rational business decision-making. The ultimate result of the institutional imperative is a follow-the-pack mentality producing industry imitators, rather than industry leaders—what Buffett calls a lemming-like approach to business.

## ALTERNATIVES TO COMMON STOCK

All these investment principles are animated in Buffett's lively essays concerning investment opportunities other than common stock, such as junk and zero-coupon bonds and preferred stock. Challenging both Wall Street and the academy, Buffett again draws on Graham's ideas to reject the "dagger thesis" advanced to defend junk bonds. The dagger thesis, using the metaphor of the intensified care an automobile driver would take facing a dagger mounted on the steering wheel, overemphasizes the disciplining effect that enormous amounts of debt in a capital structure exerts on management.

Buffett points to the large numbers of corporations that failed in the early 1990s recession under crushing debt burdens to dispute academic research showing that higher interest rates on junk bonds more than compensated for their higher default rates. He attributes this error to a flawed assumption recognizable to any first-year statistics student: that historical conditions prevalent during the study period would be identical in the future. They would not. Further illuminating the folly of junk bonds is an essay in this collection by Charlie Munger that discusses Michael Milken's approach to finance.

Wall Street tends to embrace ideas based on revenue-generating power, rather than on financial sense, a tendency that often perverts good ideas to bad ones. In a history of zero-coupon bonds, for example, Buffett shows that they can enable a purchaser to lock in a compound rate of return equal to a coupon rate that a normal bond paying periodic interest would not provide. Using zero-coupons thus for a time enabled a borrower to borrow more without need of additional free cash flow to pay the interest expense. Problems arose, however, when zero-coupon bonds started to be issued by weaker and weaker credits whose free cash flow could not sustain increasing debt obligations. Buffett laments, "as happens in Wall Street all too often, what the wise do in the beginning, fools do in the end."

The essays on preferred stock show the art of investing at its finest, emphasizing the economic characteristics of businesses, the quality of management, and the difficult judgments that are always necessary, but not always correct. A piece on unconventional investments considers applied arbitrage in allocating excess cash to vehicles such as oil, silver, and even zero-coupon bonds.

### COMMON STOCK

Buffett recalls that on the day Berkshire listed on the New York Stock Exchange in 1988, he told Jimmy Maguire, the specialist in Berkshire stock, "I will consider you an enormous success if the next trade in this stock is about two years from now." While Buffett jokes that Maguire "didn't seem to get enthused about that," he emphasizes that his mind-set when he buys any stock is "if we aren't happy owning a piece of that business with the Exchange closed, we're not happy owning it with the Exchange open." Berkshire and Buffett are investors for the long haul; Berkshire's capital structure and dividend policy prove it.

Unlike many CEOs, who desire their company's stock to trade at the highest possible prices in the market, Buffett prefers Berkshire stock to trade at or around its intrinsic value—neither materially higher nor lower. Such linkage means that business results during one period will benefit the people who owned the company during that period. Maintaining the linkage requires a shareholder group with a collective long-term, business-oriented investment philosophy, rather than a short-term, market-oriented strategy.

Buffett notes Phil Fisher's suggestion that a company is like a restaurant, offering a menu that attracts people with particular tastes. Berkshire's long-term menu emphasizes that the costs of trading activity can impair long-term results. Indeed, Buffett estimates that the transaction costs of actively traded stocks—broker commissions and market-maker spreads—often amount to 10% or more of earnings. Avoiding or minimizing such costs is necessary for long-term investment success, and Berkshire's listing on the New York Stock Exchange helped contain those costs.

Corporate dividend policy is a major capital allocation issue, always of interest to investors but infrequently explained to them. Buffett's essays clarify this subject, emphasizing that "capital allocation is crucial to business and investment management." In early 1998, Berkshire's common stock was priced in the market at over $50,000 per share and the company's book value, earnings, and intrinsic value have steadily increased well in excess of average annual rates. Yet the company has never effected a stock split, and has not paid a cash dividend in over three decades.

Apart from reflecting the long-term menu and minimization of transaction costs, Berkshire's dividend policy also reflects Buffett's conviction that a company's earnings payout versus retention decision should be based on a single test: each dollar of earnings should be retained if retention will increase market value by at least a like amount; otherwise it should be paid out. Earnings retention is justified only when "capital retained produces incremental earnings equal to, or above, those generally available to investors."

Like many of Buffett's simple rules, this one is often ignored by corporate managers, except of course when they make dividend decisions for their subsidiaries. Earnings are often retained for non-owner reasons, such as expanding the corporate empire or furnishing operational comfort for management.

Things are so different at Berkshire, Buffett said at the symposium, that under his test Berkshire "might distribute more than 100% of the earnings," to which Charlie Munger chimed in, "You're damn right." That has not been necessary, however, for throughout Buffett's stewardship at Berkshire, opportunities for superior returns on capital have been discovered, and exploited.

Share repurchases of underpriced stock can be a value-enhancing way to allocate capital, though these are not always what they seem. In the 1980s and early 1990s, share buy-backs were uncommon and Buffett credited managers who recognized that the purchase of a share priced at $1 but with a value of $2 would rarely be inferior to any other use of corporate funds. Alas, as often happens, the imitators stepped in and now you frequently see companies paying $2 to buy back shares worth $1. These value-destroying share repurchases often are intended to prop up a sagging share price or to offset the simultaneous issuing of stock under stock options exercised at much lower prices.

Stock splits are another common action in corporate America that Buffett points out disserve owner interests. Stock splits have three consequences: they increase transaction costs by promoting high share turnover; they attract shareholders with short-term, market-oriented views who unduly focus on stock market prices; and, as a result of both of those effects, they lead to prices that depart materially from intrinsic business value. With no offsetting benefits, splitting Berkshire's stock would be foolish. Not only that, Buffett adds, it would threaten to reverse over three decades of hard work that has attracted to Berkshire a shareholder group comprised of more focused and long-term investors than probably any other major public corporation.

Two important consequences have followed from Berkshire's high stock price and its dividend policy. First, the extraordinarily high share price impaired the ability of Berkshire shareholders to effect gifts of their equity interest to family members or friends, though Buffett has offered a few sensible strategies like bargain sales to donees to deal with that. Second, Wall Street engineers tried to create securities that would purport to mimic Berkshire's performance and that would be sold to people lacking an understanding of Berkshire, its business, and its investment philosophy.

In response to these consequences, Buffett and Berkshire did an ingenious thing. In mid-1996, Berkshire effected a recapitalization by creating a new class of stock, called the Class B shares, and sold it to the public. The Class B shares have 1/30th the rights of the existing Class A shares, except with respect to voting rights they have 1/200th of those of the A shares; and the Class B shares are not eligible to participate in the Berkshire charitable contributions program. Accordingly, the Class B shares should (and do) trade somewhere in the vicinity of 1/30th of the market price of the Class A shares.

The Class A shares are convertible into Class B shares, giving Berkshire shareholders a do-it-yourself mechanism to effect a stock-split to facilitate gift giving and so on. More importantly, the Berkshire recapitalization would halt the marketing of Berkshire clones that contradict all the basic principles Buffett believes in.

These clones—investment trusts that would buy and sell Berkshire shares according to demand for units in the trust—would have imposed costs on shareholders. If held by people who do not understand Berkshire's business or philosophy, they would have caused spikes in Berkshire's stock price, producing substantial deviations between price and value.

The Class B shares are designed to be attractive only to investors who share Buffett's philosophy of focused investing. For example, in connection with the offering of the Class B shares, Buffett and Munger emphasized that Berkshire stock was, at that time, not underpriced in the market. They said that neither of them would buy the Class A shares at the market price nor the Class B shares at the offering price. The message was simple: do not buy these securities unless you are prepared to hold them for the long term. The effort to attract only long-term investors to the Class B shares appears to have worked: trading volume in the shares after the offering was far below average for Big Board stocks.

Some expressed surprise at Buffett and Munger's cautionary statement, since most managers tell the market that newly-issued equity in their companies is being offered at a very good price. You should not be surprised by Buffett and Munger's disclosure, however. A company that sells its stock at a price less than its value is stealing from its existing shareholders. Quite plausibly, Buffett considers that a crime.

### MERGERS AND ACQUISITIONS

Berkshire's acquisition policy is the double-barreled approach: buying portions or all of businesses with excellent economic characteristics and run by managers Buffett and Munger like, trust, and admire. Contrary to common practice, Buffett argues that in buying all of a business, there is rarely any reason to pay a premium.

The rare cases involve businesses with franchise characteristics—those that can raise prices without impairing sales volume or market share and only require incremental capital investment to increase both. Even ordinary managers can operate franchise businesses to generate high returns on capital. The second category of rare cases is where extraordinary managers exist who can achieve the difficult feat of identifying underperforming businesses, and apply extraordinary talent to unlock hidden value.

These two categories are extremely limited, and certainly do not explain the hundreds of high-premium takeovers that occur annually. Buffett attributes high-premium takeovers outside those unusual categories to three motives of buying-managers: the thrill of an acquisition, the thrill of enhanced size, and excessive optimism about synergies.

In paying for acquisitions, Berkshire issues stock only when it receives as much in business value as it gives. This has become increasingly difficult for Berkshire to do. This is the case because Berkshire has assembled the business equivalent of the art collection at the Louvre. Enhancing the value of the existing collection by adding a single new Botticelli is difficult enough, and even more so if you have to give up part of your Rembrandt collection to get it.

It has also been difficult for managers of other companies to follow this rule, but not so much because of the wonderful collection of businesses they have. Instead, Buffett notes that sellers in stock acquisitions measure the purchase price by the market price of the buyer's stock, not by its intrinsic value. If a buyer's stock is trading at a price equal to, say, half its intrinsic value, then a buyer who goes along with that measure gives twice as much in business value as it is getting. Its manager, usually rationalizing his or her actions by arguments about synergies or size, is elevating thrill or excessive optimism above shareholder interests.

Moreover, acquisitions paid for in stock are too often (almost always) described as "buyer buys seller" or "buyer acquires seller." Buffett suggests clearer thinking would follow from saying "buyer sells part of itself to acquire seller," or something of the sort. After all, that is what is happening; and it would enable one to evaluate what the buyer is giving up to make the acquisition.

Another abuse of shares-as-currency is the practice of greenmail, the repurchase of shares from an unwanted suitor at a premium price to fend off his acquisition overtures. While share repurchases available to all shareholders can be value-enhancing, Buffett condemns this practice as simply another form of corporate robbery.

Nearly as reprehensible, a second Charlie Munger essay in this collection explains, were the cascades of leveraged buy-outs (LBOs) in the 1980s. Permissive laws made LBOs hugely profitable, Munger tells us, but the LBOs weakened corporations, put a heavy premium on cash generation to pay for enormous debt obligations, and raised the average cost of acquisitions.

Value-enhancing acquisitions are hard enough to find without the added burden of higher average costs for all of them. Indeed, most acquisitions are value-decreasing, Buffett says. Finding the best value-enhancing transactions requires concentrating on opportunity costs, measured principally against the alternative of buying small pieces of excellent businesses through stock market purchases. Such concentration is alien to the manager obsessed with synergies and size, but a vital part of Berkshire's double-barreled investment approach.

Berkshire has additional advantages in acquisitions: a high quality stock to pay with and a substantial amount of managerial autonomy to offer once a deal is done—both rare in an acquiring company, Buffett says. Buffett also puts his money where his mouth is, reminding prospective sellers that Berkshire has acquired many of its businesses from family or other closely-held groups, and inviting them to check with every previous seller about Berkshire's initial promises measured against its later actions.

## ACCOUNTING AND VALUATION

Buffett's essays provide an entertaining and illuminating tutorial on understanding and using financial information. In dissecting significant aspects of generally accepted accounting principles (GAAP), Buffett shows both their importance and limits in understanding and valuing any business or investment. Buffett demystifies key topics that highlight the important differences between accounting earnings and economic earnings, between accounting goodwill and economic goodwill, and between accounting book value and intrinsic value. These are essential tools for any investor's or manager's valuation toolbox.

The most basic point to understand about accounting is that it is a form. As a form, it can be manipulated. Buffett shows just how severe the manipulation can be with a satire written by Ben Graham in the 1930s. The advanced bookkeeping methods Graham presents enable his phantom US Steel to report "phenomenally enhanced" earnings without cash outlays or changes in operating conditions or sales. Except in its lampooning spirit, Graham's illustration of accounting chicanery is not all that different from what is often seen coming out of corporate America.

Buffett emphasizes that useful financial statements must enable a user to answer three basic questions about a business: approximately how much a company is worth, its likely ability to meet its future obligations, and how good a job its managers are doing in operating the business. Buffett laments that GAAP conventions make these determinations difficult, and indeed almost any accounting system will be hard-pressed to furnish completely accurate answers given the complexities of business. Acknowledging the monumental difficulty of inventing an accounting system superior to GAAP, Buffett articulates a range of concepts that go a longer way toward making financial information useful to investors and managers.

Consider a concept Buffett calls "look-through earnings." GAAP investment accounting calls for using the consolidation method for majority-owned equity, which means full reporting of all line items from the investee's financial statements on the parent's. For equity investments from 20% to 50%, GAAP calls for reporting the investor's proportionate share of earnings of the investee on its statements; for investments of less than 20%, GAAP provides that only dividends actually received by the investor be recorded, rather than any share of the investee's earnings. These accounting rules obscure a major factor in Berkshire's economic performance: the undistributed earnings of its investee companies are an enormous part of Berkshire's value, but would not be reported on its financial statements prepared using GAAP.

Recognizing that it is not the size of an equity investment that determines its value, but how the undistributed earnings are deployed, Buffett develops the concept of look-through earnings to gauge Berkshire's economic performance. Look-through earnings add to Berkshire's own net earnings the undistributed earnings in investee companies, less an incremental amount for taxes. Look-through earnings are not different from GAAP earnings for many businesses. But they are for Berkshire and probably are for many individual investors. Accordingly, individuals can adopt a similar approach for their own portfolios and try to design a portfolio that delivers the highest possible look-through earnings over the long term.

The difference between accounting goodwill and economic goodwill is well-known, but Buffett's lucidity makes the subject refreshing. Accounting goodwill is essentially the amount by which the purchase price of a business exceeds the fair value of the assets acquired (after deducting liabilities). It is recorded as an asset on the balance sheet and then amortized as an annual expense, usually over forty years. So the accounting goodwill assigned to that business decreases over time by the aggregate amount of that expense.

Economic goodwill is something else. It is the combination of intangible assets, like brand name recognition, that enable a business to produce earnings on tangible assets, like plant and equipment, in excess of average rates.  The amount of economic goodwill is the capitalized value of that excess.  Economic goodwill tends to increase over time, at least nominally in proportion to inflation for mediocre businesses, and more than that for businesses with solid economic or franchise characteristics.  Indeed, businesses with more economic goodwill relative to tangible assets are hurt far less by inflation than businesses with less of that.

These differences between accounting goodwill and economic goodwill entail the following insights.  First, the best guide to the value of a business's economic goodwill is what it can earn on un-leveraged net tangible assets, excluding charges for amortization of goodwill.  Therefore when a business acquires other businesses, and the acquisitions are reflected in an asset account called good-will, analysis of that business should ignore the amortization charges.  Second, since economic goodwill should be measured at its full economic cost, i.e., before amortization, evaluation of a possible business acquisition should be conducted without regard to those amortization charges as well.

Buffett emphasizes, however, that the same does not hold for depreciation charges—these should not be ignored because they are real economic costs.  He makes this point in explaining why Berkshire always shows its shareholders the results of operations with respect to acquired businesses net of any purchase price adjustments GAAP requires.

It is common on Wall Street to value businesses using a calculation of cash flows equal to *(a)* operating earnings plus *(b)* depreciation expense and other non-cash charges.  Buffett regards that calculation as incomplete.  After taking *(a)* operating earnings and adding back *(b)* non-cash charges, Buffett argues that you must then subtract something else: *(c)* required reinvestment in the business.  Buffett defines *(c)* as "the average amount of capitalized expenditures for plant and equipment, etc., that the business requires to fully maintain its long-term competitive position and its unit volume."  Buffett calls the result of *(a)* + *(b)* − *(c)* "owner earnings."

When *(b)* and *(c)* differ, cash flow analysis and owner earnings analysis differ too.  For most businesses, *(c)* usually exceeds *(b)*, so cash flow analysis usually overstates economic reality.  In all cases where *(c)* differs from *(b)*, calculation of owner earnings enables one to appraise performance more accurately than would analysis of GAAP earnings, or cash flows affected by purchase price accounting adjustments.  That is why Berkshire supplementally reports owner earnings for its acquired businesses, rather than rely solely on GAAP earnings figures, or cash flow figures.

A final example of Buffett's specialized toolkit is intrinsic value, "the discounted value of the cash that can be taken out of a business during its remaining life." Though simple to state, calculating intrinsic value is neither easy nor objective. It depends on estimation of both future cash flows and interest rate movements. But it is what ultimately matters about a business. Book value, in contrast, is easy to calculate, but of limited use. So too with market price, at least for most companies. Differences between intrinsic value and book value and market price may be hard to pin down. They can go either way, but there will almost certainly be differences.

Aesop was to fables of the ancient world what Buffett is to business essays in ours. The essayist invokes the fabulist to show that valuation has been the same across the millennia—Aesop said "a bird in the hand is worth two in the bush" and Buffett extends the principle to dollars. Valuation is counting cash, not hopes or dreams, a lesson many should have learned amid the late 1990s tech rush bubble that burst when everyone finally realized there were few birds in the bushes. It is doubtful everyone learned the lesson, however, for it has been taught repeatedly since Aesop's time and yet, well, it has been taught repeatedly since Aesop's time.

## ACCOUNTING POLICY AND TAX MATTERS

Buffett's essays on economic versus accounting goodwill and owner earnings lead to a policy position on a decades old accounting debate that periodically becomes front page news: whether mergers should be accounted for as "purchases" of one company by another or as "poolings" of previously separate companies. Riding on the difference is whether or not the combined company has to amortize its accounting goodwill as a charge against earnings for many decades. Managers prefer not to punish future earnings this way and therefore opt for pooling treatment. Accounting purists think it is the only way that makes sense and therefore want to abolish pooling and require purchase accounting for all mergers.

Buffett offers a solution that should satisfy both camps and also comports with reality. The solution is to record an asset for goodwill but not automatically requiring it to be charged against future earnings. The purists should be happy that a goodwill account is recorded and the managers should be happy that charges to future earnings would only be required if goodwill became impaired. It comports with reality because in virtually all mergers (a) one party is the purchaser and the other the seller and (b) purchased economic goodwill actually increases rather than decreases in value in the future. (Accounting standard setters eventually opted for a version of this proposal.)

GAAP has enough trouble. Yet two groups of people make it worse: those who try to overcome GAAP requirements by stretching their accounting imagination, and those who deliberately employ GAAP to facilitate financial fraud. The former is especially hard to deal with, as Buffett suggests in illustrating how debate on accounting for stock options reveals the parochialism of many executives and accountants. For example, criticizing the view against treating stock options as expenses when granted, Buffett delivers this laconic argument: "If options aren't a form of compensation, what are they? If compensation isn't an expense, what is? And, if expenses shouldn't go into the calculation of earnings, where in the world should they go?" So far, he has gotten no answers.

The quest for integrity in financial reporting is endless, with new flavors of accounting machinations developed regularly and periodically sweeping the chief financial officer (CFO) suites of corporate America. The latest product to catch on is accounting for "restructurings," a label given to a whole range of maneuvers that enable managers to engage in age-old earnings management and smoothing techniques with greater felicity and deftness than ever before. Investors beware.

Devotees of integrity in financial reporting sometimes must take matters into their own hands. Buffett does so regularly by furnishing Berkshire shareholders with information, such as segment data, that GAAP does not require but which Buffett would want to see if their positions were reversed. Sometimes the crusaders triumph, however, as Buffett shows was the case when accounting rules began to require companies to record promises to fund retiree benefits that had previously not been required.

One clear lesson from Buffett's discussions of financial information is that accounting has inherent limits, even though it is absolutely essential. Despite enormous managerial leeway in reporting earnings and potential abuse, financial information can be of great use to investors. Buffett uses it every day, and has allocated billions of dollars doing it. So it is possible to make important investment decisions on the basis of available financial information if one exercises knowledgeable judgment. That judgment may include making adjustments to determine look-through earnings, owner earnings, and intrinsic value, and to show the real costs of stock options or other obligations that GAAP does not require to be recorded on the financial statements.

Bringing this collection full circle, the concluding essays note the obvious but often overlooked tax advantages of long-term investment. Linking life's two certainties, the final essay includes one of Buffett's many jokes about his personal longevity: if enjoying life promotes longevity, he is jeopardizing Methuselah's record (969 years). At the symposium featuring this collection, someone asked what effect Buffett's death would have on Berkshire stock. Another answered, "a negative effect." Without missing a beat, Buffett quipped: "It won't be as negative for the holders as it will be for me."

---

The prominence of accounting discussions in Buffett's essays underscores that accounting policy and accounting decisions matter. That position is supported by Graham-Dodd fundamental valuation analysis. Yet it conflicts with modern finance theory's view that efficient markets will pierce accounting conventions to produce prices equal to values, and it also goes against the grain of what many MBA and JD students have been taught in the past few decades.

Buffett's essays can reeducate a generation of students, and continue the education of others. That is important because the gospel of modern finance theory that swept America in the past thirty years is still commonly preached. A lemming-like willingness to follow the crowd endures. Entailing the destruction of both leadership and independent thought, that weakness is the intellectual foe in the struggle Buffett's essays wage for intelligent and focused investing. While the battle remains to be won, this compendium is intended to aid in the quest.

# PROLOGUE[1]

In some ways, our shareholder group is a rather unusual one, and this affects our manner of reporting to you. For example, at the end of each year about 98% of the shares outstanding are held by people who also were shareholders at the beginning of the year. Therefore, in our annual report we build upon what we have told you in previous years instead of restating a lot of material. You get more useful information this way, and we don't get bored.

Furthermore, perhaps 90% of our shares are owned by investors for whom Berkshire is their largest security holding, very often far and away the largest. Many of these owners are willing to spend a significant amount of time with the annual report, and we attempt to provide them with the same information we would find useful if the roles were reversed.

In contrast, we include no narrative with our quarterly reports. Our owners and managers both have very long time-horizons in regard to this business, and it is difficult to say anything new or meaningful each quarter about events of long-term significance.

But when you do receive a communication from us, it will come from the fellow you are paying to run the business. Your Chairman has a firm belief that owners are entitled to hear directly from the CEO as to what is going on and how he evaluates the business, currently and prospectively. You would demand that in a private company; you should expect no less in a public company. A once-a-year report of stewardship should not be turned over to a staff specialist or public relations consultant who is unlikely to be in a position to talk frankly on a manager-to-owner basis.

We feel that you, as owners, are entitled to the same sort of reporting by your managers as we feel is owed to us at Berkshire Hathaway by managers of our business units. Obviously, the degree of detail must be different, particularly where information would be useful to a business competitor or the like. But the general scope, balance, and level of candor should be similar. We don't expect a public relations document when our operating managers tell us what is going on, and we don't feel you should receive such a document.

In large part, companies obtain the shareholder constituency that they seek and deserve. If they focus their thinking and com-

---

1 [1979. Footnotes throughout indicate the year of the annual report from which essays are taken. To avoid interrupting the narrative flow in this collection, omissions of text within excerpts are not indicated by ellipses or other punctuation.]

munications on short-term results or short-term stock market consequences they will, in large part, attract shareholders who focus on the same factors. And if they are cynical in their treatment of investors, eventually that cynicism is highly likely to be returned by the investment community.

Phil Fisher, a respected investor and author, once likened the policies of the corporation in attracting shareholders to those of a restaurant attracting potential customers. A restaurant could seek a given clientele—patrons of fast foods, elegant dining, Oriental food, etc.—and eventually obtain an appropriate group of devotees. If the job were expertly done, that clientele, pleased with the service, menu, and price level offered, would return consistently. But the restaurant could not change its character constantly and end up with a happy and stable clientele. If the business vacillated between French cuisine and take-out chicken, the result would be a revolving door of confused and dissatisfied customers.

So it is with corporations and the shareholder constituency they seek. You can't be all things to all men, simultaneously seeking different owners whose primary interests run from high current yield to long-term capital growth to stock market pyrotechnics, etc.

The reasoning of managements that seek large trading activity in their shares puzzles us. In effect, such managements are saying that they want a good many of the existing clientele continually to desert them in favor of new ones—because you can't add lots of new owners (with new expectations) without losing lots of former owners.

We much prefer owners who like our service and menu and who return year after year. It would be hard to find a better group to sit in the Berkshire Hathaway shareholder "seats" than those already occupying them. So we hope to continue to have a very low turnover among our owners, reflecting a constituency that understands our operation, approves of our policies, and shares our expectations. And we hope to deliver on those expectations.

# I. CORPORATE GOVERNANCE

Many annual meetings are a waste of time, both for shareholders and for management. Sometimes that is true because management is reluctant to open up on matters of business substance. More often a non-productive session is the fault of shareholder participants who are more concerned about their own moment on stage than they are about the affairs of the corporation. What should be a forum for business discussion becomes a forum for theatrics, spleen-venting and advocacy of issues. (The deal is irresistible: for the price of one share you get to tell a captive audience your ideas as to how the world should be run.) Under such circumstances, the quality of the meeting often deteriorates from year to year as the antics of those interested in themselves discourage attendance by those interested in the business.

Berkshire's meetings are a different story. The number of shareholders attending grows a bit each year and we have yet to experience a silly question or an ego-inspired commentary.[2] Instead, we get a wide variety of thoughtful questions about the business. Because the annual meeting is the time and place for these, Charlie and I are happy to answer them all, no matter how long it takes. (We cannot, however, respond to written or phoned questions at other times of the year; one-person-at-a-time reporting is a poor use of management time in a company with [thousands of] shareholders.) The only business matters that are off limits at the annual meeting are those about which candor might cost our company real money. Our activities in securities would be the main example.[3]

## A. Owner-Related Business Principles[4]

1. *Although our form is corporate, our attitude is partnership. Charlie Munger and I think of our shareholders as owner-partners, and of ourselves as managing partners. (Because of the size of our shareholdings we are also, for better or worse, controlling partners.) We do not view the company itself as the ultimate owner of our business assets but instead view the company as a conduit through which our shareholders own the assets.*

---

[2] [Subsequent letters sometimes report on the turnout at prior annual meetings. The turnout went from 12 at the 1975 meeting to approximately 7,500 at the 1997 meeting to over 15,000 in the early 2000s, with steady increases since 1984 averaging about 40% annually.]

[3] [Introductory essay, 1984.]

[4] [1996 Owner's Manual—originally 1983, and annually beginning in 1988.]

Charlie and I hope that you do not think of yourself as merely owning a piece of paper whose price wiggles around daily and that is a candidate for sale when some economic or political event makes you nervous. We hope you instead visualize yourself as a part owner of a business that you expect to stay with indefinitely, much as you might if you owned a farm or apartment house in partnership with members of your family. For our part, we do not view Berkshire shareholders as faceless members of an ever-shifting crowd, but rather as co-venturers who have entrusted their funds to us for what may well turn out to be the remainder of their lives.

The evidence suggests that most Berkshire shareholders have indeed embraced this long-term partnership concept. The annual percentage turnover in Berkshire's shares is a small fraction of that occurring in the stocks of other major American corporations, even when the shares I own are excluded from the calculation.

In effect, our shareholders behave in respect to their Berkshire stock much as Berkshire itself behaves in respect to companies in which it has an investment. As owners of, say, Coca-Cola or Gillette shares, we think of Berkshire as being a non-managing partner in two extraordinary businesses, in which we measure our success by the long-term progress of the companies rather than by the month-to-month movements of their stocks. In fact, we would not care in the least if several years went by in which there was no trading, or quotation of prices, in the stocks of those companies. If we have good long-term expectations, short-term price changes are meaningless for us except to the extent they offer us an opportunity to increase our ownership at an attractive price.

2. *In line with Berkshire's owner-orientation, most of our directors have a major portion of their net worth invested in the company. We eat our own cooking.*

Charlie's family has 90% or more of its net worth in Berkshire shares; my wife, Susie, and I have more than 99%. In addition, many of my relatives—my sisters and cousins, for example—keep a huge portion of their net worth in Berkshire stock.

Charlie and I feel totally comfortable with this eggs-in-one-basket situation because Berkshire itself owns a wide variety of truly extraordinary businesses. Indeed, we believe that Berkshire is close to being unique in the quality and diversity of the businesses in which it owns either a controlling interest or a minority interest of significance.

Charlie and I cannot promise you results. But we can guarantee that your financial fortunes will move in lockstep with ours for whatever period of time you elect to be our partner. We have no interest in large salaries or options or other means of gaining an "edge" over you. We want to make money only when our partners do and in exactly the same proportion. Moreover, when I do something dumb, I want you to be able to derive some solace from the fact that my financial suffering is proportional to yours.

3.  *Our long-term economic goal (subject to some qualifications mentioned later) is to maximize Berkshire's average annual rate of gain in intrinsic business value on a per-share basis. We do not measure the economic significance or performance of Berkshire by its size; we measure by per-share progress. We are certain that the rate of per-share progress will diminish in the future—a greatly enlarged capital base will see to that. But we will be disappointed if our rate does not exceed that of the average large American corporation.*

Since that was written at year end 1983, our intrinsic value (a topic I'll discuss a bit later)[5] has increased at an annual rate of about 25%, a pace that has definitely surprised both Charlie and me. Nevertheless the principle just stated remains valid: Operating with large amounts of capital as we do today, we cannot come close to performing as well as we once did with much smaller sums. The best rate of gain in intrinsic value we can even hope for is an average of 15% per annum, and we may well fall far short of that target. Indeed, we think very few large businesses have a chance of compounding intrinsic value at 15% per annum over an extended period of time. So it may be that we will end up meeting our stated goal—being above average—with gains that fall significantly short of 15%.

4.  *Our preference would be to reach our goal by directly owning a diversified group of businesses that generate cash and consistently earn above-average returns on capital. Our second choice is to own parts of similar businesses, attained primarily through purchases of marketable common stocks by our insurance subsidiaries. The price and availability of businesses and the need for insurance capital determine any given year's capital allocation.*

As has usually been the case, it is easier today to buy small pieces of outstanding businesses via the stock market than to buy similar businesses in their entirety on a negotiated basis. Neverthe-

---

5 [*See* the essay Intrinsic Value, Book Value, and Market Price in Part VI.E.]

less, we continue to prefer the 100% purchase, and in some years we get lucky: In 1995, in fact, we made three acquisitions. Though there will be dry years also, we expect to make a number of acquisitions in the decades to come, and our hope is that they will be large. If these purchases approach the quality of those we have made in the past, Berkshire will be well served.

The challenge for us is to generate ideas as rapidly as we generate cash. In this respect, a depressed stock market is likely to present us with significant advantages. For one thing, it tends to reduce the prices at which entire companies become available for purchase. Second, a depressed market makes it easier for our insurance companies to buy small pieces of wonderful businesses—including additional pieces of business we already own—at attractive prices. And third, some of those same wonderful businesses, such as Coca-Cola and Wells Fargo, are consistent buyers of their own shares, which means that they, and we, gain from the cheaper prices at which they can buy.

Overall, Berkshire and its long-term shareholders benefit from a sinking stock market much as a regular purchaser of food benefits from declining food prices. So when the market plummets—as it will from time to time—neither panic nor mourn. It's good news for Berkshire.

5. *Because of our two-pronged approach to business ownership and because of the limitations of conventional accounting, consolidated reported earnings may reveal relatively little about our true economic performance. Charlie and I, both as owners and managers, virtually ignore such consolidated numbers. However, we will also report to you the earnings of each major business we control, numbers we consider of great importance. These figures, along with other information we will supply about the individual businesses, should generally aid you in making judgments about them.*

To state things simply, we try to give you in the annual report the numbers and other information that really matter. Charlie and I pay a great deal of attention to how well our businesses are doing, and we also work to understand the environment in which each business is operating. For example, is one of our businesses enjoying an industry tailwind or is it facing a headwind? Charlie and I need to know exactly which situation prevails and to adjust our expectations accordingly. We will also pass along our conclusions to you.

Over time, practically all of our businesses have exceeded our expectations. But occasionally we have disappointments, and we will try to be as candid in informing you about those as we are in describing the happier experiences. When we use unconventional measures to chart our progress . . . we will try to explain these concepts and why we regard them as important. In other words, we believe in telling you how we think so that you can evaluate not only Berkshire's businesses but also assess our approach to management and capital allocation.

6. *Accounting consequences do not influence our operating or capital-allocation decisions. When acquisition costs are similar, we much prefer to purchase $2 of earnings that is not reportable by us under standard accounting principles than to purchase $1 of earnings that is reportable. This is precisely the choice that often faces us since entire businesses (whose earnings will be fully reportable) frequently sell for double the pro-rata price of small portions (whose earnings will be largely unreportable). In aggregate and over time, we expect the unreported earnings to be fully reflected in our intrinsic business value through capital gains.*

We attempt to offset the shortcomings of conventional accounting by regularly reporting "look-through" earnings. The look-through numbers include Berkshire's own reported operating earnings, excluding capital gains and purchase-accounting adjustments (an explanation of which occurs later in this message) plus Berkshire's share of the undistributed earnings of our major investees—amounts that are not included in Berkshire's figures under conventional accounting. From these undistributed earnings of our investees we subtract the tax we would have owed had the earnings been paid to us as dividends. We also exclude capital gains, purchase-accounting adjustments and extraordinary charges or credits from the investee numbers.

We have found over time that the undistributed earnings of our investees, in aggregate, have been as fully as beneficial to Berkshire as if they had been distributed to us (and therefore had been included in the earnings we officially report). This pleasant result has occurred because most of our investees are engaged in truly outstanding businesses that can often employ incremental capital to great advantage, either by putting it to work in their businesses or by repurchasing their shares. Obviously, every capital decision that our investees have made has not benefitted us as shareholders, but overall we have garnered far more than a dollar of value for each dollar they have retained. We consequently regard look-through earnings as realistically portraying our yearly gain from operations.

7.  *We use debt sparingly and, when we do borrow, we attempt to structure our loans on a long-term fixed-rate basis. We will reject interesting opportunities rather than over-leverage our balance sheet. This conservatism has penalized our results but it is the only behavior that leaves us comfortable, considering our fiduciary obligations to policyholders, lenders and the many equity holders who have committed unusually large portions of their net worth to our care. (As one of the Indianapolis "500" winners said: "To finish first, you must first finish.")*

The financial calculus that Charlie and I employ would never permit our trading a good night's sleep for a shot at a few extra percentage points of return. I've never believed in risking what my family and friends have and need in order to pursue what they don't have and don't need.

Besides, Berkshire has access to two low-cost, non-perilous sources of leverage that allow us to safely own far more assets than our equity capital alone would permit: deferred taxes and "float," the funds of others that our insurance business holds because it receives premiums before needing to pay out losses. Both of these funding sources have grown rapidly and now total about $12 billion.

Better yet, this funding to date has been cost-free. Deferred tax liabilities bear no interest. And as long as we can break even in our insurance underwriting—which we have done, on the average, during our 29 years in the business—the cost of the float developed from that operation is zero. Neither item, it should be understood, is equity; these are real liabilities. But they are liabilities without covenants or due dates attached to them. In effect, they give us the benefit of debt—an ability to have more assets working for us—but saddle us with none of its drawbacks.

Of course, there is no guarantee that we can obtain our float in the future at no cost. But we feel our chances of attaining that goal are as good as those of anyone in the insurance business. Not only have we reached the goal in the past (despite a number of important mistakes by your Chairman), but have now, with our acquisition of GEICO, materially improved our prospects for getting there in the future.

8.  *A managerial "wish list" will not be filled at shareholder expense. We will not diversify by purchasing entire businesses at control prices that ignore long-term economic consequences to our shareholders. We will only do with your money what we would do with our own, weighing fully the values you can obtain by diversify-*

*ing your own portfolios through direct purchases in the stock market.*

Charlie and I are interested only in acquisitions that we believe will raise the *per-share* intrinsic value of Berskhire's stock. The size of our paychecks or our offices will never be related to the size of Berkshire's balance sheet.

9. *We feel noble intentions should be checked periodically against results. We test the wisdom of retaining earnings by assessing whether retention, over time, delivers shareholders at least $1 of market value for each $1 retained. To date, this test has been met. We will continue to apply it on a five-year rolling basis. As our net worth grows, it is more difficult to use retained earnings wisely.*

We continue to pass the test, but the challenges of doing so have grown more difficult. If we reach the point that we can't create extra value by retaining earnings, we will pay them out and let our shareholders deploy the funds.

10. *We will issue common stock only when we receive as much in business value as we give. This rule applies to all forms of issuance—not only mergers or public stock offerings, but stock-for-debt swaps, stock options, and convertible securities as well. We will not sell small portions of your company—and that is what the issuance of shares amounts to—on a basis inconsistent with the value of the entire enterprise.*

When we sold the Class B shares, we stated that Berkshire stock was not undervalued—and some people found that shocking. That reaction was not well-founded. Shock should have registered instead had we issued shares when our stock *was* undervalued. Managements that say or imply during a public offering that their stock is undervalued are usually being economical with the truth or uneconomical with their existing shareholders' money: Owners unfairly lose if their managers deliberately sell assets for 80¢ that in fact are worth $1. We didn't commit that kind of crime in our recent offering and we never will.

11. *You should be fully aware of one attitude Charlie and I share that hurts our financial performance: Regardless of price, we have no interest at all in selling any good businesses that Berkshire owns. We are also very reluctant to sell sub-par businesses as long as we expect them to generate at least some cash and as long as we feel good about their managers and labor relations. We hope not to repeat the capital-allocation mistakes that led us into such sub-par businesses. And we react with great caution to suggestions that our poor businesses can be restored to satisfactory profitability by major*

*capital expenditures. (The projections will be dazzling and the advocates sincere, but, in the end, major additional investment in a terrible industry usually is about as rewarding as struggling in quicksand.) Nevertheless, gin rummy managerial behavior (discard your least promising business at each turn) is not our style. We would rather have our overall results penalized a bit than engage in that kind of behavior.*

We continue to avoid gin rummy behavior. True, we closed our textile business in the mid-1980s after 20 years of struggling with it, but only because we felt it was doomed to run never-ending operating losses. We have not, however, given thought to selling operations that would command very fancy prices nor have we dumped our laggards, though we focus hard on curing the problems that cause them to lag.

12.   *We will be candid in our reporting to you, emphasizing the pluses and minuses important in appraising business value. Our guideline is to tell you the business facts that we would want to know if our positions were reversed. We owe you no less. Moreover, as a company with a major communications business, it would be inexcusable for us to apply lesser standards of accuracy, balance and incisiveness when reporting on ourselves than we would expect our news people to apply when reporting on others. We also believe candor benefits us as managers: The CEO who misleads others in public may eventually mislead himself in private.*

At Berkshire you will find no "big bath" accounting maneuvers or restructuring. And we won't "smooth" quarterly or annual results: If earnings figures are lumpy when they reach headquarters, they will be lumpy when they reach you. Finally, when the numbers are a very rough "guesstimate," as they necessarily must be in insurance reserving, we will try to be both consistent and conservative in our approach.

We will be communicating with you in several ways. Through the annual report, I try to give all shareholders as much value-defining information as can be conveyed in a document kept to reasonable length. We also try to convey a liberal quantity of condensed but important information in our quarterly reports, though I don't write those (one recital a year is enough). Still another important occasion for communication is our Annual Meeting, at which Charlie and I are delighted to spend five hours or more answering questions about Berkshire. But there is one way we *can't* communicate: on a one-on-one basis. That isn't feasible given Berkshire's many thousands of owners.

In all of our communications, we try to make sure that no single shareholder gets an edge: We do not follow the usual practice of giving earnings "guidance" to analysts or large shareholders. Our goal is to have all of our owners updated at the same time.

13.  *Despite our policy of candor we will discuss our activities in marketable securities only to the extent legally required. Good investment ideas are rare, valuable and subject to competitive appropriation just as good product or business acquisition ideas are. Therefore we normally will not talk about our investment ideas. This ban extends even to securities we have sold (because we may purchase them again) and to stocks we are incorrectly rumored to be buying. If we deny those reports but say "no comment" on other occasions, the no-comments become confirmation.*

Though we continue to be unwilling to talk about specific stocks, we freely discuss our business and investment philosophy. I benefitted enormously from the intellectual generosity of Ben Graham, the greatest teacher in the history of finance, and I believe it appropriate to pass along what I learned from him, even if that creates new and able investment competitors for Berkshire just as Ben's teachings did for him.

## AN ADDED PRINCIPLE

*To the extent possible, we would like each Berkshire shareholder to record a gain or loss in market value during his period of ownership that is proportional to the gain or loss in per-share intrinsic value recorded by the company during that holding period. For this to come about, the relationship between the intrinsic value and the market price of a Berkshire share would need to remain constant, and by our preferences at 1-to-1. As that implies, we would rather see Berkshire's stock price at a* **fair** *level than a* **high** *level.* Obviously, Charlie and I can't control Berkshire's price. But by our policies and communications, we can encourage informed, rational behavior by owners that, in turn, will tend to produce a stock price that is also rational. Our it's-as-bad-to-be-overvalued-as-to-be-undervalued approach may disappoint some shareholders, particularly those poised to sell. We believe, however, that it affords Berkshire the best prospect of attracting long-term investors who seek to profit from the progress of the company rather than from the investment mistakes of their partners.

## B.   *Full and Fair Disclosure*[6]

At Berkshire, full reporting means giving you the information that we would wish you to give to us if our positions were reversed. What Charlie and I would want under that circumstance would be all the important facts about current operations as well as the CEO's frank view of the long-term economic characteristics of the business. We would expect both a lot of financial details and a discussion of any significant data we would need to interpret what was presented.

When Charlie and I read reports, we have no interest in pictures of personnel, plants or products. References to EBITDA make us shudder—does management think the tooth fairy pays for capital expenditures?[7] We're very suspicious of accounting methodology that is vague or unclear, since too often that means management wishes to hide something. And we don't want to read messages that a public relations department or consultant has turned out. Instead, we expect a company's CEO to explain in his or her own words what's happening.

For us, fair reporting means getting information to our 300,000 "partners" simultaneously, or as close to that mark as possible. We therefore put our annual and quarterly financials on the Internet between the close of the market on a Friday and the following morning. By our doing that, shareholders and other interested investors have timely access to these important releases and also have a reasonable amount of time to digest the information they include before the markets open on Monday.

We applaud the work that Arthur Levitt, Jr., until recently Chairman of the SEC, has done in cracking down on the corporate practice of "selective disclosure" that had spread like cancer in recent years. Indeed, it had become virtually standard practice for major corporations to "guide" analysts or large holders to earnings expectations that were intended either to be on the nose or a tiny bit below what the company truly expected to earn. Through the selectively dispersed hints, winks and nods that companies engaged in, speculatively-minded institutions and advisors were given an information edge over investment-oriented individuals. This was corrupt behavior, unfortunately embraced by both Wall Street and corporate America.

---

6  [2000.]

7  [*See* the essay Owner Earnings and the Cash Flow Fallacy in Part VI.D.]

Thanks to Chairman Levitt, whose general efforts on behalf of investors were both tireless and effective, corporations are now required to treat all of their owners equally. The fact that this reform came about because of coercion rather than conscience should be a matter of shame for CEOs and their investor relations departments.

One further thought while I'm on my soapbox: Charlie and I think it is both deceptive and dangerous for CEOs to predict growth rates for their companies. They are, of course, frequently egged on to do so by both analysts and their own investor relations departments. They should resist, however, because too often these predictions lead to trouble.

It's fine for a CEO to have his own internal goals and, in our view, it's even appropriate for the CEO to publicly express some hopes about the future, if these expectations are accompanied by sensible caveats. But for a major corporation to predict that its per-share earnings will grow over the long term at, say, 15% annually is to court trouble.

That's true because a growth rate of that magnitude can only be maintained by a very small percentage of large businesses. Here's a test: Examine the record of, say, the 200 highest earning companies from 1970 to 1980 and tabulate how many have increased per-share earnings by 15% annually since those dates. You will find that only a handful have. I would wager you a very significant sum that fewer than 10 of the 200 most profitable companies in 2000 will attain 15% annual growth in earnings-per-share over the next 20 years.

The problem arising from lofty predictions is not just that they spread unwarranted optimism. Even more troublesome is the fact that they corrode CEO behavior. Over the years, Charlie and I have observed many instances in which CEOs engaged in uneconomic operating maneuvers so that they could meet earnings targets they had announced. Worse still, after exhausting all that operating acrobatics would do, they sometimes played a wide variety of accounting games to "make the numbers." These accounting shenanigans have a way of snowballing: Once a company moves earnings from one period to another, operating shortfalls that occur thereafter require it to engage in further accounting maneuvers that must be even more "heroic." These can turn fudging into fraud. (More money, it has been noted, has been stolen with the point of a pen than at the point of a gun.)

Charlie and I tend to be leery of companies run by CEOs who woo investors with fancy predictions. A few of these managers will prove prophetic—but others will turn out to be congenital optimists, or even charlatans. Unfortunately, it's not easy for investors to know in advance which species they are dealing with.

### C.   *Boards and Managers*[8]

[The performance of CEOs of investee companies], which we have observed at close range, contrasts vividly with that of many CEOs, which we have fortunately observed from a safe distance. Sometimes these CEOs clearly do not belong in their jobs; their positions, nevertheless, are usually secure. The supreme irony of business management is that it is far easier for an inadequate CEO to keep his job than it is for an inadequate subordinate.

If a secretary, say, is hired for a job that requires typing ability of at least 80 words a minute and turns out to be capable of only 50 words a minute, she will lose her job in no time. There is a logical standard for this job; performance is easily measured; and if you can't make the grade, you're out. Similarly, if new sales people fail to generate sufficient business quickly enough, they will be let go. Excuses will not be accepted as a substitute for orders.

However, a CEO who doesn't perform is frequently carried indefinitely. One reason is that performance standards for his job seldom exist. When they do, they are often fuzzy or they may be waived or explained away, even when the performance shortfalls are major and repeated. At too many companies, the boss shoots the arrow of managerial performance and then hastily paints the bullseye around the spot where it lands.

Another important, but seldom recognized, distinction between the boss and the foot soldier is that the CEO has no immediate superior whose performance is itself getting measured. The sales manager who retains a bunch of lemons in his sales force will soon be in hot water himself. It is in his immediate self-interest to promptly weed out his hiring mistakes. Otherwise, he himself may be weeded out. An office manager who has hired inept secretaries faces the same imperative.

But the CEO's boss is a Board of Directors that seldom measures itself and is infrequently held to account for substandard corporate performance. If the Board makes a mistake in hiring, and perpetuates that mistake, so what? Even if the company is taken

---

8 [Divided by hash lines: 1988; 1993; 1986; 1998.]

over because of the mistake, the deal will probably bestow substantial benefits on the outgoing Board members. (The bigger they are, the softer they fall.)

Finally, relations between the Board and the CEO are expected to be congenial. At board meetings, criticism of the CEO's performance is often viewed as the social equivalent of belching. No such inhibitions restrain the office manager from critically evaluating the substandard typist.

These points should not be interpreted as a blanket condemnation of CEOs or Boards of Directors: Most are able and hard-working, and a number are truly outstanding. But the management failings that Charlie and I have seen make us thankful that we are linked with the managers of our three permanent holdings. They love their businesses, they think like owners, and they exude integrity and ability.

---

At our annual meetings, someone usually asks "What happens to this place if you get hit by a truck?" I'm glad they are still asking the question in this form. It won't be too long before the query becomes: "What happens to this place if you *don't* get hit by a truck?"

Such questions, in any event, raise a reason for me to discuss corporate governance, a hot topic during the past year. In general, I believe that directors have stiffened their spines recently and that shareholders are now being treated somewhat more like true owners than was the case not long ago. Commentators on corporate governance, however, seldom make any distinction among three fundamentally different manager/owner situations that exist in publicly-held companies. Though the legal responsibility of directors is identical throughout, their ability to effect change differs in each of the cases. Attention usually falls on the first case, because it prevails on the corporate scene. Since Berkshire falls into the second category, however, and will someday fall into the third, we will discuss all three variations.

The first, and by far most common, board situation is one in which a corporation has no controlling shareholder. In that case, I believe directors should behave as if there is a single absentee owner, whose long-term interest they should try to further in all proper ways. Unfortunately, "long-term" gives directors a lot of wiggle room. If they lack either integrity or the ability to think independently, directors can do great violence to shareholders while still claiming to be acting in their long-term interest. But assume the board is functioning well and must deal with a management that is mediocre or worse. Directors then have the responsibility for changing that management, just as an intelligent owner would do if he were present. And if able but greedy managers over-reach and try to dip too deeply into the shareholders' pockets, directors must slap their hands.

In this plain-vanilla case, a director who sees something he doesn't like should attempt to persuade the other directors of his view. If he is successful, the board will have the muscle to make the appropriate change. Suppose, though, that the unhappy director can't get other directors to agree with him. He should then feel free to make his views known to the absentee owners. Directors seldom do that, of course. The temperament of many directors would in fact be incompatible with critical behavior of that sort. But I see nothing improper in such actions, assuming the issues are serious. Naturally, the complaining director can expect a vigorous rebuttal from the unpersuaded directors, a prospect that should discourage the dissenter from pursuing trivial or non-rational causes.

For the boards just discussed, I believe the directors ought to be relatively few in number—say, ten or less—and ought to come mostly from the outside. The outside board members should establish standards for the CEO's performance and should also periodically meet, without his being present, to evaluate his performance against those standards.

The requisites for board membership should be business savvy, interest in the job, and owner-orientation. Too often, directors are selected simply because they are prominent or add diversity to the board. That practice is a mistake. Furthermore, mistakes in selecting directors are particularly serious because appointments are so hard to undo: The pleasant but vacuous director need never worry about job security.

The second case is that existing at Berkshire, where the controlling owner is also the manager. At some companies, this arrangement is facilitated by the existence of two classes of stock endowed with disproportionate voting power. In these situations, it's obvious that the board does not act as an agent between owners and management and that the directors cannot effect change except through persuasion. Therefore, if the owner/manager is mediocre or worse—or is over-reaching—there is little a director can do about it except object. If the directors having no connections to the owner/manager make a unified argument, it may well have some effect. More likely it will not.

If change does not come, and the matter is sufficiently serious, the outside directors should resign. Their resignation will signal their doubts about management, and it will emphasize that no outsider is in a position to correct the owner/manager's shortcomings.

The third governance case occurs when there is a controlling owner who is not involved in management. This case, examples of which are Hershey Foods and Dow Jones, puts the outside directors in a potentially useful position. If they become unhappy with either the competence or integrity of the manager, they can go directly to the owner (who may also be on the board) and report their dissatisfaction. This situation is ideal for an outside director, since he need make his case only to a single, presumably interested owner, who can forthwith effect change if the argument is persuasive. Even so, the dissatisfied director has only that single course of action. If he remains unsatisfied about a critical matter, he has no choice but to resign.

Logically, the third case should be the most effective in insuring first-class management. In the second case the owner is not going to fire himself, and in the first case, directors often find it very difficult to deal with mediocrity or mild over-reaching. Unless the unhappy directors can win over a majority of the board—an awkward social and logistical task, particularly if management's behavior is merely odious, not egregious—their hands are effectively tied. In practice, directors trapped in situations of this kind usually convince themselves that by staying around they can do at least some good. Meanwhile, management proceeds unfettered.

In the third case, the owner is neither judging himself nor burdened with the problem of garnering a majority. He can also insure that outside directors are selected who will bring useful qualities to the board. These directors, in turn, will know that the good advice they give will reach the right ears, rather than being stifled by a recalcitrant management. If the controlling owner is intelligent and self-confident, he will make decisions in respect to management that are meritocratic and pro-shareholder. Moreover—and this is critically important—he can readily correct any mistake he makes.

At Berkshire we operate in the second mode now and will for as long as I remain functional. My health, let me add, is excellent. For better or worse, you are likely to have me as an owner/manager for some time.

After my death, all of my stock will go to my wife, Susie, should she survive me, or to a foundation if she dies before I do. In neither case will taxes and bequests require the sale of consequential amounts of stock.

When my stock is transferred to either my wife or the foundation, Berkshire will enter the third governance mode, going forward with a vitally interested, but non-management, owner and with a management that must perform for that owner. In preparation for that time, Susie was elected to the board a few years ago, and in 1993 our son, Howard, joined the board. These family members will not be managers of the company in the future, but they will represent the controlling interest should anything happen to me. Most of our other directors are also significant owners of Berkshire stock, and each has a strong owner-orientation. All in all, we're prepared for "the truck."

---

Charlie and I really have only two jobs. One is to attract and keep outstanding managers to run our various operations.[9] This hasn't been all that difficult. Usually the managers came with the companies we bought, having demonstrated their talents throughout careers that spanned a wide variety of business circumstances. They were managerial stars long before they knew us, and our main contribution has been to not get in their way. This approach seems elementary: if my job were to manage a golf team—and if Jack Nicklaus or Arnold Palmer were willing to play for me—neither would get a lot of directives from me about how to swing.

Some of our key managers are independently wealthy (we hope they all become so), but that poses no threat to their continued interest: they work because they love what they do and relish the thrill of outstanding performance. They unfailingly think like owners (the highest compliment we can pay a manager) and find all aspects of their business absorbing.

(Our prototype for occupational fervor is the Catholic tailor who used his small savings of many years to finance a pilgrimage to the Vatican. When he returned, his parish held a special meeting to get his first-hand account of the Pope. "Tell us," said the eager faithful, "just what sort of fellow is he?" Our hero wasted no words: "He's a forty-four medium.")

Charlie and I know that the right players will make almost any team manager look good. We subscribe to the philosophy of

---

[9] [The other is capital allocation, discussed in Parts II and VI.]

Ogilvy & Mather's founding genius, David Ogilvy: "If each of us hires people who are smaller than we are, we shall become a company of dwarfs. But, if each of us hires people who are bigger than we are, we shall become a company of giants."

A by-product of our managerial style is the ability it gives us to easily expand Berkshire's activities. We've read management treatises that specify exactly how many people should report to any one executive, but they make little sense to us. When you have able managers of high character running businesses about which they are passionate, you can have a dozen or more reporting to you and still have time for an afternoon nap. Conversely, if you have even one person reporting to you who is deceitful, inept or uninterested, you will find yourself with more than you can handle. Charlie and I could work with double the number of managers we now have, so long as they had the rare qualities of the present ones.

We intend to continue our practice of working only with people whom we like and admire. This policy not only maximizes our chances for good results, it also ensures us an extraordinarily good time. On the other hand, working with people who cause your stomach to churn seems much like marrying for money—probably a bad idea under any circumstances, but absolute madness if you are already rich.

———————

At Berkshire we feel that telling outstanding CEOs, such as Tony [Nicely of GEICO], how to run their companies would be the height of foolishness. Most of our managers wouldn't work for us if they got a lot of backseat driving. (Generally, they don't have to work for *anyone*, since 75% or so are independently wealthy.) Besides, they are the Mark McGwires of the business world and need no advice from us as to how to hold the bat or when to swing.

Nevertheless, Berkshire's ownership may make even the best of managers more effective. First, we eliminate all of the ritualistic and nonproductive activities that normally go with the job of CEO. Our managers are totally in charge of their personal schedules. Second, we give each a simple mission: Just run your business as if: (1) you own 100% of it; (2) it is the only asset in the world that you and your family have or will ever have; and (3) you can't sell or merge it for at least a century. As a corollary, we tell them they should not let any of their decisions be affected even slightly by accounting considerations. We want our managers to think about what counts, not how it will be counted.

Very few CEOs of public companies operate under a similar mandate, mainly because they have owners who focus on short-term prospects and reported earnings. Berkshire, however, has a shareholder base–which it will have for decades to come–that has the longest investment horizon to be found in the public-company universe. Indeed, a majority of our shares are held by investors who expect to die still holding them. We can therefore ask our CEOs to manage for maximum long-term value, rather than for next quarter's earnings. We certainly don't ignore the current results of our businesses–in most cases, they are of great importance–but we *never* want them to be achieved at the expense of our building ever-greater competitive strengths.

I believe the GEICO story demonstrates the benefits of Berkshire's approach. Charlie and I haven't taught Tony a thing–and never will–but we *have* created an environment that allows him to apply all of his talents to what's important. He does not have to devote his time or energy to board meetings, press interviews, presentations by investment bankers or talks with financial analysts. Furthermore, he need never spend a moment thinking about financing, credit ratings or "Street" expectations for earnings per share. Because of our ownership structure, he also knows that this operational framework will endure for decades to come. In this environment of freedom, both Tony and his company can convert their almost limitless potential into matching achievements.

### D.  *The Anxieties of Plant Closings*[10]

In July we decided to close our textile operation, and by yearend this unpleasant job was largely completed. The history of this business is instructive.

When Buffett Partnership, Ltd., an investment partnership of which I was general partner, bought control of Berkshire Hathaway 21 years ago, it had an accounting net worth of $22 million, all devoted to the textile business. The company's intrinsic business value, however, was considerably less because the textile assets were unable to earn returns commensurate with their accounting value. Indeed, during the previous nine years (the period in which Berkshire and Hathaway operated as a merged company) aggregate sales of $530 million had produced an aggregate loss of $10 million. Profits had been reported from time to time but the net effect was always one step forward, two steps back.

---

[10] [1985.]

At the time we made our purchase, southern textile plants—largely non-union—were believed to have an important competitive advantage. Most northern textile operations had closed and many people thought we would liquidate our business as well.

We felt, however, that the business would be run much better by a long-time employee whom we immediately selected to be president, Ken Chace. In this respect we were 100% correct: Ken and his recent successor, Garry Morrison, have been excellent managers, every bit the equal of managers at our more profitable businesses.

In early 1967 cash generated by the textile operation was used to fund our entry into insurance via the purchase of National Indemnity Company. Some of the money came from earnings and some from reduced investment in textile inventories, receivables, and fixed assets. This pullback proved wise: although much improved by Ken's management, the textile business never became a good earner, not even in cyclical upturns.

Further diversification for Berkshire followed, and gradually the textile operation's depressing effect on our overall return diminished as the business became a progressively smaller portion of the corporation. We remained in the business for reasons that I stated in the 1978 annual report (and summarized at other times also): "(1) our textile businesses are very important employers in their communities, (2) management has been straightforward in reporting on problems and energetic in attacking them, (3) labor has been cooperative and understanding in facing our common problems, and (4) the business should average modest cash returns relative to investment." I further said, "As long as these conditions prevail—and we expect that they will—we intend to continue to support our textile business despite more attractive alternative uses for capital."

It turned out that I was very wrong about (4). Though 1979 was moderately profitable, the business thereafter consumed major amounts of cash. By mid-1985 it became clear, even to me, that this condition was almost sure to continue. Could we have found a buyer who would continue operations, I would have certainly preferred to sell the business rather than liquidate it, even if that meant somewhat lower proceeds for us. But the economics that were finally obvious to me were also obvious to others, and interest was nil.

I won't close down businesses of sub-normal profitability merely to add a fraction of a point to our corporate rate of return.

However, I also feel it inappropriate for even an exceptionally profitable company to fund an operation once it appears to have unending losses in prospect. Adam Smith would disagree with my first proposition, and Karl Marx would disagree with my second; the middle ground is the only position that leaves me comfortable.

I should reemphasize that Ken and Garry have been resourceful, energetic and imaginative in attempting to make our textile operation a success. Trying to achieve sustainable profitability, they reworked product lines, machinery configurations and distribution arrangements. We also made a major acquisition, Waumbec Mills, with the expectation of important synergy (a term widely used in business to explain an acquisition that otherwise makes no sense). But in the end nothing worked and I should be faulted for not quitting sooner. A recent *Business Week* article stated that 250 textile mills have closed since 1980. Their owners were not privy to any information that was unknown to me; they simply processed it more objectively. I ignored Comte's advice—"the intellect should be the servant of the heart, but not its slave"—and believed what I preferred to believe.

The domestic textile industry operates in a commodity business, competing in a world market in which substantial excess capacity exists. Much of the trouble we experienced was attributable, both directly and indirectly, to competition from foreign countries whose workers are paid a small fraction of the U.S. minimum wage. But that in no way means that our labor force deserves any blame for our closing. In fact, in comparison with employees of American industry generally, our workers were poorly paid, as has been the case throughout the textile business. In contract negotiations, union leaders and members were sensitive to our disadvantageous cost position and did not push for unrealistic wage increases or unproductive work practices. To the contrary, they tried just as hard as we did to keep us competitive. Even during our liquidation period they performed superbly. (Ironically, we would have been better off financially if our union had behaved unreasonably some years ago; we then would have recognized the impossible future that we faced, promptly closed down, and avoided significant future losses.)

Over the years, we had the option of making large capital expenditures in the textile operation that would have allowed us to somewhat reduce variable costs. Each proposal to do so looked like an immediate winner. Measured by standard return-on-investment tests, in fact, these proposals usually promised greater economic benefits than would have resulted from comparable expenditures in our highly-profitable candy and newspaper businesses.

But the promised benefits from these textile investments were illusory. Many of our competitors, both domestic and foreign, were stepping up to the same kind of expenditures and, once enough companies did so, their reduced costs became the baseline for reduced prices industrywide. Viewed individually, each company's capital investment decision appeared cost-effective and rational; viewed collectively, the decisions neutralized each other and were irrational (just as happens when each person watching a parade decides he can see a little better if he stands on tiptoes). After each round of investment, all the players had more money in the game and returns remained anemic.

Thus, we faced a miserable choice: huge capital investment would have helped to keep our textile business alive, but would have left us with terrible returns on ever-growing amounts of capital. After the investment, moreover, the foreign competition would still have retained a major, continuing advantage in labor costs. A refusal to invest, however, would make us increasingly non-competitive, even measured against domestic textile manufacturers. I always thought myself in the position described by Woody Allen in one of his movies: "More than any other time in history, mankind faces a crossroads. One path leads to despair and utter hopelessness, the other to total extinction. Let us pray we have the wisdom to choose correctly."

For an understanding of how the to-invest-or-not-to-invest dilemma plays out in a commodity business, it is instructive to look at Burlington Industries, by far the largest U.S. textile company both 21 years ago and now. In 1964 Burlington had sales of $1.2 billion against our $50 million. It had strengths in both distribution and production that we could never hope to match and also, of course, had an earnings record far superior to ours. Its stock sold at 60 at the end of 1964; ours was 13.

Burlington made a decision to stick to the textile business, and in 1985 had sales of about $2.8 billion. During the 1964-85 period, the company made capital expenditures of about $3 billion, far more than any other U.S. textile company and more than $200-per-share on that $60 stock. A very large part of the expenditures, I am sure, was devoted to cost improvement and expansion. Given Burlington's basic commitment to stay in textiles, I would also surmise that the company's capital decisions were quite rational.

Nevertheless, Burlington has lost sales volume in real dollars and has far lower returns on sales and equity now than 20 years ago. Split 2-for-1 in 1965, the stock now sells at 34—on an adjusted basis, just a little over its $60 price in 1964. Meanwhile, the CPI has more than tripled. Therefore, each share commands about one-third the purchasing power it did at the end of 1964. Regular dividends have been paid but they, too, have shrunk significantly in purchasing power.

This devastating outcome for the shareholders indicates what can happen when much brain power and energy are applied to a faulty premise. The situation is suggestive of Samuel Johnson's horse: "A horse that can count to ten is a remarkable horse—not a remarkable mathematician." Likewise, a textile company that allocates capital brilliantly within its industry is a remarkable textile company—but not a remarkable business.

My conclusion from my own experiences and from much observation of other businesses is that a good managerial record (measured by economic returns) is far more a function of what business boat you get into than it is of how effectively you row (though intelligence and effort help considerably, of course, in any business, good or bad). Should you find yourself in a chronically-leaking boat, energy devoted to changing vessels is likely to be more productive than energy devoted to patching leaks.

### E.   *An Owner-Based Approach to Corporate Charity*[11]

A recent survey reported that about 50% of major American companies match charitable contributions made by directors (sometimes by a factor of three to one). In effect, these representatives of the owners direct funds to their favorite charities, and never consult the owners as to their charitable preferences. (I wonder how they would feel if the process were reversed and shareholders could invade the directors' pockets for charities favored by the shareholders.) When A takes money from B to give to C and A is a legislator, the process is called taxation. But when A is an officer or director of a corporation, it is called philanthropy. We continue to believe that contributions, aside from those with quite clear direct benefits to the company, should reflect the charitable preferences of owners rather than those of officers and directors.

---

[11] [Divided by hash lines: 1987; 1981 (reprinted 1988); 1981; 1990-93; 1993.]

On September 30, 1981 Berkshire received a tax ruling from the U.S. Treasury Department that, in most years, should produce a significant benefit for charities of your choice.

Each Berkshire shareholder—on a basis proportional to the number of shares of Berkshire that he owns—will be able to designate recipients of charitable contributions by our company. You'll name the charity; Berkshire will write the check. The ruling states that there will be no personal tax consequences to our shareholders from making such designations.

Thus, our owners now can exercise a perquisite that, although routinely exercised by the owners in closely-held businesses, is almost exclusively exercised by the managers in more widely-held businesses.

In a widely-held corporation the executives ordinarily arrange all charitable donations, with no input at all from shareholders, in two main categories:

(1) Donations considered to benefit the corporation directly in an amount roughly commensurate with the cost of the donation; and

(2) Donations considered to benefit the corporation indirectly through hard-to-measure, long-delayed feedback effects of various kinds.

I and other Berkshire executives have arranged in the past, as we will arrange in the future, all charitable donations in the first category. However, the aggregate level of giving in such category has been quite low, and very likely will remain quite low, because not many gifts can be shown to produce roughly commensurate direct benefits to Berkshire.

In the second category, Berkshire's charitable gifts have been virtually nil, because I am not comfortable with ordinary corporate practice and had no better practice to substitute. What bothers me about ordinary corporate practice is the way gifts tend to be made based more on who does the asking and how corporate peers are responding than on an objective evaluation of the donee's activities. Conventionality often overpowers rationality.

A common result is the use of the stockholder's money to implement the charitable inclinations of the corporate manager, who usually is heavily influenced by specific social pressures on him. Frequently there is an added incongruity; many corporate managers deplore governmental allocation of the taxpayer's dollar but embrace enthusiastically their own allocation of the shareholder's dollar.

For Berkshire, a different model seems appropriate. Just as I wouldn't want you to implement your personal judgments by writing checks on my bank account for charities of your choice, I feel it inappropriate to write checks on your corporate "bank account" for charities of my choice. Your charitable preferences are as good as mine and, for both you and me, funds available to foster charitable interests in a tax-deductible manner reside largely at the corporate level rather than in our own hands.

Under such circumstances, I believe Berkshire should imitate more closely-held companies, not larger public companies. If you and I each own 50% of a corporation, our charitable decision making would be simple. Charities very directly related to the operations of the business would have first claim on our available charitable funds. Any balance available after the "operations-related" contributions would be divided among various charitable interests of the two of us, on a basis roughly proportional to our ownership interest. If the manager of our company had some suggestions, we would listen carefully—but the final decision would be ours. Despite our corporate form, in this aspect of the business we probably would behave as if we were a partnership.

Wherever feasible, I believe in maintaining such a partnership frame of mind, even though we operate through a large, fairly widely-held corporation. Our Treasury ruling will allow such partnership-like behavior in this area.

I am pleased that Berkshire donations can become owner-directed. It is ironic, but understandable, that a large and growing number of major corporations have charitable policies pursuant to which they will match gifts made by their employees (and—brace yourself for this one—many even match gifts made by directors) but none, to my knowledge, has a plan matching charitable gifts by owners. I say "understandable" because much of the stock of many large corporations is owned on a "revolving door" basis by institutions that have short-term investment horizons, and that lack a long-term owner's perspective.

Our own shareholders are a different breed. [A]t the end of each year, more than 98% of our shares are owned by people who were shareholders at the beginning of the year. This long-term commitment to the business reflects an owner mentality which, as your manager, I intend to acknowledge in all feasible ways. The designated contributions policy is an example of that intent.

Our new program enabling shareholders to designate the recipients of corporate charitable contributions was greeted with extraordinary enthusiasm. Of 932,206 shares eligible for participation (shares where the name of the actual owner appeared on our stockholder record), 95.6% responded. Even excluding Buffett-related shares, the response topped 90%.

In addition, more than 3% of our shareholders voluntarily wrote letters or notes, all but one approving of the program. Both the level of participation and of commentary surpass any shareholder response we have witnessed, even when such response has been intensively solicited by corporate staff and highly-paid professional proxy organizations. In contrast, your extraordinary level of response occurred without even the nudge of a company-provided return envelope. This self-propelled behavior speaks well for the program, and speaks well for our shareholders.

Apparently the owners of our corporation like both possessing and exercising the ability to determine where gifts of their funds shall be made. The "father-knows-best" school of corporate governance will be surprised to find that none of our shareholders sent in a designation sheet with instructions that the officers of Berkshire—in their superior wisdom, of course—make the decision on charitable funds applicable to his shares. Nor did anyone suggest that his share of our charitable funds be used to match contributions made by our corporate directors to charities of the directors' choice (a popular, proliferating and non-publicized policy at many large corporations).

All told, $1,783,655 of shareholder-designated contributions were distributed to about 675 charities. In addition, Berkshire and subsidiaries continue to make certain contributions pursuant to local level decisions made by our operating managers.

There will be some years, perhaps two or three out of ten, when contributions by Berkshire will produce substandard tax deductions—or none at all. In those years we will not effect our shareholder-designated charitable program. In all other years we expect to inform you about October 10th of the amount per share that you may designate. A reply form will accompany the notice, and you will be given about three weeks to respond with your designation.

The designated-contributions idea, along with many other ideas that have turned out well for us, was conceived by Charlie Munger, Vice Chairman of Berkshire. Irrespective of titles, Charlie and I work as partners in managing all controlled companies.

To almost a sinful degree, we enjoy our work as managing partners. And we enjoy having you as our financial partners.

---

In addition to the shareholder-designated contributions that Berkshire distributes, managers of our operating businesses make contributions, including merchandise, averaging [between $1.5 million and $2.5 million] annually. These contributions support local charities, such as The United Way, and produce roughly commensurate benefits for our businesses.

However, neither our operating managers nor officers of the parent company use Berkshire funds to make contributions to broad national programs or charitable activities of special personal interest to them, except to the extent they do so as shareholders. If your employees, including your CEO, wish to give to their alma maters or other institutions to which they feel a personal attachment, we believe they should use their own money, not yours.

---

Let me add that our program is easy to administer. Last fall, for two months, we borrowed one person from National Indemnity to help us implement the instructions that came from our 7,500 registered shareholders. I'd guess that the average corporate program in which employee gifts are matched incurs far greater administrative costs. Indeed, our entire corporate overhead is less than half the size of our charitable contributions. (Charlie, however, insists that I tell you that $1.4 million of our $4.9 million overhead is attributable to our corporate jet, The Indefensible.)[12]

---

[12] [Typesetting in original] [The 1986 letter contained the following:]

We bought a corporate jet last year. [Typesetting in original] What you have heard about such planes is true: they are very expensive and a luxury in situations like ours where little travel to out-of-the-way places is required. And planes not only cost a lot to operate, they cost a lot just to look at. Pre-tax, cost of capital plus depreciation on a new $15 million plane probably runs $3 million annually. On our own plane, bought for $850,000 used, such costs run close to $200,000 annually.

Cognizant of such figures, your Chairman, unfortunately, has in the past made a number of rather intemperate remarks about corporate jets. Accordingly, prior to our purchase, I was forced into my Galileo mode. I promptly experienced the necessary "counter-revelation" and travel is now considerably easier—and considerably costlier—than in the past. Whether Berkshire will get its money's worth from the plane is an open question, but I will work at achieving some business triumph that I can (no matter how dubiously) attribute to it. I'm afraid Ben Franklin had my number. Said he: "So convenient a thing it is to be a reasonable creature, since it enables one to find or make a reason for everything one has a mind to do."

[The 1989 letter contained the following:]

Last summer we sold the corporate jet that we purchased for $850,000 three years ago and bought another used jet for $6.7 million. [Noting an amusing anecdote of Carl Sagan

Below is a list showing the largest categories to which our shareholders have steered their contributions.

(a) 347 churches and synagogues received 569 gifts

(b) 238 colleges and universities received 670 gifts

(c) 244 K-12 schools (about two-thirds secular, one-third religious) received 525 gifts

(d) 288 institutions dedicated to art, culture or the humanities received 447 gifts

(e) 180 religious social-service organizations (split about equally between Christian and Jewish) received 411 gifts

(f) 445 secular social-service organizations (about 40% youth-related) received 759 gifts

(g) 153 hospitals received 261 gifts

(h) 186 health-related organizations (American Heart Association, American Cancer Society, etc.) received 320 gifts

Three things about this list seem particularly interesting to me. First, to some degree it indicates what people choose to give money to when they are acting of their own accord, free of pressure from solicitors or emotional appeals from charities. Second, the contributions programs of publicly-held companies almost never allow gifts to churches and synagogues, yet clearly these institutions are what many shareholders would like to support. Third, the gifts made by our shareholders display conflicting philosophies: 130 gifts were directed to organizations that believe in making abortions readily available for women and 30 gifts were directed to organizations (other than churches) that discourage or are opposed to abortion.

Last year I told you that I was thinking of raising the amount that Berkshire shareholders can give under our designated-contri-

---

about obstacles that impede exponential growth of bacteria—referred to in the Epilogue below, some readers] will understandably panic: If our net worth continues to increase at current rates, and the cost of replacing planes also continues to rise at the now-established rate of 100% compounded annually, it will not be long before Berkshire's entire net worth is consumed by its jet.

Charlie doesn't like it when I equate the jet with bacteria; he feels it's degrading to the bacteria. His idea of traveling in style is an air-conditioned bus, a luxury he steps up to only when bargain fares are in effect. My own attitude toward the jet can be summarized by the prayer attributed, apocryphally I'm sure, to St. Augustine as he contemplated leaving a life of secular pleasures to become a priest. Battling the conflict between intellect and glands, he pled: "Help me, Oh Lord, to become chaste—but not yet."

Naming the plane has not been easy. I initially suggested "The Charles T. Munger." Charlie countered with "The Aberration." We finally settled on "The Indefensible."

[The 1998 letter indicates that Buffett sold the Berkshire plane and now does all his flying with Berkshire's flight services businesses.]

butions program and asked for your comments. We received a few well-written letters opposing the entire idea, on the grounds that it was our job to run the business and not our job to force shareholders into making charitable gifts. Most of the shareholders responding, however, noted the tax efficiency of the plan and urged us to increase the designated amount. Several shareholders who have given stock to their children or grandchildren told me that they consider the program a particularly good way to get youngsters thinking at an early age about the subject of giving. These people, in other words, perceive the program to be an educational, as well as philanthropic, tool. The bottom line is that we did raise the amount in 1993, from $8 per share to $10.[13]

### F.  *A Principled Approach to Executive Pay*[14]

When returns on capital are ordinary, an earn-more-by-putting-up-more record is no great managerial achievement. You can get the same result personally while operating from your rocking chair. Just quadruple the capital you commit to a savings account and you will quadruple your earnings. You would hardly expect hosannas for that particular accomplishment. Yet, retirement announcements regularly sing the praises of CEOs who have, say, quadrupled earnings of their widget company during their reign—with no one examining whether this gain was attributable simply to many years of retained earnings and the workings of compound interest.

If the widget company consistently earned a superior return on capital throughout the period, or if capital employed only doubled during the CEO's reign, the praise for him may be well deserved. But if return on capital was lackluster and capital employed increased in pace with earnings, applause should be withheld. A savings account in which interest was reinvested would achieve the same year-by-year increase in earnings—and, at only 8% interest, would quadruple its annual earnings in 18 years.

The power of this simple math is often ignored by companies to the detriment of their shareholders. Many corporate compensa-

---

13 [Each annual letter states the approximate percentage of eligible shares that participated in the shareholder-designated contributions program, the dollar amount of the contributions, and the number of recipients. The percentage of participating shares always exceeds 95% and usually exceeds 97%; the annual dollar amount rises steadily, from $1-2 million in the early 1980s to around $20 million in the early 2000s; the number of different charities grew from fewer than 1,000 to nearly 4,000 in the same period; and aggregate giving through the program by the early 2000s was closing in on $200 million.]

14 [Divided by hash lines: 1985; 1994; 1991.]

tion plans reward managers handsomely for earnings increases produced solely, or in large part, by retained earnings—i.e., earnings withheld from owners. For example, ten-year, fixed-price stock options are granted routinely, often by companies whose dividends are only a small percentage of earnings.

An example will illustrate the inequities possible under such circumstances. Let's suppose that you had a $100,000 savings account earning 8% interest and "managed" by a trustee who could decide each year what portion of the interest you were to be paid in cash. Interest not paid out would be "retained earnings" added to the savings account to compound. And let's suppose that your trustee, in his superior wisdom, set the "pay-out ratio" at one-quarter of the annual earnings.

Under these assumptions, your account would be worth $179,084 at the end of ten years. Additionally, your annual earnings would have increased about 70% from $8,000 to $13,515 under this inspired management. And, finally, your "dividends" would have increased commensurately, rising regularly from $2,000 in the first year to $3,378 in the tenth year. Each year, when your manager's public relations firm prepared his annual report to you, all of the charts would have had lines marching skyward.

Now, just for fun, let's push our scenario one notch further and give your trustee-manager a ten-year fixed-price option on part of your "business" (i.e., your savings account) based on its fair value in the first year. With such an option, your manager would reap a substantial profit at your expense—just from having held on to most of your earnings. If he were both Machiavellian and a bit of a mathematician, your manager might also have cut the pay-out ratio once he was firmly entrenched.

This scenario is not as farfetched as you might think. Many stock options in the corporate world have worked in exactly that fashion: they have gained in value simply because management retained earnings, not because it did well with the capital in its hands.

Managers actually apply a double standard to options. Leaving aside warrants (which deliver the issuing corporation immediate and substantial compensation), I believe it is fair to say that nowhere in the business world are ten-year, fixed-price options on all or a portion of a business granted to outsiders. Ten months, in fact, would be regarded as extreme. It would be particularly unthinkable for managers to grant a long-term option on a business that was regularly adding to its capital. Any outsider wanting to secure such an option would be required to pay fully for capital added during the option period.

The unwillingness of managers to do-unto-outsiders, however, is not matched by an unwillingness to do-unto-themselves. (Negotiating with one's self seldom produces a bar room brawl.) Managers regularly engineer ten-year, fixed-price options for themselves and associates that, first, totally ignore the fact that retained earnings automatically build value and, second, ignore the carrying cost of capital. As a result, these managers end up profiting much as they would have had they had an option on that savings account that was automatically building up in value.

Of course, stock options often go to talented, value-adding managers and sometimes deliver them rewards that are perfectly appropriate. (Indeed, managers who are really exceptional almost always get far less than they should.) But when the result is equitable, it is accidental. Once granted, the option is blind to individual performance. Because it is irrevocable and unconditional (so long as a manager stays in the company), the sluggard receives rewards from his options precisely as does the star. A managerial Rip Van Winkle, ready to doze for ten years, could not wish for a better "incentive" system.

(I can't resist commenting on one long-term option given an "outsider": that granted the U.S. Government on Chrysler shares as partial consideration for the government's guarantee of some life-saving loans. When these options worked out well for the government, Chrysler sought to modify the payoff, arguing that the rewards to the government were both far greater than intended and outsize[d] in relation to its contribution to Chrysler's recovery. The company's anguish over what it saw as an imbalance between payoff and performance made national news. That anguish may well be unique: to my knowledge, no managers—anywhere—have been similarly offended by unwarranted payoffs arising from options granted to themselves or their colleagues.)

Ironically, the rhetoric about options frequently describes them as desirable because they put managers and owners in the same financial boat. In reality, the boats are far different. No owner has ever escaped the burden of capital costs, whereas a holder of a fixed-price option bears no capital costs at all. An owner must weigh upside potential against downside risk; an option holder has no downside. In fact, the business project in which you would wish to have an option frequently is a project in which you would reject ownership. (I'll be happy to accept a lottery ticket as a gift—but I'll never buy one.)

In dividend policy also, the option holders' interests are best served by a policy that may ill serve the owner. Think back to the savings account example. The trustee, holding his option, would benefit from a no-dividend policy. Conversely, the owner of the account should lean to a total payout so that he can prevent the option-holding manager from sharing in the account's retained earnings.[15]

Despite their shortcomings, options can be appropriate under some circumstances. My criticism relates to their indiscriminate use and, in that connection, I would like to emphasize three points:

First, stock options are inevitably tied to the overall performance of a corporation. Logically, therefore, they should be awarded only to those managers with overall responsibility. Managers with limited areas of responsibility should have incentives that pay off in relation to results under their control. The .350 hitter expects, and also deserves, a big payoff for his performance—even if he plays for a cellar-dwelling team. And the .150 hitter should get no reward—even if he plays for a pennant winner. Only those with overall responsibility for the team should have their rewards tied to its results.

Second, options should be structured carefully. Absent special factors, they should have built into them a retained-earnings or carrying-cost factor. Equally important, they should be priced realistically. When managers are faced with offers for their companies, they unfailingly point out how unrealistic market prices can be as an index of real value. But why, then, should these same depressed prices be the valuations at which managers sell portions of their businesses to themselves? (They may go further: officers and directors sometimes consult the Tax Code to determine the *lowest* prices at which they can, in effect, sell part of the business to insiders. While they're at it, they often elect plans that produce the *worst* tax result for the company.) Except in highly unusual cases, owners are not well served by the sale of part of their business at a bargain price—whether the sale is to outsiders or to insiders. The obvious conclusion: options should be priced at true business value.

Third, I want to emphasize that some managers whom I admire enormously—and whose operating records are far better than mine—disagree with me regarding fixed-price options. They have

---

15 [*See* the essay Dividend Policy and Share Repurchases in Part IV.C.]

built corporate cultures that work, and fixed-price options have been a tool that helped them. By their leadership and example, and by the use of options as incentives, these managers have taught their colleagues to think like owners. Such a culture is rare and when it exists should perhaps be left intact—despite inefficiencies and inequities that may infest the option program. "If it ain't broke, don't fix it" is preferable to "purity at any price".

At Berkshire, however, we use an incentive-compensation system that rewards key managers for meeting targets in their own bailiwicks. If See's does well, that does not produce incentive compensation at the News—nor vice versa. Neither do we look at the price of Berkshire stock when we write bonus checks. We believe good unit performance should be rewarded whether Berkshire stock rises, falls, or stays even. Similarly, we think average performance should earn no special rewards even if our stock should soar. "Performance", furthermore, is defined in different ways depending upon the underlying economics of the business: in some our managers enjoy tailwinds not of their own making, in others they fight unavoidable headwinds.

The rewards that go with this system can be large. At our various business units, top managers sometimes receive incentive bonuses of five times their base salary, or more, and it would appear possible that one manager's bonus could top $2 million in 1986. (I hope so.) We do not put a cap on bonuses, and the potential for rewards is not hierarchical. The manager of a relatively small unit can earn far more than the manager of a larger unit if results indicate he should. We believe, further, that such factors as seniority and age should not affect incentive compensation (though they sometimes influence basic compensation.) A 20 year-old who can hit .300 is as valuable to us as a 40 year-old performing as well.

Obviously, all Berkshire managers can use their bonus money (or other funds, including borrowed money) to buy our stock in the market. Many have done just that—and some now have large holdings. By accepting both the risks and the carrying cost that go with outright purchases, these managers truly walk in the shoes of owners.

———————

At Berkshire, we try to be as logical about compensation as about capital allocation. For example, we compensate Ralph Schey based upon the results of Scott Fetzer rather than those of Berkshire. What could make more sense, since he's responsible for one operation but not the other? A cash bonus or a stock option tied to the fortunes of Berkshire would provide totally capricious rewards to Ralph. He could, for example, be hitting home runs at Scott Fetzer while Charlie and I rang up mistakes at Berkshire, thereby negating his efforts many times over. Conversely, why should option profits or bonuses be heaped upon Ralph if good things are occurring in other parts of Berkshire but Scott Fetzer is lagging?

In setting compensation, we like to hold out the promise of large carrots, but make sure their delivery is tied directly to results in the area that a manager controls. When capital invested in an operation is significant, we also both charge managers a high rate for incremental capital they employ and credit them at an equally high rate for capital they release.

The product of this money's-not-free approach is definitely visible at Scott Fetzer. If Ralph can employ incremental funds at good returns, it pays him to do so: His bonus increases when earnings on additional capital exceed a meaningful hurdle charge. But our bonus calculation is symmetrical: If incremental investment yields sub-standard returns, the shortfall is costly to Ralph as well as to Berkshire. The consequence of this two-way arrangement is that it pays Ralph—and pays him well—to send to Omaha any cash he can't advantageously use in his business.

It has become fashionable at public companies to describe almost every compensation plan as aligning the interests of management with those of shareholders. In our book, alignment means being a partner in both directions, not just on the upside. Many "alignment" plans flunk this basic test, being artful forms of "heads I win, tails you lose."

A common form of misalignment occurs in the typical stock option arrangement, which does not periodically increase the option price to compensate for the fact that retained earnings are building up the wealth of the company. Indeed, the combination of a ten-year option, a low dividend payout, and compound interest can provide lush gains to a manager who has done no more than tread water in his job. A cynic might even note that when payments to owners are held down, the profit to the option-holding manager increases. I have yet to see this vital point spelled out in a proxy statement asking shareholders to approve an option plan.

I can't resist mentioning that our compensation arrangement with Ralph Schey was worked out in about five minutes, immediately upon our purchase of Scott Fetzer and without the "help" of lawyers or compensation consultants. This arrangement embodies a few very simple ideas—not the kind of terms favored by consultants who cannot easily send a large bill unless they have established that you have a large problem (and one, of course, that requires an annual review). Our agreement with Ralph has never been changed. It made sense to him and to me in 1986, and it makes sense now. Our compensation arrangements with the managers of all our other units are similarly simple, though the terms of each agreement vary to fit the economic characteristics of the business at issue, the existence in some cases of partial ownership of the unit by managers, etc.

In all instances, we pursue rationality. Arrangements that pay off in capricious ways, unrelated to a manager's personal accomplishments, may well be welcomed by certain managers. Who, after all, refuses a free lottery ticket? But such arrangements are wasteful to the company and cause the manager to lose focus on what should be his real areas of concern. Additionally, irrational behavior at the parent may well encourage imitative behavior at subsidiaries.

At Berkshire, only Charlie and I have the managerial responsibility for the entire business. Therefore, we are the only parties who should logically be compensated on the basis of what the enterprise does as a whole. Even so, that is not a compensation arrangement we desire. We have carefully designed both the company and our jobs so that we do things we enjoy with people we like. Equally important, we are forced to do very few boring or unpleasant tasks. We are the beneficiaries as well of the abundant array of material and psychic perks that flow to the heads of corporations. Under such idyllic conditions, we don't expect shareholders to ante up loads of compensation for which we have no possible need.

Indeed, if we were not paid at all, Charlie and I would be delighted with the cushy jobs we hold. At bottom, we subscribe to Ronald Reagan's creed: "It's probably true that hard work never killed anyone, but I figure why take the chance."

---

We made a sizable acquisition in 1991—the H.H. Brown Shoe Co., the leading North American manufacturer of work shoes and boots, and it has a history of earning unusually fine margins on sales and assets. Shoes are a tough business—of the billion pairs purchased in the United States each year, about 85% are imported—and most manufacturers in the industry do poorly. The wide range of styles and sizes that producers offer causes inventories to be heavy; substantial capital is also tied up in receivables.

A distinguishing characteristic of H.H. Brown is one of the most unusual compensation systems I've encountered—but one that warms my heart: A number of key managers are paid an annual salary of $7,800, to which is added a designated percentage of the profits of the company after these are reduced by a charge for capital employed. These managers therefore truly stand in the shoes of owners. In contrast, most managers talk the talk but don't walk the walk, choosing instead to employ compensation systems that are long on carrots but short on sticks (and that almost invariably treat equity capital as if it were cost-free). The arrangement at Brown, in any case, has served both the company and its managers exceptionally well, which should be no surprise: Managers eager to bet heavily on their abilities usually have plenty of ability to bet on.

## II. CORPORATE FINANCE AND INVESTING

We bought all of our [Washington Post Company ("WPC")] holdings in mid-1973 at a price of not more than one-fourth of the then per-share business value of the enterprise. Calculating the price/value ratio required no unusual insights. Most security analysts, media brokers, and media executives would have estimated WPC's intrinsic business value at $400 to $500 million just as we did. And its $100 million stock market valuation was published daily for all to see. Our advantage, rather, was attitude: we had learned from Ben Graham that the key to successful investing was the purchase of shares in good businesses when market prices were at a large discount from underlying business values.

Most institutional investors in the early 1970s, on the other hand, regarded business value as of only minor relevance when they were deciding the prices at which they would buy or sell. This now seems hard to believe. However, these institutions were then under the spell of academics at prestigious business schools who were preaching a newly-fashioned theory: the stock market was totally efficient, and therefore calculations of business value—and even thought, itself—were of no importance in investment activities. (We are enormously indebted to those academics: what could be more advantageous in an intellectual contest—whether it be bridge, chess, or stock selection—than to have opponents who have been taught that thinking is a waste of energy?)[16]

### A.  *Mr. Market*[17]

Whenever Charlie and I buy common stocks for Berkshire's insurance companies (leaving aside arbitrage purchases, discussed [in the next essay]) we approach the transaction as if we were buying into a private business. We look at the economic prospects of the business, the people in charge of running it, and the price we must pay. We do not have in mind any time or price for sale. Indeed, we are willing to hold a stock indefinitely so long as we expect the business to increase in intrinsic value at a satisfactory rate. When investing, we view ourselves as business analysts—not as market analysts, not as macroeconomic analysts, and not even as security analysts.

Our approach makes an active trading market useful, since it periodically presents us with mouth-watering opportunities. But by

---

16 [Introductory essay, 1985.]
17 [Divided by hash lines: 1987; 1997.]

no means is it essential: a prolonged suspension of trading in the securities we hold would not bother us any more than does the lack of daily quotations on World Book or Fechheimer. Eventually, our economic fate will be determined by the economic fate of the business we own, whether our ownership is partial or total.

Ben Graham, my friend and teacher, long ago described the mental attitude toward market fluctuations that I believe to be most conducive to investment success. He said that you should imagine market quotations as coming from a remarkably accommodating fellow named Mr. Market who is your partner in a private business. Without fail, Mr. Market appears daily and names a price at which he will either buy your interest or sell you his.

Even though the business that the two of you own may have economic characteristics that are stable, Mr. Market's quotations will be anything but. For, sad to say, the poor fellow has incurable emotional problems. At times he feels euphoric and can see only the favorable factors affecting the business. When in that mood, he names a very high buy-sell price because he fears that you will snap up his interest and rob him of imminent gains. At other times he is depressed and can see nothing but trouble ahead for both the business and the world. On these occasions he will name a very low price, since he is terrified that you will unload your interest on him.

Mr. Market has another endearing characteristic: He doesn't mind being ignored. If his quotation is uninteresting to you today, he will be back with a new one tomorrow. Transactions are strictly at your option. Under these conditions, the more manic-depressive his behavior, the better for you.

But, like Cinderella at the ball, you must heed one warning or everything will turn into pumpkins and mice: Mr. Market is there to serve you, not to guide you. It is his pocketbook, not his wisdom, that you will find useful. If he shows up some day in a particularly foolish mood, you are free to either ignore him or to take advantage of him, but it will be disastrous if you fall under his influence. Indeed, if you aren't certain that you understand and can value your business far better than Mr. Market you don't belong in the game. As they say in poker, "If you've been in the game 30 minutes and you don't know who the patsy is, *you're* the patsy."

Ben's Mr. Market allegory may seem out-of-date in today's investment world, in which most professionals and academicians talk of efficient markets, dynamic hedging and betas. Their interest in such matters is understandable, since techniques shrouded in mystery clearly have value to the purveyor of investment advice.

After all, what witch doctor has ever achieved fame and fortune by simply advising "Take two aspirins"?

The value of market esoterica to the consumer of investment advice is a different story. In my opinion, investment success will not be produced by arcane formulae, computer programs or signals flashed by the price behavior of stocks and markets. Rather an investor will succeed by coupling good business judgment with an ability to insulate his thoughts and behavior from the super-contagious emotions that swirl about the marketplace. In my own efforts to stay insulated, I have found it highly useful to keep Ben's Mr. Market concept firmly in mind.

Following Ben's teachings, Charlie and I let our marketable equities tell us by their operating results—not by their daily, or even yearly, price quotations—whether our investments are successful. The market may ignore business success for a while, but eventually will confirm it. As Ben said: "In the short run, the market is a voting machine but in the long run it is a weighing machine." The speed at which a business's success is recognized, furthermore, is not that important as long as the company's intrinsic value is increasing at a satisfactory rate. In fact, delayed recognition can be an advantage: It may give us the chance to buy more of a good thing at a bargain price.

Sometimes, of course, the market may judge a business to be more valuable than the underlying facts would indicate it is. In such a case, we will sell our holdings. Sometimes, also, we will sell a security that is fairly valued or even undervalued because we require funds for a still more undervalued investment or one we believe we understand better.

We need to emphasize, however, that we do not sell holdings just because they have appreciated or because we have held them for a long time. (Of Wall Street maxims the most foolish may be "You can't go broke taking a profit.") We are quite content to hold any security indefinitely, so long as the prospective return on equity capital of the underlying business is satisfactory, management is competent and honest, and the market does not overvalue the business.

However, our insurance companies own three marketable common stocks that we would not sell even though they became far overpriced in the market. In effect, we view these investments exactly like our successful controlled businesses—a permanent part of Berkshire rather than merchandise to be disposed of once Mr. Market offers us a sufficiently high price. To that, I will add one qualifier: These stocks are held by our insurance companies and we would, if absolutely necessary, sell portions of our holdings to pay extraordinary insurance losses. We intend, however, to manage our affairs so that sales are never required.

A determination to have and to hold, which Charlie and I share, obviously involves a mixture of personal and financial considerations. To some, our stand may seem highly eccentric. (Charlie and I have long followed David Ogilvy's advice: "Develop your eccentricities while you are young. That way, when you get old, people won't think you're going ga-ga.") Certainly, in the transaction-fixated Wall Street of recent years, our posture must seem odd: To many in that arena, both companies and stocks are seen only as raw material for trades.

Our attitude, however, fits our personalities and the way we want to live our lives. Churchill once said, "You shape your houses and then they shape you." We know the manner in which we wish to be shaped. For that reason, we would rather achieve a return of X while associating with people whom we strongly like and admire than realize 110% of X by exchanging these relationships for uninteresting or unpleasant ones.

––––––––––––

A short quiz: If you plan to eat hamburgers throughout your life and are not a cattle producer, should you wish for higher or lower prices for beef? Likewise, if you are going to buy a car from time to time but are not an auto manufacturer, should you prefer higher or lower car prices? These questions, of course, answer themselves.

But now for the final exam: If you expect to be a net saver during the next five years, should you hope for a higher or lower stock market during that period? Many investors get this one wrong. Even though they are going to be net buyers of stocks for many years to come, they are elated when stock prices rise and depressed when they fall. In effect, they rejoice because prices have risen for the "hamburgers" they will soon be buying. This reaction makes no sense. Only those who will be sellers of equities in the near future should be happy at seeing stocks rise. Prospective purchasers should much prefer sinking prices.

For shareholders of Berkshire who do not expect to sell, the choice is even clearer. To begin with, our owners are automatically saving even if they spend every dime they personally earn: Berkshire "saves" for them by retaining all earnings, thereafter using these savings to purchase businesses and securities. Clearly, the more cheaply we make these buys, the more profitable our owners' indirect savings program will be.

Furthermore, through Berkshire you own major positions in companies that consistently repurchase their shares. The benefits that these programs supply us grow as prices fall: When stock prices are low, the funds that an investee spends on repurchases increase our ownership of that company by a greater amount than is the case when prices are higher. For example, the repurchases that Coca-Cola, The Washington Post and Wells Fargo made in past years at very low prices benefitted Berkshire far more than do today's repurchases, made at loftier prices.

[Since at the end of every year, almost all Berkshire shares are held by the same investors who owned them at the start of the year, Berkshire shareholders are] savers. They should therefore rejoice when markets decline and allow both us and our investees to deploy funds more advantageously.

So smile when you read a headline that says "Investors lose as market falls." Edit it in your mind to "Disinvestors lose as market falls–but investors gain." Though writers often forget this truism, there is a buyer for every seller and what hurts one necessarily helps the other. (As they say in golf matches: "Every putt makes *someone* happy.")

We gained enormously from the low prices placed on many equities and businesses in the 1970s and 1980s. Markets that then were hostile to investment transients were friendly to those taking up permanent residence. In recent years, the actions we took in those decades have been validated, but we have found few new opportunities. In its role as a corporate "saver," Berkshire continually looks for ways to sensibly deploy capital, but it may be some time before we find opportunities that get us truly excited.

## B.  *Arbitrage*[18]

[O]ur insurance subsidiaries sometimes engage in arbitrage as an alternative to holding short-term cash equivalents. We prefer, of course, to make major long-term commitments, but we often have more cash than good ideas. At such times, arbitrage sometimes promises much greater returns than Treasury Bills and, equally important, cools any temptation we may have to relax our standards for long-term investments. (Charlie's signoff after we've

---

[18] [Divided by hash lines: 1988; 1989.]

talked about an arbitrage commitment is usually: "Okay, at least it will keep you out of bars.")

During 1988 we made unusually large profits from arbitrage, measured both by absolute dollars and rate of return. Our pre-tax gain was about $78 million on average invested funds of about $147 million.

This level of activity makes some detailed discussion of arbitrage and our approach to it appropriate. Once, the word applied only to the simultaneous purchase and sale of securities or foreign exchange in two different markets. The goal was to exploit tiny price differentials that might exist between, say, Royal Dutch stock trading in guilders in Amsterdam, pounds in London, and dollars in New York. Some people might call this scalping: it won't surprise you that practitioners opted for the French term, arbitrage.

Since World War I the definition of arbitrage—or "risk arbitrage," as it is now sometimes called—has expanded to include the pursuit of profits from an announced corporate event such as sale of the company, merger, recapitalization, reorganization, liquidation, self-tender, etc. In most cases the arbitrageur expects to profit regardless of the behavior of the stock market. The major risk he usually faces instead is that the announced event won't happen.

Some offbeat opportunities occasionally arise in the arbitrage field. I participated in one of these when I was 24 and working in New York for Graham-Newman Corp. Rockwood & Co., a Brooklyn-based chocolate products company of limited profitability, had adopted LIFO inventory valuation in 1941 when cocoa was selling for 5 cents per pound. In 1954 a temporary shortage of cocoa caused the price to soar to over 60 cents. Consequently Rockwood wished to unload its valuable inventory—quickly, before the price dropped. But if the cocoa had simply been sold off, the company would have owed close to a 50% tax on the proceeds.

The 1954 Tax Code came to the rescue. It contained an arcane provision that eliminated the tax otherwise due on LIFO profits if inventory was distributed to shareholders as part of a plan reducing the scope of a corporation's business. Rockwood decided to terminate one of its businesses, the sale of cocoa butter, and said 13 million pounds of its cocoa bean inventory was attributable to that activity. Accordingly, the company offered to repurchase its stock in exchange for the cocoa beans it no longer needed, paying 80 pounds of beans for each share.

For several weeks I busily bought shares, sold beans, and made periodic stops at Schroeder Trust to exchange stock certificates for warehouse receipts. The profits were good and my only expense was subway tokens.

The architect of Rockwood's restructuring was an unknown, but brilliant Chicagoan, Jay Pritzker, then 32. If you're familiar with Jay's subsequent record, you won't be surprised to hear the action worked out rather well for Rockwood's continuing shareholders also. From shortly before the tender until shortly after it, Rockwood stock appreciated from 15 to 100, even though the company was experiencing large operating losses. Sometimes there is more to stock valuation than price-earnings ratios.

In recent years, most arbitrage operations have involved takeovers, friendly and unfriendly. With acquisition fever rampant, with anti-trust challenges almost non-existent, and with bids often ratcheting upward, arbitrageurs have prospered mightily. They have not needed special talents to do well; the trick, à la Peter Sellers in the movie, has simply been "Being There." In Wall Street the old proverb has been reworded: "Give a man a fish and you feed him for a day. Teach him how to arbitrage and you feed him forever." (If, however, he studied at the Ivan Boesky School of Arbitrage, it may be a state institution that supplies his meals.)

To evaluate arbitrage situations you must answer four questions: (1) How likely is it that the promised event will indeed occur? (2) How long will your money be tied up? (3) What chance is there that something still better will transpire—a competing takeover bid, for example? and (4) What will happen if the event does not take place because of anti-trust action, financing glitches, etc.?

Arcata Corp., one of our more serendipitous arbitrage experiences, illustrates the twists and turns of the business. On September 28, 1981 the directors of Arcata agreed in principle to sell the company to Kohlberg Kravis Roberts & Co. (KKR), then and now a major leveraged-buyout firm. Arcata was in the printing and forest products businesses and had one other thing going for it: In 1978 the U.S. Government had taken title to 10,700 acres of Arcata timber, primarily old-growth redwood, to expand Redwood National Park. The government had paid $97.9 million, in several installments, for this acreage, a sum Arcata was contesting as grossly inadequate. The parties also disputed the interest rate that should apply to the period between the taking of the property and final payment for it. The enabling legislation stipulated 6% simple interest; Arcata argued for a much higher and compounded rate.

   Buying a company with a highly-speculative, large-sized claim in litigation creates a negotiating problem, whether the claim is on behalf of or against the company. To solve this problem, KKR offered $37.00 per Arcata share plus two-thirds of any additional amounts paid by the government for the redwood lands.

   Appraising this arbitrage opportunity, we had to ask ourselves whether KKR would consummate the transaction since, among other things, its offer was contingent upon its obtaining "satisfactory financing." A clause of this kind is always dangerous for the seller: It offers an easy exit for a suitor whose ardor fades between proposal and marriage. However, we were not particularly worried about this possibility because KKR's past record for closing had been good.

   We also had to ask ourselves what would happen if the KKR deal did fall through, and here we also felt reasonably comfortable: Arcata's management and directors had been shopping the company for some time and were clearly determined to sell. If KKR went away, Arcata would likely find another buyer, though of course, the price might be lower.

   Finally, we had to ask ourselves what the redwood claim might be worth. Your Chairman, who can't tell an elm from an oak, had no trouble with that one: He coolly evaluated the claim at somewhere between zero and a whole lot.

   We started buying Arcata stock, then around $33.50, on September 30 and in eight weeks purchased about 400,000 shares, or 5% of the company. The initial announcement said that the $37.00 would be paid in January, 1982. Therefore, if everything had gone perfectly, we would have achieved an annual rate of return of about 40%—not counting the redwood claim, which would have been frosting.

   All did not go perfectly. In December it was announced that the closing would be delayed a bit. Nevertheless, a definitive agreement was signed on January 4. Encouraged, we raised our stake, buying at around $38.00 per share and increasing our holdings to 655,000 shares, or over 7% of the company. Our willingness to pay up—even though the closing had been postponed—reflected our leaning toward "a whole lot" rather than "zero" for the redwoods.

   Then, on February 25 the lenders said they were taking a "second look" at financing terms "in view of the severely depressed housing industry and its impact on Arcata's outlook." The stockholders' meeting was postponed again, to April. An Arcata spokesman said he "did not think the fate of the acquisition itself was imperiled." When arbitrageurs hear such reassurances, their minds flash to the old saying: "He lied like a finance minister on the eve of devaluation."

On March 12 KKR said its earlier deal wouldn't work, first cutting its offer to $33.50, then two days later raising it to $35.00. On March 15, however, the directors turned this bid down and accepted another group's offer of $37.50 plus one-half of any redwood recovery. The shareholders okayed the deal, and the $37.50 was paid on June 4.

We received $24.6 million versus our cost of $22.9 million; our average holding period was close to six months. Considering the trouble this transaction encountered, our 15% annual rate of return—excluding any value for the redwood claim—was more than satisfactory.

But the best was yet to come. The trial judge appointed two commissions, one to look at the timber's value, the other to consider the interest rate questions. In January 1987, the first commission said the redwoods were worth $275.7 million and the second commission recommended a compounded, blended rate of return working out to about 14%.

In August 1987 the judge upheld these conclusions, which meant a net amount of about $600 million would be due Arcata. The government then appealed. In 1988, though, before this appeal was heard, the claim was settled for $519 million. Consequently, we received an additional $29.48 per share, or about $19.3 million. We will get another $800,000 or so in 1989.

Berkshire's arbitrage activities differ from those of many arbitrageurs. First, we participate in only a few, and usually very large, transactions each year. Most practitioners buy into a great many deals—perhaps 50 or more per year. With that many irons in the fire, they must spend most of their time monitoring both the progress of deals and the market movements of the related stocks. This is not how Charlie nor I wish to spend our lives. (What's the sense in getting rich just to stare at a ticker tape all day?)

Because we diversify so little, one particularly profitable or unprofitable transaction will affect our yearly result from arbitrage far more than it will the typical arbitrage operation. So far, Berkshire has not had a really bad experience. But we will—and when it happens we'll report the gory details to you.

The other way we differ from some arbitrage operations is that we participate only in transactions that have been publicly an-

nounced. We do not trade on rumors or try to guess takeover candidates. We just read the newspapers, think about a few of the big
propositions, and go by our own sense of probabilities.

At year end, our only major arbitrage position was 3,342,000
shares of RJR Nabisco with a cost of $281.8 million and a market
value of $304.5 million. In January we increased our holdings to
roughly four million shares and in February we eliminated our position. About three million shares were accepted when we ten-
dered our holdings to KKR, which acquired RJR, and the returned
shares were promptly sold in the market. Our pre-tax profit was a
better-than-expected $64 million.

Earlier, another familiar face turned up in the RJR bidding
contest: Jay Pritzker, who was part of a First Boston group that
made a tax-oriented offer. To quote Yogi Berra; "It was déjà vu all
over again."

During most of the time when we normally would have been
purchasers of RJR, our activities in the stock were restricted because of Salomon's participation in a bidding group. Customarily,
Charlie and I, though we are directors of Salomon, are walled off
from information about its merger and acquisition work. We have
asked that it be that way: The information would do us no good
and could, in fact, occasionally inhibit Berkshire's arbitrage
operations.

However, the unusually large commitment that Salomon proposed to make in the RJR deal required that all directors be fully
informed and involved. Therefore, Berkshire's purchases of RJR
were made at only two times: first, in the few days immediately
following management's announcement of buyout plans, before
Salomon became involved; and considerably later, after the RJR
board made its decision in favor of KKR. Because we could not
buy at other times, our directorships cost Berkshire significant
money.

Considering Berkshire's good results in 1988, you might expect us to pile into arbitrage during 1989. Instead, we expect to be
on the sidelines.

One pleasant reason is that our cash holdings are down—because our position in equities that we expect to hold for a very long
time is substantially up. As regular readers of this report know,
our new commitments are not based on a judgment about short-
term prospects for the stock market. Rather, they reflect an opinion about long-term business prospects for specific companies. We
do not have, never have had, and never will have an opinion about

where the stock market, interest rates, or business activity will be a year from now.

Even if we had a lot of cash we probably would do little in arbitrage in 1989. Some extraordinary excesses have developed in the takeover field. As Dorothy says: "Toto, I have a feeling we're not in Kansas any more."

We have no idea how long the excesses will last, nor do we know what will change the attitudes of government, lender and buyer that fuel them. But we do know that the less the prudence with which others conduct their affairs, the greater the prudence with which we should conduct our own affairs. We have no desire to arbitrage transactions that reflect the unbridled—and, in our view, often unwarranted—optimism of both buyers and lenders. In our activities, we will heed the wisdom of Herb Stein: "If something can't go on forever, it will end."

---

We told you last year that we expected to do little in arbitrage during 1989, and that's the way it turned out. Arbitrage positions are a substitute for short-term cash equivalents, and during part of the year we held relatively low levels of cash. In the rest of the year we had a fairly good-sized cash position and even so chose not to engage in arbitrage. The main reason was corporate transactions that made no economic sense to us; arbitraging such deals comes too close to playing the greater-fool game. (As Wall Streeter Ray DeVoe says: "Fools rush in where angels fear to trade.") We will engage in arbitrage from time to time—sometimes on a large scale—but only when we like the odds.

## C. *Debunking Standard Dogma*[19]

The preceding discussion about arbitrage makes a small discussion of "efficient market theory" (EMT) also seem relevant. This doctrine became highly fashionable—indeed, almost holy scripture—in academic circles during the 1970s. Essentially, it said that analyzing stocks was useless because all public information about them was appropriately reflected in their prices. In other words, the market always knew everything. As a corollary, the professors who taught EMT said that someone throwing darts at the stock tables could select a stock portfolio having prospects just as good as one selected by the brightest, most hard-working security analyst. Amazingly, EMT was embraced not only by academics,

---

[19] [Divided by hash lines: 1988; 1988; 1993; 1986; 1991; 1987.]

but by many investment professionals and corporate managers as well. Observing correctly that the market was *frequently* efficient, they went on to conclude incorrectly that it was *always* efficient. The difference between these propositions is night and day.

In my opinion, the continuous 63-year arbitrage experience of Graham-Newman Corp., Buffett Partnership, and Berkshire illustrates just how foolish EMT is. (There's plenty of other evidence, also.) While at Graham-Newman, I made a study of its earnings from arbitrage during the entire 1926-1956 lifespan of the company. Unleveraged returns averaged 20% per year. Starting in 1956, I applied Ben Graham's arbitrage principles, first at Buffett Partnership and then Berkshire. Though I've not made an exact calculation, I have done enough work to know that the 1956-1988 returns averaged well over 20%. (Of course, I operated in an environment far more favorable than Ben's; he had 1929-1932 to contend with.)

All of the conditions are present that are required for a fair test of portfolio performance: (1) the three organizations traded hundreds of different securities while building this 63-year record; (2) the results are not skewed by a few fortunate experiences; (3) we did not have to dig for obscure facts or develop keen insights about products or managements—we simply acted on highly-publicized events; and (4) our arbitrage positions were a clearly identified universe—they have not been selected by hindsight.

Over the 63 years, the general market delivered just under a 10% annual return, including dividends. That means $1,000 would have grown to $405,000 if all income had been reinvested. A 20% rate of return, however, would have produced $97 million. That strikes us a statistically-significant differential that might, conceivably, arouse one's curiosity.

Yet proponents of the theory have never seemed interested in discordant evidence of this type. True, they don't talk quite as much about their theory today as they used to. But no one, to my knowledge, has ever said he was wrong, no matter how many thousands of students he has sent forth misinstructed. EMT, moreover, continues to be an integral part of the investment curriculum at major business schools. Apparently, a reluctance to recant, and thereby to demystify the priesthood, is not limited to theologians.

Naturally the disservice done students and gullible investment professionals who have swallowed EMT has been an extraordinary service to us and other followers of Graham. In any sort of a contest—financial, mental, or physical—it's an enormous advantage to have opponents who have been taught that it's useless to even try. From a selfish point of view, Grahamites should probably endow chairs to ensure the perpetual teaching of EMT.

All this said, a warning is appropriate. Arbitrage has looked easy recently. But this is not a form of investing that guarantees profits of 20% a year or, for that matter, profits of any kind. As noted, the market is reasonably efficient much of the time: For every arbitrage opportunity we seized in that 63-year period, many more were foregone because they seemed properly-priced.

An investor cannot obtain superior profits from stocks by simply committing to a specific investment category or style. He can earn them only by carefully evaluating facts and continuously exercising discipline. Investing in arbitrage situations, per se, is no better a strategy than selecting a portfolio by throwing darts.

---

[W]hen we own portions of outstanding businesses with outstanding managements, our favorite holding period is forever. We are just the opposite of those who hurry to sell and book profits when companies perform well but who tenaciously hang on to businesses that disappoint. Peter Lynch aptly likens such behavior to cutting the flowers and watering the weeds.

---

[W]e continue to think that it is usually foolish to part with an interest in a business that is both understandable and durably wonderful. Business interests of that kind are simply too hard to replace.

Interestingly, corporate managers have no trouble understanding that point when they are focusing on a business they operate: A parent company that owns a subsidiary with superb long-term economics is not likely to sell that entity regardless of price. "Why," the CEO would ask, "should I part with my crown jewel?" Yet that same CEO, when it comes to running his personal investment portfolio, will offhandedly—and even impetuously—move from business to business when presented with no more than superficial arguments by his broker for doing so. The worst of these is perhaps, "You can't go broke taking a profit." Can you imagine a CEO using this line to urge his board to sell a star subsidiary? In our view, what makes sense in business also makes sense in stocks: An investor should ordinarily hold a small piece of an outstanding business with the same tenacity that an owner would exhibit if he owned all of that business.

Earlier I mentioned the financial results that could have been achieved by investing $40 in The Coca-Cola Co. in 1919.[20] In 1938, more than 50 years after the introduction of Coke, and long after the drink was firmly established as an American icon, *Fortune* did an excellent story on the company. In the second paragraph the writer reported: "Several times every year a weighty and serious investor looks long and with profound respect at Coca-Cola's record, but comes regretfully to the conclusion that he is looking too late. The specters of saturation and competition rise before him."

Yes, competition there was in 1938 and in 1993 as well. But it's worth noting that in 1938 The Coca-Cola Co. sold 207 million cases of soft drinks (if its gallonage then is converted into the 192-ounce cases used for measurement today) and in 1993 it sold about 10.7 billion cases, a 50-fold increase in physical volume from a company that in 1938 was already dominant in its very major industry. Nor was the party over in 1938 for an investor: Though the $40 invested in 1919 in one share had (with dividends reinvested) turned into $3,277 by the end of 1938, a fresh $40 then invested in Coca-Cola stock would have grown to $25,000 by year end 1993.

I can't resist one more quote from that 1938 *Fortune* story: "It would be hard to name any company comparable in size to Coca-Cola and selling, as Coca-Cola does, an unchanged product that can point to a ten-year record anything like Coca-Cola's." In the 55 years that have since passed, Coke's product line has broadened somewhat, but it's remarkable how well that description still fits.

Charlie and I decided long ago that in an investment lifetime it's too hard to make hundreds of smart decisions. That judgment became ever more compelling as Berkshire's capital mushroomed and the universe of investments that could significantly affect our results shrank dramatically. Therefore, we adopted a strategy that required our being smart—and not too smart at that—only a very few times. Indeed, we'll now settle for one good idea a year. (Charlie says it's my turn.)

The strategy we've adopted precludes our following standard diversification dogma. Many pundits would therefore say the strat-

---

[20] [A separate paragraph from this 1993 letter provided as follows:]

Let me add a lesson from history: Coke went public in 1919 at $40 per share. By the end of 1920 the market, coldly reevaluating Coke's future prospects, had battered the stock down by more than 50%, to $19.50. At year end 1993, that single share, with dividends reinvested, was worth more than $2.1 million. As Ben Graham said: "In the short-run, the market is a voting machine—reflecting a voter-registration test that requires only money, not intelligence or emotional stability—but in the long-run, the market is a weighing machine."

egy must be riskier than that employed by more conventional investors. We disagree. We believe that a policy of portfolio concentration may well *decrease* risk if it raises, as it should, both the intensity with which an investor thinks about a business and the comfort-level he must feel with its economic characteristics before buying into it. In stating this opinion, we define risk, using dictionary terms, as "the possibility of loss or injury."

Academics, however, like to define investment "risk" differently, averring that it is the relative volatility of a stock or portfolio of stocks—that is, their volatility as compared to that of a large universe of stocks. Employing data bases and statistical skills, these academics compute with precision the "beta" of a stock—its relative volatility in the past—and then build arcane investment and capital-allocation theories around this calculation. In their hunger for a single statistic to measure risk, however, they forget a fundamental principle: It is better to be approximately right than precisely wrong.

For owners of a business—and that's the way we think of shareholders—the academics' definition of risk is far off the mark, so much so that it produces absurdities. For example, under beta-based theory, a stock that has dropped very sharply compared to the market—as had Washington Post when we bought it in 1973—becomes "riskier" at the lower price than it was at the higher price. Would that description have then made any sense to someone who was offered the entire company at a vastly-reduced price?

In fact, the true investor *welcomes* volatility. Ben Graham explained why in Chapter 8 of *The Intelligent Investor*. There he introduced "Mr. Market," an obliging fellow [noted above] who shows up every day to either buy from you or sell to you, whichever you wish. The more manic-depressive this chap is, the greater the opportunities available to the investor. That's true because a wildly fluctuating market means that irrationally low prices will periodically be attached to solid businesses. It is impossible to see how the availability of such prices can be thought of as increasing the hazards for an investor who is totally free to either ignore the market or exploit its folly.

In assessing risk, a beta purist will disdain examining what a company produces, what its competitors are doing, or how much borrowed money the business employs. He may even prefer not to know the company's name. What he treasures is the price history of its stock. In contrast, we'll happily forgo knowing the price history and instead will seek whatever information will further our understanding of the company's business. After we buy a stock, consequently, we would not be disturbed if markets closed for a year or two. We don't need a daily quote on our 100% position in See's or H.H. Brown to validate our well-being. Why, then, should we need a quote on our 7% interest in Coke?

In our opinion, the real risk an investor must assess is whether his aggregate after-tax receipts from an investment (including those he receives on sale) will, over his prospective holding period, give him at least as much purchasing power as he had to begin with, plus a modest rate of interest on that initial stake. Though this risk cannot be calculated with engineering precision, it can in some cases be judged with a degree of accuracy that is useful. The primary factors bearing upon this evaluation are:

    (1) The certainty with which the long-term economic characteristics of the business can be evaluated;

    (2) The certainty with which management can be evaluated, both as to its ability to realize the full potential of the business and to wisely employ its cash flows;

    (3) The certainty with which management can be counted on to channel the reward from the business to the shareholders rather than to itself;

    (4) The purchase price of the business;

    (5) The levels of taxation and inflation that will be experienced and that will determine the degree by which an investor's purchasing-power return is reduced from his gross return.

These factors will probably strike many analysts as unbearably fuzzy since they cannot be extracted from a data base of any kind. But the difficulty of precisely quantifying these matters does not negate their importance nor is it insuperable. Just as Justice Stewart found it impossible to formulate a test for obscenity but nevertheless asserted, "I know it when I see it," so also can investors—in an inexact but useful way—"see" the risks inherent in certain investments without reference to complex equations or price histories.

Is it really so difficult to conclude that Coca-Cola and Gillette possess far less business risk over the long term than, say, any computer company or retailer? Worldwide, Coke sells about 44% of all soft drinks, and Gillette has more than a 60% share (in value) of the blade market. Leaving aside chewing gum, in which Wrigley is dominant, I know of no other significant businesses in which the leading company has long enjoyed such global power.

Moreover, both Coke and Gillette have actually increased their worldwide shares of market in recent years. The might of their brand names, the attributes of their products, and the strength of their distribution systems give them an enormous competitive advantage, setting up a protective moat around their economic castles. The average company, in contrast, does battle daily without any such means of protection. As Peter Lynch says, stocks of companies selling commodity-like products should come with a warning label: "Competition may prove hazardous to human wealth."

The competitive strengths of a Coke or Gillette are obvious to even the casual observer of business. Yet the beta of their stocks is similar to that of a great many run-of-the-mill companies who possess little or no competitive advantage. Should we conclude from this similarity that the competitive strength of Coke and Gillette gains them nothing when business risk is being measured? Or should we conclude that the risk in owning a piece of a company— its stock—is somehow divorced from the long-term risk inherent in its business operations? We believe neither conclusion makes sense and that equating beta with investment risk makes no sense.

The theoretician bred on beta has no mechanism for differentiating the risk inherent in, say, a single-product toy company selling pet rocks or hula hoops from that of another toy company whose sole product is Monopoly or Barbie. But it's quite possible for ordinary investors to make such distinctions if they have a reasonable understanding of consumer behavior and the factors that create long-term competitive strength or weakness. Obviously, every investor will make mistakes. But by confining himself to a relatively few, easy-to-understand cases, a reasonably intelligent, informed and diligent person can judge investment risks with a useful degree of accuracy.

In many industries, of course, Charlie and I can't determine whether we are dealing with a "pet rock" or a "Barbie." We couldn't solve this problem, moreover, even if we were to spend years intensely studying those industries. Sometimes our own intellectual shortcomings would stand in the way of understanding, and in other cases the nature of the industry would be the roadblock. For example, a business that must deal with fast-moving technology is not going to lend itself to reliable evaluations of its long-term economics. Did we foresee thirty years ago what would transpire in the television-manufacturing or computer industries? Of course not. (Nor did most of the investors and corporate managers who enthusiastically entered those industries.) Why, then, should Charlie and I now think we can predict the future of other rapidly-evolving businesses? We'll stick instead with the easy cases. Why search for a needle buried in a haystack when one is sitting in plain sight?

Of course, some investment strategies—for instance, our efforts in arbitrage over the years—require wide diversification. If significant risk exists in a single transaction, overall risk should be reduced by making that purchase one of many mutually-independent commitments. Thus, you may consciously purchase a risky investment—one that indeed has a significant possibility of causing loss or injury—if you believe that your gain, weighted for probabilities, considerably exceeds your loss, comparably weighted, and if you can commit to a number of similar, but unrelated opportunities. Most venture capitalists employ this strategy. Should you choose to pursue this course, you should adopt the outlook of the casino that owns a roulette wheel, which will want to see lots of action because it is favored by probabilities, but will refuse to accept a single, huge bet.

Another situation requiring wide diversification occurs when an investor who does not understand the economics of specific businesses nevertheless believes it in his interest to be a long-term owner of American industry. That investor should both own a large number of equities and space out his purchases. By periodically investing in an index fund, for example, the know-nothing investor can actually out-perform most investment professionals. Paradoxically, when "dumb" money acknowledges its limitations, it ceases to be dumb.

On the other hand, if you are a know-something investor, able to understand business economics and to find five to ten sensibly-priced companies that possess important long-term competitive advantages, conventional diversification makes no sense for you. It is apt simply to hurt your results and increase your risk. I cannot understand why an investor of that sort elects to put money into a business that is his 20th favorite rather than simply adding that money to his top choices—the businesses he understands best and that present the least risk, along with the greatest profit potential. In the words of the prophet Mae West: "Too much of a good thing can be wonderful."

———————————

We should note that we expect to keep permanently our three primary holdings, Capital Cities/ABC, Inc., GEICO Corporation, and The Washington Post.[21]  Even if these securities were to appear significantly overpriced, we would not anticipate selling them, just as we would not sell See's or Buffalo Evening News if someone were to offer us a price far above what we believe those businesses are worth.

This attitude may seem old-fashioned in a corporate world in which activity has become the order of the day.  The modern manager refers to his "portfolio" of businesses—meaning that all of them are candidates for "restructuring" whenever such a move is dictated by Wall Street preferences, operating conditions or a new corporate "concept." (Restructuring is defined narrowly, however: it extends only to dumping offending businesses, not to dumping the officers and directors who bought the businesses in the first place.  "Hate the sin but love the sinner" is a theology as popular with the Fortune 500 as it is with the Salvation Army.)

Investment managers are even more hyperkinetic: their behavior during trading hours makes whirling dervishes appear sedated by comparison.  Indeed, the term "institutional investor" is becoming one of those self-contradictions called an oxymoron, comparable to "jumbo shrimp," "lady mudwrestler" and "inexpensive lawyer."

Despite the enthusiasm for activity that has swept business and financial America, we will stick with our 'til-death-do-us-part policy.  It's the only one with which Charlie and I are comfortable, it produces decent results, and it lets our managers and those of our investees run their businesses free of distractions.

———————————

Our stay-put behavior reflects our view that the stock market serves as a relocation center at which money is moved from the active to the patient.  (With tongue only partly in check, I suggest that recent events indicate that the much-maligned "idle rich" have received a bad rap: They have maintained or increased their wealth while many of the "energetic rich"—aggressive real estate operators, corporate acquirers, oil drillers, etc.—have seen their fortunes disappear.)

We continually search for large businesses with understandable, enduring and mouth-watering economics that are run by able and shareholder-oriented managements.  This focus doesn't guarantee results: We both have to buy at a sensible price and get busi-

———————————

21 [Berkshire's Capital Cities/ABC holdings left the "primary and permanent" category following its 1996 acquisition, for stock and cash, by The Walt Disney Company.]

ness performance from our companies that validates our assessment. But this investment approach—searching for the superstars—offers us our only chance for real success. Charlie and I are simply not smart enough, considering the large sums we work with, to get great results by adroitly buying and selling portions of far-from-great businesses. Nor do we think many others can achieve long-term investment success by flitting from flower to flower. Indeed, we believe that according the name "investors" to institutions that trade actively is like calling someone who repeatedly engages in one-night stands a romantic.

If my universe of business possibilities was limited, say, to private companies in Omaha, I would, first, try to assess the long-term economic characteristics of each business; second, assess the quality of the people in charge of running it; and, third, try to buy into a few of the best operations at a sensible price. I certainly would not wish to own an equal part of every business in town. Why, then, should Berkshire take a different tack when dealing with the larger universe of public companies? And since finding great businesses and outstanding managers is so difficult, why should we discard proven products? (I was tempted to say "the real thing.") Our motto is: "If at first you do succeed, quit trying."

John Maynard Keynes, whose brilliance as a practicing investor matched his brilliance in thought, wrote a letter to a business associate, F.C. Scott, on August 15, 1934 that says it all: "As time goes on, I get more and more convinced that the right method in investment is to put fairly large sums into enterprises which one thinks one knows something about and in the management of which one thoroughly believes. It is a mistake to think that one limits one's risk by spreading too much between enterprises about which one knows little and has no reason for special confidence. One's knowledge and experience are definitely limited and there are seldom more than two or three enterprises at any given time in which I personally feel myself entitled to put *full* confidence."

---

During 1987 the stock market was an area of much excitement but little net movement: The Dow advanced 2.3% for the year. You are aware, of course, of the roller coaster ride that produced this minor change. Mr. Market was on a manic rampage until October and then experienced a sudden, massive seizure.

We have "professional" investors, those who manage many billions, to thank for most of this turmoil. Instead of focusing on what businesses will do in the years ahead, many prestigious money managers now focus on what they expect other money managers to do in the days ahead. For them, stocks are merely tokens in a game, like the thimble and flatiron in Monopoly.

An extreme example of what their attitude leads to is "portfolio insurance," a money-management strategy that many leading investment advisors embraced in 1986-1987. This strategy—which is simply an exotically-labeled version of the small speculator's stop-loss order—dictates that ever-increasing portions of a stock portfolio, or their index-future equivalents, be sold as prices decline. The strategy says nothing else matters: A downtick of a given magnitude automatically produces a huge sell order. According to the Brady Report, $60 billion to $90 billion of equities were poised on this hair trigger in mid-October of 1987.

If you've thought that investment advisors were hired to invest, you may be bewildered by this technique. After buying a farm, would a rational owner next order his real estate agent to start selling off pieces of it whenever a neighboring property was sold at a lower price? Or would you sell your house to whatever bidder was available at 9:31 on some morning merely because at 9:30 a similar house sold for less than it would have brought on the previous day?

Moves like that, however, are what portfolio insurance tells a pension fund or university to make when it owns a portion of enterprises such as Ford or General Electric. The less these companies are being valued at, says this approach, the more vigorously they should be sold. As a "logical" corollary, the approach commands the institutions to repurchase these companies—*I'm not making this up*—once their prices have rebounded significantly. Considering that huge sums are controlled by managers following such Alice-in-Wonderland practices, is it any surprise that markets sometimes behave in aberrational fashion?

Many commentators, however, have drawn an incorrect conclusion upon observing recent events: They are fond of saying that the small investor has no chance in a market now dominated by the erratic behavior of the big boys. This conclusion is dead wrong: Such markets are ideal for any investor—small or large—so long as he sticks to his investment knitting. Volatility caused by money managers who speculate irrationally with huge sums will offer the true investor more chances to make intelligent investment moves. He can be hurt by such volatility only if he is forced, by either financial or psychological pressures, to sell at untoward times.

### D. *"Value" Investing: A Redundancy*[22]

We really don't see many fundamental differences between the purchase of a controlled business and the purchase of marketable holdings. In each case we try to buy into businesses with favorable long-term economics. Our goal is to find an outstanding business at a sensible price, not a mediocre business at a bargain price. Charlie and I have found that making silk purses out of silk is the best that we can do; with sow's ears, we fail.

(It must be noted that your Chairman, always a quick study, required only 20 years to recognize how important it was to buy good businesses. In the interim, I searched for "bargains"—and had the misfortune to find some. My punishment was an education in the economics of short-line farm implement manufacturers, third-place department stores, and New England textile manufacturers.)

Of course, Charlie and I may misread the fundamental economics of a business. When that happens, we will encounter problems whether that business is a wholly-owned subsidiary or a marketable security, although it is usually far easier to exit from the latter. (Indeed, businesses can be misread: Witness the European reporter who, after being sent to this country to profile Andrew Carnegie, cabled his editor, "My God, you'll never believe the sort of money there is in running libraries.")

In making both control purchases and stock purchases, we try to buy not only good businesses, but ones run by high-grade, talented and likeable managers. If we make a mistake about the managers we link up with, the controlled company offers a certain advantage because we have the power to effect change. In practice, however, this advantage is somewhat illusory: Management changes, like marital changes, are painful, time-consuming and chancy. In any event, at our three marketable-but-permanent holdings, this point is moot: With Tom Murphy and Dan Burke at Cap Cities, Bill Snyder and Lou Simpson at GEICO, and Kay Graham and Dick Simmons at The Washington Post, we simply couldn't be in better hands.

I would say that the controlled company offers two main advantages. First, when we control a company we get to allocate capital, whereas we are likely to have little or nothing to say about this process with marketable holdings. This point can be important because the heads of many companies are not skilled in capital alloca-

---

22 [Divided by hash lines: 1987; 1992; 1985.]

tion. Their inadequacy is not surprising. Most bosses rise to the top because they have excelled in an area such as marketing, production, engineering, administration—or, sometimes, institutional politics.

Once they become CEOs, they face new responsibilities. They now must make capital allocation decisions, a critical job that they may have never tackled and that is not easily mastered. To stretch the point, it's as if the final step for a highly-talented musician was not to perform at Carnegie Hall but, instead, to be named Chairman of the Federal Reserve.

The lack of skill that many CEOs have at capital allocation is no small matter: After ten years on the job, a CEO whose company annually retains earnings equal to 10% of net worth will have been responsible for the deployment of more than 60% of all the capital at work in the business.

CEOs who recognize their lack of capital-allocation skills (which not all do) will often try to compensate by turning to their staffs, management consultants, or investment bankers. Charlie and I have frequently observed the consequences of such "help." On balance, we feel it is more likely to accentuate the capital-allocation problem than to solve it.

In the end, plenty of unintelligent capital allocation takes place in corporate America. (That's why you hear so much about "restructuring.") Berkshire, however, has been fortunate. At the companies that are our major non-controlled holdings, capital has generally been well-deployed and, in some cases, brilliantly so.

The second advantage of a controlled company over a marketable security has to do with taxes. Berkshire, as a corporate holder, absorbs some significant tax costs through the ownership of partial positions that we do not when our ownership is 80% or greater. Such tax disadvantages have long been with us, but changes in the tax code caused them to increase significantly during [1986]. As a consequence, a given business result can now deliver Berkshire financial results that are as much as 50% better if they come from an 80%-or-greater holding rather than from a lesser holding.

The disadvantages of owning marketable securities are sometimes offset by a huge advantage: Occasionally the stock market offers us the chance to buy non-controlling pieces of extraordinary businesses at truly ridiculous prices—dramatically below those commanded in negotiated transactions that transfer control. For example, we purchased our Washington Post stock in 1973 at $5.63

per share, and per-share operating earnings in 1987 after taxes were $10.30. Similarly, our GEICO stock was purchased in 1976, 1979 and 1980 at an average of $6.67 per share, and after-tax operating earnings per share last year were $9.01. In cases such as these, Mr. Market has proven to be a mighty good friend.

------

Our equity-investing strategy remains little changed from what it was when we said in the 1977 annual report: "We select our marketable equity securities in much the way we would evaluate a business for acquisition in its entirety. We want the business to be one (a) that we can understand; (b) with favorable long-term prospects; (c) operated by honest and competent people; and (d) available at a very attractive price." We have seen cause to make only one change in this creed: Because of both market conditions and our size, we now substitute "an attractive price" for "a very attractive price."

But how, you will ask, does one decide what's "attractive"? In answering this question, most analysts feel they must choose between two approaches customarily thought to be in opposition: "value" and "growth." Indeed, many investment professionals see any mixing of the two terms as a form of intellectual cross-dressing.

We view that as fuzzy thinking (in which, it must be confessed, I myself engaged some years ago). In our opinion, the two approaches are joined at the hip: Growth is *always* a component in the calculation of value, constituting a variable whose importance can range from negligible to enormous and whose impact can be negative as well as positive.

In addition, we think the very term "value investing" is redundant. What is "investing" if it is not the act of seeking value at least sufficient to justify the amount paid? Consciously paying more for a stock than its calculated value—in the hope that it can soon be sold for a still-higher price—should be labeled speculation (which is neither illegal, immoral nor—in our view—financially fattening).

Whether appropriate or not, the term "value investing" is widely used. Typically, it connotes the purchase of stocks having attributes such as a low ratio of price to book value, a low price-earnings ratio, or a high dividend yield. Unfortunately, such characteristics, even if they appear in combination, are far from determinative as to whether an investor is indeed buying something for what it is worth and is therefore truly operating on the principle of obtaining value in his investments. Correspondingly, opposite characteristics—a high ratio of price to book value, a high price-earnings ratio, and a low dividend yield—are in no way inconsistent with a "value" purchase.

Similarly, business growth, per se, tells us little about value. It's true that growth often has a positive impact on value, sometimes one of spectacular proportions. But such an effect is far from certain. For example, investors have regularly poured money into the domestic airline business to finance profitless (or worse) growth. For these investors, it would have been far better if Orville had failed to get off the ground at Kitty Hawk: The more the industry has grown, the worse the disaster for owners.

Growth benefits investors only when the business in point can invest at incremental returns that are enticing—in other words, only when each dollar used to finance the growth creates over a dollar of long-term market value. In the case of a low-return business requiring incremental funds, growth hurts the investor.

In *The Theory of Investment Value*, written over 50 years ago, John Burr Williams set forth the equation for value, which we condense here: *The value of any stock, bond or business today is determined by the cash inflows and outflows—discounted at an appropriate interest rate—that can be expected to occur during the remaining life of the asset.* Note that the formula is the same for stocks as for bonds. Even so, there is an important, and difficult to deal with, difference between the two: A bond has a coupon and maturity date that define future cash flows; but in the case of equities, the investment analyst must himself estimate the future "coupons." Furthermore, the quality of management affects the bond coupon only rarely—chiefly when management is so inept or dishonest that payment of interest is suspended. In contrast, the ability of management can dramatically affect the equity "coupons."

The investment shown by the discounted-flows-of-cash calculation to be the cheapest is the one that the investor should purchase—irrespective of whether the business grows or doesn't, displays volatility or smoothness in its earnings, or carries a high price or low [price] in relation to its current earnings and book value. Moreover, though the value equation has usually shown equities to be cheaper than bonds, that result is not inevitable: When bonds are calculated to be the more attractive investment, they should be bought.

Leaving the question of price aside, the best business to own is one that over an extended period can employ large amounts of incremental capital at very high rates of return. The worst business to own is one that must, or *will*, do the opposite—that is, consistently employ ever-greater amounts of capital at very low rates of return. Unfortunately, the first type of business is very hard to find: Most high-return businesses need relatively little capital. Shareholders of such a business usually will benefit if it pays out most of its earnings in dividends or makes significant stock repurchases.

Though the mathematical calculations required to evaluate equities are not difficult, an analyst—even one who is experienced and intelligent—can easily go wrong in estimating future "coupons." At Berkshire, we attempt to deal with this problem in two ways. First, we try to stick to businesses we believe we understand. That means they must be relatively simple and stable in character. If a business is complex or subject to constant change, we're not smart enough to predict future cash flows. Incidentally, that shortcoming doesn't bother us. What counts for most people in investing is not how much they know, but rather how realistically they define what they don't know. An investor needs to do very few things right as long as he or she avoids big mistakes.

Second, and equally important, we insist on a margin of safety in our purchase price. If we calculate the value of a common stock to be only slightly higher than its price, we're not interested in buying. We believe this margin-of-safety principle, so strongly emphasized by Ben Graham, to be the cornerstone of investment success.

[A]n intelligent investor in common stocks will do better in the secondary market than he will do buying new issues. The reason has to do with the way prices are set in each instance. The secondary market, which is periodically ruled by mass folly, is constantly setting a "clearing" price. No matter how foolish that price may be, it's what counts for the holder of a stock or bond who needs or wishes to sell, of whom there are always going to be a few at any moment. In many instances, shares worth $x$ in business value have sold in the market for $\frac{1}{2}x$ or less.

The new-issue market, on the other hand, is ruled by controlling stockholders and corporations, who can usually select the timing of offerings or, if the market looks unfavorable, can avoid an offering altogether. Understandably, these sellers are not going to offer any bargains, either by way of a public offering or in a negotiated transaction: It's rare you'll find $x$ for $\frac{1}{2}x$ here. Indeed, in the case of common-stock offerings, selling shareholders are often motivated to unload only when they feel the market is overpaying. (These sellers, of course, would state that proposition somewhat differently, averring instead that they simply resist selling when the market is underpaying for their goods.)

———————

Right after year end, Berkshire purchased 3 million shares of Capital Cities/ABC, Inc. ("Cap Cities") at $172.50 per share, the market price of such shares at the time the commitment was made early in March, 1985. I've been on record for many years about the management of Cap Cities: I think it is the best of any publicly-owned company in the country. And Tom Murphy and Dan Burke are not only great managers, they are precisely the sort of fellows that you would want your daughter to marry. It is a privilege to be associated with them—and also a lot of fun, as any of you who know them will understand.

Our purchase of stock helped Cap Cities finance the $3.5 billion acquisition of American Broadcasting Companies. For Cap Cities, ABC is a major undertaking whose economics are likely to be unexciting over the next few years. This bothers us not an iota; we can be very patient. (No matter how great the talent or effort, some things just take time: you can't produce a baby in one month by getting nine women pregnant.)

As evidence of our confidence, we have executed an unusual agreement: for an extended period Tom, as CEO (or Dan, should he be CEO) votes our stock. This arrangement was initiated by Charlie and me, not by Tom. We also have restricted ourselves in various ways regarding sale of our shares. The object of these restrictions is to make sure that our block does not get sold to anyone who is a large holder (or intends to become a large holder) without the approval of management, an arrangement similar to ones we initiated some years ago at GEICO and Washington Post.

Since large blocks frequently command premium prices, some might think we have injured Berkshire financially by creating such restrictions. Our view is just the opposite. We feel the long-term economic prospects for these businesses—and, thus, for ourselves as owners—are enhanced by the arrangements. With them in place, the first-class managers with whom we have aligned ourselves can focus their efforts entirely upon running the businesses and maximizing long-term values for owners. Certainly this is much better than having those managers distracted by "revolving-door capitalists" hoping to put the company "in play." (Of course, some managers place their own interests above those of the company and its owners and deserve to be shaken up—but, in making investments, we try to steer clear of this type.)

Today, corporate instability is an inevitable consequence of widely-diffused ownership of voting stock. At any time a major holder can surface, usually mouthing reassuring rhetoric but frequently harboring uncivil intentions. By circumscribing our blocks of stock as we often do, we intend to promote stability where it otherwise might be lacking. That kind of certainty, combined with a good manager and a good business, provides excellent soil for a rich financial harvest. That's the economic case for our arrangements.

The human side is just as important. We don't want managers we like and admire—and who have welcomed a major financial commitment by us—to ever lose any sleep wondering whether surprises might occur because of our large ownership. I have told them there will be no surprises, and these agreements put Berkshire's signature where my mouth is. That signature also means the managers have a corporate commitment and therefore need not worry if my personal participation in Berkshire's affairs ends prematurely (a term I define as any age short of three digits).

Our Cap Cities purchase was made at a full price, reflecting the very considerable enthusiasm for both media stocks and media properties that has developed in recent years (and that, in the case of some property purchases, has approached a mania). It's no field for bargains. However, our Cap Cities investment allies us with an exceptional combination of properties and people—and we like the opportunity to participate in size.

Of course, some of you probably wonder why we are now buying Cap Cities at $172.50 per share given that your Chairman, in a characteristic burst of brilliance, sold Berkshire's holdings in the same company at $43 per share in 1978-80. Anticipating your question, I spent much of 1985 working on a snappy answer that would reconcile these acts.

A little more time, please.

## E.　*Intelligent Investing*[23]

Inactivity strikes us as intelligent behavior. Neither we nor most business managers would dream of feverishly trading highly-profitable subsidiaries because a small move in the Federal Reserve's discount rate was predicted or because some Wall Street pundit had reversed his views on the market. Why, then, should we behave differently with our minority positions in wonderful

---

[23] [Divided by hash lines: 1996; 1999; 1997.]

businesses? The art of investing in public companies successfully is little different from the art of successfully acquiring subsidiaries. In each case you simply want to acquire, at a sensible price, a business with excellent economics and able, honest management. Thereafter, you need only monitor whether these qualities are being preserved.

When carried out capably, an investment strategy of that type will often result in its practitioner owning a few securities that will come to represent a very large portion of his portfolio. This investor would get a similar result if he followed a policy of purchasing an interest in, say, 20% of the future earnings of a number of outstanding college basketball stars. A handful of these would go on to achieve NBA stardom, and the investor's take from them would soon dominate his royalty stream. To suggest that this investor should sell off portions of his most successful investments simply because they have come to dominate his portfolio is akin to suggesting that the Bulls trade Michael Jordan because he has become so important to the team.

In studying the investments we have made in both subsidiary companies and common stocks, you will see that we favor businesses and industries unlikely to experience major change. The reason for that is simple: Making either type of purchase, we are searching for operations that we believe are virtually certain to possess enormous competitive strength ten or twenty years from now. A fast-changing industry environment may offer the chance for huge wins, but it precludes the certainty we seek.

I should emphasize that, as citizens, Charlie and I welcome change: Fresh ideas, new products, innovative processes and the like cause our country's standard of living to rise, and that's clearly good. As investors, however, our reaction to a fermenting industry is much like our attitude toward space exploration: We applaud the endeavor but prefer to skip the ride.

Obviously all businesses change to some extent. Today, See's is different in many ways from what it was in 1972 when we bought it: It offers a different assortment of candy, employs different machinery and sells through different distribution channels. But the reasons why people today buy boxed chocolates, and why they buy them from us rather than from someone else, are virtually unchanged from what they were in the 1920s when the See family was building the business. Moreover, these motivations are not likely to change over the next 20 years, or even 50.

We look for similar predictability in marketable securities. Take Coca-Cola: The zeal and imagination with which Coke products are sold has burgeoned under Roberto Goizueta, who has done an absolutely incredible job in creating value for his shareholders. Aided by Don Keough and Doug Ivester, Roberto has rethought and improved every aspect of the company. But the fundamentals of the business—the qualities that underlie Coke's competitive dominance and stunning economics—have remained constant through the years.

I was recently studying the 1896 report of Coke (and you think that you are behind in your reading!). At that time Coke, though it was already the leading soft drink, had been around for only a decade. But its blueprint for the next 100 years was already drawn. Reporting sales of $148,000 that year, Asa Candler, the company's president, said: "We have not lagged in our efforts to go into all the world teaching that Coca-Cola is the article, par excellence, for the health and good feeling of all people." Though "health" may have been a reach, I love the fact that Coke still relies on Candler's basic theme today—a century later. Candler went on to say, just as Roberto could now, "No article of like character has ever so firmly entrenched itself in public favor." Sales of syrup that year, incidentally, were 116,492 gallons versus about 3.2 billion in 1996.

I can't resist one more Candler quote: "Beginning this year about March 1st . . . we employed ten traveling salesmen by means of which, with systematic correspondence from the office, we covered almost the territory of the Union." That's my kind of sales force.

Companies such as Coca-Cola and Gillette might well be labeled "The Inevitables." Forecasters may differ a bit in their predictions of exactly how much soft drink or shaving-equipment business these companies will be doing in ten or twenty years. Nor is our talk of inevitability meant to play down the vital work that these companies must continue to carry out, in such areas as manufacturing, distribution, packaging and product innovation. In the end, however, no sensible observer—not even these companies' most vigorous competitors, assuming they are assessing the matter honestly—questions that Coke and Gillette will dominate their fields worldwide for an investment lifetime. Indeed, their dominance will probably strengthen. Both companies have significantly expanded their already huge shares of market during the past ten years, and all signs point to their repeating that performance in the next decade.

Obviously many companies in high-tech businesses or embryonic industries will grow much faster in percentage terms than will The Inevitables. But I would rather be certain of a good result than hopeful of a great one.

Of course, Charlie and I can identify only a few Inevitables, even after a lifetime of looking for them. Leadership alone provides no certainties: Witness the shocks some years back at General Motors, IBM and Sears, all of which had enjoyed long periods of seeming invincibility. Though some industries or lines of business exhibit characteristics that endow leaders with virtually insurmountable advantages, and that tend to establish Survival of the Fattest as almost a natural law, most do not. Thus, for every Inevitable, there are dozens of Impostors, companies now riding high but vulnerable to competitive attacks. Considering what it takes to be an Inevitable, Charlie and I recognize that we will never be able to come up with a Nifty Fifty or even a Twinkling Twenty. To the Inevitables in our portfolio, therefore, we add a few "Highly Probables."

You can, of course, pay too much for even the best of businesses. The overpayment risk surfaces periodically and, in our opinion, may now be quite high for the purchasers of virtually all stocks, The Inevitables included. Investors making purchases in an overheated market need to recognize that it may often take an extended period for the value of even an outstanding company to catch up with the price they paid.

A far more serious problem occurs when the management of a great company gets sidetracked and neglects its wonderful base business while purchasing other businesses that are so-so or worse. When that happens, the suffering of investors is often prolonged. Unfortunately, that is precisely what transpired years ago at both Coke and Gillette. (Would you believe that a few decades back they were growing shrimp at Coke and exploring for oil at Gillette?) Loss of focus is what most worries Charlie and me when we contemplate investing in businesses that in general look outstanding. All too often, we've seen value stagnate in the presence of hubris or of boredom that caused the attention of managers to wander. That's not going to happen again at Coke and Gillette, however—not given their current and prospective managements.

\*  \*  \*  \*  \*

Let me add a few thoughts about your own investments. Most investors, both institutional and individual, will find that the best way to own common stocks is through an index fund that charges minimal fees. Those following this path are sure to beat the net results (after fees and expenses) delivered by the great majority of investment professionals.

Should you choose, however, to construct your own portfolio, there are a few thoughts worth remembering. Intelligent investing is not complex, though that is far from saying that it is easy. What an investor needs is the ability to correctly evaluate selected businesses. Note that word "selected": You don't have to be an expert on every company, or even many. You only have to be able to evaluate companies within your circle of competence. The size of that circle is not very important; knowing its boundaries, however, is vital.

To invest successfully, you need not understand beta, efficient markets, modern portfolio theory, option pricing, or emerging markets. You may, in fact, be better off knowing nothing of these. That, of course, is not the prevailing view at most business schools, whose finance curriculum tends to be dominated by such subjects. In our view, though, investment students need only two well-taught courses—How to Value a Business, and How to Think About Market Prices.

Your goal as an investor should simply be to purchase, at a rational price, a part interest in an easily-understandable business whose earnings are virtually certain to be materially higher five, ten and twenty years from now. Over time, you will find only a few companies that meet these standards—so when you see one that qualifies, you should buy a meaningful amount of stock. You must also resist the temptation to stray from your guidelines: If you aren't willing to own a stock for ten years, don't even think about owning it for ten minutes. Put together a portfolio of companies whose aggregate earnings march upward over the years, and so also will the portfolio's market value.

Though it's seldom recognized, this is the exact approach that has produced gains for Berkshire shareholders: Our look-through earnings have grown at a good clip over the years, and our stock price has risen correspondingly. Had those gains in earnings not materialized, there would have been little increase in Berkshire's value.

––––––––––––

[S]everal of the companies in which we have large investments had disappointing business results last year. Nevertheless, we believe these companies have important competitive advantages that will endure over time. This attribute, which makes for good long-term investment results, is one Charlie and I occasionally believe we can identify. More often, however, we can't–not at least with a high degree of conviction. This explains, by the way, why we don't own stocks of tech companies, even though we share the general view that our society will be transformed by their products and services. Our problem–which we can't solve by studying up–is that we have no insights into which participants in the tech field possess a truly *durable* competitive advantage.

Our lack of tech insights, we should add, does not distress us. After all, there are a great many business areas in which Charlie and I have no special capital-allocation expertise. For instance, we bring nothing to the table when it comes to evaluating patents, manufacturing processes or geological prospects. So we simply don't get into judgments in those fields.

If we have a strength, it is in recognizing when we are operating well within our circle of competence and when we are approaching the perimeter. Predicting the long-term economics of companies that operate in fast-changing industries is simply far beyond our perimeter. If others claim predictive skill in those industries–and seem to have their claims validated by the behavior of the stock market–we neither envy nor emulate them. Instead, we just stick with what we understand. If we stray, we will have done so inadvertently, not because we got restless and substituted hope for rationality. Fortunately, it's almost certain there will be opportunities from time to time for Berkshire to do well within the circle we've staked out.

Right now, the prices of the fine businesses we already own are just not that attractive. In other words, we feel much better about the businesses than their stocks. That's why we haven't added to our present holdings. Nevertheless, we haven't yet scaled back our portfolio in a major way: If the choice is between a questionable business at a comfortable price or a comfortable business at a questionable price, we much prefer the latter. What really gets our attention, however, is a comfortable business at a comfortable price.

Our reservations about the prices of securities we own apply also to the general level of equity prices. We have never attempted to forecast what the stock market is going to do in the next month or the next year, and we are not trying to do that now. But [as of late 1999] equity investors currently seem wildly optimistic in their expectations about future returns.

We see the growth in corporate profits as being largely tied to the business done in the country (GDP), and we see GDP growing at a real rate of about 3%. In addition, we have hypothesized 2% inflation. Charlie and I have no particular conviction about the accuracy of 2%. However, it's the market's view: Treasury Inflation-Protected Securities (TIPS) yield about two percentage points less than the standard treasury bond, and if you believe inflation rates are going to be higher than that, you can profit by simply buying TIPS and shorting Governments.

If profits do indeed grow along with GDP, at about a 5% rate, the valuation placed on American business is unlikely to climb by much more than that. Add in something for dividends, and you emerge with returns from equities that are dramatically less than most investors have either experienced in the past or expect in the future. If investor expectations become more realistic–and they almost certainly will–the market adjustment is apt to be severe, particularly in sectors in which speculation has been concentrated.

Berkshire will someday have opportunities to deploy major amounts of cash in equity markets–we are confident of that. But, as the song goes, "Who knows where or when?" Meanwhile, if anyone starts explaining to you what is going on in the truly-manic portions of this "enchanted" market, you might remember still another line of song: "Fools give you reasons, wise men never try."

———————————

[At times when prices are high for both businesses and stocks], we try to exert a Ted Williams kind of discipline. In his book *The Science of Hitting*, Ted explains that he carved the strike zone into 77 cells, each the size of a baseball. Swinging only at balls in his "best" cell, he knew, would allow him to bat .400; reaching for balls in his "worst" spot, the low outside corner of the strike zone, would reduce him to .230. In other words, waiting for the fat pitch would mean a trip to the Hall of Fame; swinging indiscriminately would mean a ticket to the minors.

If they are in the strike zone at all, the business "pitches" we now see are just catching the lower outside corner. If we swing, we will be locked into low returns. But if we let all of today's balls go by, there can be no assurance that the next ones we see will be more to our liking. Perhaps the attractive prices of the past were the aberrations, not the full prices of today. Unlike Ted, we can't be called out if we resist three pitches that are barely in the strike zone; nevertheless, just standing there, day after day, with my bat on my shoulder is not my idea of fun.

### F.   Cigar Butts and the Institutional Imperative[24]

To quote Robert Benchley, "Having a dog teaches a boy fidelity, perseverance, and to turn around three times before lying down." Such are the shortcomings of experience. Nevertheless, it's a good idea to review past mistakes before committing new ones. So let's take a quick look at the last 25 years.

• My first mistake, of course, was in buying control of Berkshire. Though I knew its business—textile manufacturing—to be unpromising, I was enticed to buy because the price looked cheap. Stock purchases of that kind had proved reasonably rewarding in my early years, though by the time Berkshire came along in 1965 I was becoming aware that the strategy was not ideal.

If you buy a stock at a sufficiently low price, there will usually be some hiccup in the fortunes of the business that gives you a chance to unload at a decent profit, even though the long-term performance of the business may be terrible. I call this the "cigar butt" approach to investing. A cigar butt found on the street that has only one puff left in it may not offer much of a smoke, but the "bargain purchase" will make that puff all profit.

Unless you are a liquidator, that kind of approach to buying businesses is foolish. First, the original "bargain" price probably will not turn out to be such a steal after all. In a difficult business, no sooner is one problem solved than another surfaces—never is there just one cockroach in the kitchen. Second, any initial advantage you secure will be quickly eroded by the low return that the business earns. For example, if you buy a business for $8 million that can be sold or liquidated for $10 million and promptly take either course, you can realize a high return. But the investment will disappoint if the business is sold for $10 million in ten years and in the interim has annually earned and distributed only a few percent on cost. Time is the friend of the wonderful business, the enemy of the mediocre.

You might think this principle is obvious, but I had to learn it the hard way—in fact, I had to learn it several times over. Shortly after purchasing Berkshire, I acquired a Baltimore department store, Hochschild, Kohn, buying through a company called Diversified Retailing that later merged with Berkshire. I bought at a substantial discount from book value, the people were first-class, and the deal included some extras—unrecorded real estate values and a significant LIFO inventory cushion. How could I miss? So-o-o—

---

[24] [1989.]

three years later I was lucky to sell the business for about what I had paid. After ending our corporate marriage to Hochschild, Kohn, I had memories like those of the husband in the country song, "My Wife Ran Away With My Best Friend and I Still Miss Him a Lot."

• That leads right into a related lesson: Good jockeys will do well on good horses, but not on broken-down nags. Both Berkshire's textile business and Hochschild, Kohn had able and honest people running them. The same managers employed in a business with good economic characteristics would have achieved fine records. But they were never going to make any progress while running in quicksand.[25]

I've said many times that when a management with a reputation for brilliance tackles a business with a reputation for bad economics, it is the reputation of the business that remains intact. I just wish I hadn't been so energetic in creating examples. My behavior has matched that admitted by Mae West: "I was Snow White, but I drifted."

• A further related lesson: Easy does it. After 25 years of buying and supervising a great variety of businesses, Charlie and I have *not* learned how to solve difficult business problems. What we have learned is to avoid them. To the extent we have been successful, it is because we concentrated on identifying one-foot hurdles that we could step over rather than because we acquired any ability to clear seven-footers.

The finding may seem unfair, but in both business and investments it is usually far more profitable to simply stick with the easy and obvious than it is to resolve the difficult. On occasion, tough problems *must* be tackled as was the case when we started our Sunday paper in Buffalo. In other instances, a great investment opportunity occurs when a marvelous business encounters a one-time huge, but solvable, problem as was the case many years back at both American Express and GEICO. Overall, however, we've done better by avoiding dragons than by slaying them.

• My most surprising discovery: the overwhelming importance in business of an unseen force that we might call "the institutional imperative." In business school, I was given no hint of the imperative's existence and I did not intuitively understand it when I entered the business world. I thought then that decent, intelligent, and experienced managers would automatically make rational bus-

---

[25] [*See* the essay The Anxieties of Plant Closings in Part I.D.]

iness decisions. But I learned over time that isn't so. Instead, rationality frequently wilts when the institutional imperative comes into play.

For example: (1) As if governed by Newton's First Law of Motion, an institution will resist any change in its current direction; (2) Just as work expands to fill available time, corporate projects or acquisitions will materialize to soak up available funds; (3) Any business craving of the leader, however foolish, will be quickly supported by detailed rate-of-return and strategic studies prepared by his troops; and (4) The behavior of peer companies, whether they are expanding, acquiring, setting executive compensation or whatever, will be mindlessly imitated.

Institutional dynamics, not venality or stupidity, set businesses on these courses, which are too often misguided. After making some expensive mistakes because I ignored the power of the imperative, I have tried to organize and manage Berkshire in ways that minimize its influence. Furthermore, Charlie and I have attempted to concentrate our investments in companies that appear alert to the problem.

• After some other mistakes, I learned to go into business only with people whom I like, trust, and admire. As I noted before, this policy of itself will not ensure success: A second-class textile or department-store company won't prosper simply because its managers are men that you would be pleased to see your daughter marry. However, an owner—or investor—can accomplish wonders if he manages to associate himself with such people in businesses that possess decent economic characteristics. Conversely, we do not wish to join with managers who lack admirable qualities, no matter how attractive the prospects of their business. We've never succeeded in making a good deal with a bad person.

• Some of my worst mistakes were not publicly visible. These were stock and business purchases whose virtues I understood and yet didn't make. It's no sin to miss a great opportunity outside one's area of competence. But I have passed on a couple of really big purchases that were served up to me on a platter and that I was fully capable of understanding. For Berkshire's shareholders, myself included, the cost of this thumb-sucking has been huge.

• Our consistently-conservative financial policies may appear to have been a mistake, but in my view were not. In retrospect, it is clear that significantly higher, though still conventional, leverage ratios at Berkshire would have produced considerably better returns on equity than the 23.8% we have actually averaged. Even in

1965, perhaps we could have judged there to be a 99% probability that higher leverage would lead to nothing but good. Correspondingly, we might have seen only a 1% chance that some shock factor, external or internal, would cause a conventional debt ratio to produce a result falling somewhere between temporary anguish and default.

We wouldn't have liked those 99:1 odds—and never will. A small chance of distress or disgrace cannot, in our view, be offset by a large chance of extra returns. If your actions are sensible, you are certain to get good results; in most such cases, leverage just moves things along faster. Charlie and I have never been in a big hurry: We enjoy the process far more than the proceeds—though we have learned to live with those also.

## III.  ALTERNATIVES TO COMMON STOCK

In addition to our three permanent common stock holdings, we hold large quantities of marketable securities in our insurance companies. In selecting these, we can choose among five major categories: (1) long-term common stock investments, (2) medium-term fixed-income securities, (3) long-term fixed income securities, (4) short-term cash equivalents, and (5) short-term arbitrage commitments [as discussed in the essay Arbitrage in Part II.B].

We have no particular bias when it comes to choosing from these categories. We just continuously search among them for the highest after-tax returns as measured by "mathematical expectation," limiting ourselves always to investment alternatives we think we understand. Our criteria have nothing to do with maximizing immediately reportable earnings; our goal, rather, is to maximize eventual net worth.[26]

### A.   *Junk Bonds*[27]

Lethargy bordering on sloth remains the cornerstone of our investment style: This year we neither bought nor sold a share of five of our six major holdings. The exception was Wells Fargo, a superbly-managed, high-return banking operation in which we increased our ownership to just under 10%, the most we can own without the approval of the Federal Reserve Board. About one-sixth of our position was bought in 1989, the rest in 1990.

The banking business is no favorite of ours. When assets are twenty times equity—a common ratio in this industry—mistakes that involve only a small portion of assets can destroy a major portion of equity. And mistakes have been the rule rather than the exception at many major banks. Most have resulted from a managerial failing that we described last year when discussing the "institutional imperative:" the tendency of executives to mindlessly imitate the behavior of their peers, no matter how foolish it may be to do so. In their lending, many bankers played follow-the-leader with lemming-like zeal; now they are experiencing a lemming-like fate.

Because leverage of 20:1 magnifies the effects of managerial strengths and weaknesses, we have no interest in purchasing shares

---

26 [Introductory essay, 1987; repeated without the first sentence in 1988 and 1989.]

27 [Divided by hash lines: 1990; 1990 Wesco Financial Corporation Letter to Shareholders, by Charles T. Munger. Reprinted with permission.]

of a poorly-managed bank at a "cheap" price. Instead, our only interest is in buying into well-managed banks at fair prices.

With Wells Fargo, we think we have obtained the best managers in the business, Carl Reichardt and Paul Hazen. In many ways the combination of Carl and Paul reminds me of another—Tom Murphy and Dan Burke at Capital Cities/ABC. First, each pair is stronger than the sum of its parts because each partner understands, trusts and admires the other. Second, both managerial teams pay able people well, but abhor having a bigger head count than is needed. Third, both attack costs as vigorously when profits are at record levels as when they are under pressure. Finally, both stick with what they understand and let their abilities, not their egos, determine what they attempt. (Thomas J. Watson Sr. of IBM followed the same rule: "I'm no genius," he said. "I'm smart in spots—but I stay around those spots.")

Our purchases of Wells Fargo in 1990 were helped by a chaotic market in bank stocks. The disarray was appropriate: Month by month the foolish loan decisions of once well-regarded banks were put on public display. As one huge loss after another was unveiled—often on the heels of managerial assurances that all was well—investors understandably concluded that no bank's numbers were to be trusted. Aided by their flight from bank stocks, we purchased our 10% interest in Wells Fargo for $290 million, less than five times after-tax earnings, and less than three times pre-tax earnings.

Wells Fargo is big—it has $56 billion in assets—and has been earning more than 20% on equity and 1.25% on assets. Our purchase of one-tenth of the bank may be thought of as roughly equivalent to our buying 100% of a $5 billion bank with identical financial characteristics. But were we to make such a purchase, we would have to pay about twice the $290 million we paid for Wells Fargo. Moreover, that $5 billion bank, commanding a premium price, would present us with another problem: We would not be able to find a Carl Reichardt to run it. In recent years, Wells Fargo executives have been more avidly recruited than any others in the banking business; no one however, has been able to hire the dean.

Of course, ownership of a bank—or about any other business—is far from riskless. California banks face the specific risk of a major earthquake, which might wreak enough havoc on borrowers to in turn destroy the banks lending to them. A second risk is systemic—the possibility of a business contraction or financial panic so severe that it would endanger almost every highly-leveraged institution, no matter how intelligently run. Finally, the market's major fear of the moment is that West Coast real estate values will tumble because of overbuilding and deliver huge losses to banks that have financed the expansion. Because it is a leading real estate lender, Wells Fargo is thought to be particularly vulnerable.

None of these eventualities can be ruled out. The probability of the first two occurring, however, is low and even a meaningful drop in real estate values is unlikely to cause major problems for well-managed institutions. Consider some mathematics: Wells Fargo currently earns well over $1 billion pre-tax annually after expensing more than $300 million for loan losses. If 10% of all $48 billion of the bank's loans—not just its real estate loans—were hit by problems in 1991, and these produced losses (including foregone interest) averaging 30% of principal, the company would roughly break even.

A year like that—which we consider only a low-level possibility, not a likelihood—would not distress us. In fact, at Berkshire we would love to acquire businesses or invest in capital projects that produced no return for a year, but that could then be expected to earn 20% on growing equity. Nevertheless, fears of a California real estate disaster similar to that experienced in New England caused the price of Wells Fargo stock to fall almost 50% within a few months during 1990. Even though we had bought some shares at the prices prevailing before the fall, we welcomed the decline because it allowed us to pick up many more shares at the new, panic prices.

We will be buying businesses—or small parts of businesses, called stocks—year in, year out as long as I live (and longer, if Berkshire's directors attend the seances I have scheduled). Given these intentions, declining prices for businesses benefit us, and rising prices hurt us.

The most common cause of low prices is pessimism—sometimes pervasive, sometimes specific to a company or industry. We *want* to do business in such an environment, not because we like pessimism but because we like the prices it produces. It's optimism that is the enemy of the rational buyer.

None of this means, however, that a business or stock is an intelligent purchase simply because it is unpopular; a contrarian approach is just as foolish as a follow-the-crowd strategy. What's required is thinking rather than polling. Unfortunately, Bertrand Russell's observation about life in general applies with unusual force in the financial world: "Most men would rather die than think. Many do."

* * * * *

Our other major portfolio change last year was large additions to our holdings of RJR Nabisco bonds, securities that we first bought in late 1989. At year end 1990 we had $440 million invested in these securities, an amount that approximated market value. (As I write this, however, their market value has risen by more than $150 million.)

Just as buying into the banking business is unusual for us, so is the purchase of below-investment-grade bonds. But opportunities that interest us and that are also large enough to have a worthwhile impact on Berkshire's results are rare. Therefore, we will look at any category of investment, so long as we understand the business we're buying into and believe that price and value may differ significantly. (Woody Allen, in another context, pointed out the advantage of open-mindedness: "I can't understand why more people aren't bi-sexual because it doubles your chances for a date on Saturday night.")

In the past we have bought a few below-investment-grade bonds with success, though these were all old-fashioned "fallen angels"—bonds that were initially of investment grade but that were downgraded when the issuers fell on bad times.

A kind of bastardized fallen angel burst onto the investment scene in the 1980s—"junk bonds" that were far below investment-grade when issued. As the decade progressed, new offerings of manufactured junk became ever junkier and ultimately the predictable outcome occurred: Junk bonds lived up to their name. In 1990—even before the recession dealt its blows—the financial sky became dark with the bodies of failing corporations.

The disciples of debt assured us that this collapse wouldn't happen: Huge debt, we were told, would cause operating managers to focus their efforts as never before, much as a dagger mounted on the steering wheel of a car could be expected to make its driver proceed with intensified care. We'll acknowledge that such an attention-getter would produce a very alert driver. But another certain consequence would be a deadly—and unnecessary—accident if the car hit even the tiniest pothole or sliver of ice. The roads of business are riddled with potholes; a plan that requires dodging them all is a plan for disaster.

In the final chapter of *The Intelligent Investor* Ben Graham forcefully rejected the dagger thesis: "Confronted with a challenge to distill the secret of sound investment into three words, we venture the motto, Margin of Safety." Forty-two years after reading that, I still think those are the right three words. The failure of investors to heed this simple message caused them staggering losses as the 1990s began.

At the height of the debt mania, capital structures were concocted that guaranteed failure: In some cases, so much debt was issued that even highly favorable business results could not produce the funds to service it. One particularly egregious "kill-'em-at-birth" case a few years back involved the purchase of a mature television station in Tampa, bought with so much debt that the interest on it exceeded the station's *gross revenues*. Even if you assume that all labor, programs and services were donated rather than purchased, this capital structure required revenues to explode—or else the station was doomed to go broke. (Many of the bonds that financed the purchase were sold to now-failed savings and loan associations; as a taxpayer, you are picking up the tab for this folly.)

All of this seems impossible now. When these misdeeds were done, however, dagger-selling investment bankers pointed to the "scholarly" research of academics, which reported that over the years the higher interest rates received from low-grade bonds had more than compensated for their higher rate of default. Thus, said the friendly salesmen, a diversified portfolio of junk bonds would produce greater net returns than would a portfolio of high-grade bonds. (Beware of past-performance "proofs" in finance: If history books were the key to riches, the Forbes 400 would consist of librarians.)

There was a flaw in the salesmen's logic—one that a first-year student in statistics is taught to recognize. An assumption was being made that the universe of newly-minted junk bonds was identical to the universe of low-grade fallen angels and that, therefore, the default experience of the latter group was meaningful in predicting the default experience of the new issues. (That was an error similar to checking the historical death rate from Kool-Aid before drinking the version served at Jonestown.)

The universes were of course dissimilar in several vital respects. For openers, the manager of a fallen angel almost invariably yearned to regain investment-grade status and worked toward that goal. The junk-bond operator was usually an entirely different breed. Behaving much as a heroin user might, he devoted his energies not to finding a cure for his debt-ridden condition, but rather to finding another fix. Additionally, the fiduciary sensitivities of the executives managing the typical fallen angel were often, though not always, more finely developed than were those of the junk-bond-issuing financiopath.

Wall Street cared little for such distinctions. As usual, the Street's enthusiasm for an idea was proportional not to its merit, but rather to the revenue it would produce. Mountains of junk bonds were sold by those who didn't care to those who didn't think—and there was no shortage of either.

Junk bonds remain a mine field, even at prices that today are often a small fraction of issue price. As we said last year, we have never bought a new issue of a junk bond. (The only time to buy these is on a day with no "y" in it.) We are, however, willing to look at the field, now that it is in disarray.

In the case of RJR Nabisco, we feel the Company's credit is considerably better than was generally perceived for a while and that the yield we receive, as well as the potential for capital gain, more than compensates for the risk we incur (though that is far from nil). RJR has made asset sales at favorable prices, has added major amounts of equity, and in general is being run well.

However, as we survey the field, most low-grade bonds still look unattractive. The handiwork of the Wall Street of the 1980s is even worse than we had thought: Many important businesses have been mortally wounded. We will, though, keep looking for opportunities as the junk market continues to unravel.

———————

It is interesting to compare Wesco's approach (deliberate non-diversification of investments in an attempt to be more skillful per transaction) with an approach promoted for years by Michael Milken to help sell junk bonds. The Milken approach, supported by theories of many finance professors, argued that (1) market prices were efficient in a world where investors get paid extra for enduring volatility (wide swings in outcomes); (2) therefore, the prices at which new issues of junk bonds came to market were fair in a probabilistic sense (meaning that the high promised interest rates covered increased statistical expectancy of loss) and also provided some premium return to cover volatility exposure; and (3) therefore, if a savings and loan association (or other institution) arranged diversification, say, by buying, without much examination, a large part of each new Milken issue of junk bonds, the association would work itself into the sure-to-get-better-than-average-results position of a gambling house proprietor with a "house" edge. This type of theorizing has now wreaked havoc at institutions, governed by true-believers, which backed their conclusions by buying Milken's "bonds." Contrary to the theorizing, widely diversified purchases of such "bonds" have in most cases produced dismal results. We can all understand why Milken behaved as he did and believed what he had to believe in order to maintain an endurable self-image. But how can we explain why anyone else believed that Milken was paid 5% commissions to put "bond" buyers in the position of the house in Las Vegas? We suggest this cause: many of the foolish buyers, and their advisers, were trained by finance professors who pushed beloved models (efficient market theory and modern portfolio theory) way too far, while they ignored other models that would have warned of danger. This is a common type of "expert" error.

### B.   *Zero-Coupon Bonds*[28]

Berkshire issued $902.6 million principal amount of Zero-Coupon Convertible Subordinated Debentures, which are now listed on the New York Stock Exchange. Salomon Brothers handled the underwriting in superb fashion, providing us helpful advice and a flawless execution.

Most bonds, of course, require regular payments of interest, usually semi-annually. A zero-coupon bond, conversely, requires no current interest payments; instead, the investor receives his yield by purchasing the security at a significant discount from maturity value. The effective interest rate is determined by the original issue price, the maturity value, and the amount of time between issuance and maturity.

In our case, the bonds were issued at 44.314% of maturity value and are due in 15 years. For investors purchasing the bonds, that is the mathematical equivalent of a 5.5% current payment compounded semi-annually. Because we received only 44.31 cents on the dollar, our proceeds from this offering were $400 million (less about $9.5 million of offering expenses).

The bonds were issued in denominations of $10,000 and each bond is convertible into .4515 shares of Berkshire Hathaway. Because a $10,000 bond cost $4,431, this means that the conversion price was $9,815 per Berkshire share, a 15% premium to the mar-

---

[28] [1989.]

ket price then existing. Berkshire can call the bonds at any time after September 28, 1992 at their accreted value (the original issue price plus 5.5% compounded semi-annually) and on two specified days, September 28 of 1994 and 1999, the bondholders can require Berkshire to buy the securities at their accreted value.

For tax purposes, Berkshire is entitled to deduct the 5.5% interest accrual each year, even though we make no payments to the bondholders. Thus the net effect to us, resulting from the reduced taxes, is positive cash flow. That is a very significant benefit. Some unknowable variables prevent us from calculating our exact effective rate of interest, but under all circumstances it will be well below 5.5%. There is meanwhile a symmetry to the tax law: Any taxable holder of the bonds must pay tax each year on the 5.5% interest, even though he receives no cash.

Neither our bonds nor those of certain other companies that issued similar bonds last year (notably Loews and Motorola) resemble the great bulk of zero-coupon bonds that have been issued in recent years. Of these, Charlie and I have been, and will continue to be, outspoken critics. As I will later explain, such bonds have often been used in the most deceptive of ways and with deadly consequences to investors. But before we tackle that subject, let's travel back to Eden, to a time when the apple had not yet been bitten.

If you're my age you bought your first zero-coupon bonds during World War II, by purchasing the famous Series E U.S. Savings Bond, the most widely-sold bond issue in history. (After the war, these bonds were held by one out of two U.S. households.) Nobody, of course, called the Series E a zero-coupon bond, a term in fact that I doubt had been invented. But that's precisely what the Series E was.

These bonds came in denominations as small as $18.75. That amount purchased a $25 obligation of the United States government due in 10 years, terms that gave the buyer a compounded annual return of 2.9%. At the time, this was an attractive offer: the 2.9% rate was higher than that generally available on Government bonds and the holder faced no market-fluctuation risk, since he could at any time cash in his bonds with only a minor reduction in interest.

A second form of zero-coupon U.S. Treasury issue, also benign and useful, surfaced in the last decade. One problem with a normal bond is that even though it pays a given interest rate—say 10%—the holder cannot be assured that a compounded 10% return will be realized. For that rate to materialize, each semi-annual coupon must be reinvested at 10% as it is received. If current interest rates are, say, only 6% or 7% when these coupons come due, the holder will be unable to compound his money over the life of the bond at the advertised rate. For pension funds or other investors with long-term liabilities, "reinvestment risk" of this type can be a serious problem. Savings Bonds might have solved it, except that they are issued only to individuals and are unavailable in large denominations. What big buyers needed was huge quantities of "Savings Bond Equivalents."

Enter some ingenious and, in this case, highly useful investment bankers (led, I'm happy to say, by Salomon Brothers). They created the instrument desired by "stripping" the semi-annual coupons from standard Government issues. Each coupon, once detached, takes on the essential character of a Savings Bond since it represents a single sum due sometime in the future. For example, if you strip the 40 semi-annual coupons from a U.S. Government Bond due in the year 2010, you will have 40 zero-coupon bonds, with maturities from six months to 20 years, each of which can then be bundled with other coupons of like maturity and marketed. If current interest rates are, say, 10% for all maturities, the six-month issue will sell for 95.24% of maturity value and the 20-year issue will sell for 14.20%. The purchaser of any given maturity is thus guaranteed a compounded rate of 10% for his entire holding period. Stripping of government bonds has occurred on a large scale in recent years, as long-term investors, ranging from pension funds to individual IRA accounts, recognized these high-grade, zero-coupon issues to be well suited to their needs.

But as happens in Wall Street all too often, what the wise do in the beginning, fools do in the end. In the last few years zero-coupon bonds (and their functional equivalent, pay-in-kind bonds, which distribute additional PIK bonds semi-annually as interest instead of paying cash) have been issued in enormous quantities by ever-junkier credits. To these issuers, zero (or PIK) bonds offer one overwhelming advantage: It is impossible to default on a promise to pay nothing. Indeed, if LDC governments had issued no debt in the 1970s other than long-term zero-coupon obligations, they would now have a spotless record as debtors.

This principle at work—that you need not default for a long time if you solemnly promise to pay nothing for a long time—has not been lost on promoters and investment bankers seeking to finance ever-shakier deals. But its acceptance by lenders took a while: When the leveraged buy-out craze began some years back, purchasers could borrow only on a reasonably sound basis, in which conservatively-estimated free cash flow—that is, operating earnings plus depreciation and amortization less normalized capital expenditures—was adequate to cover both interest and modest reductions in debt.

Later, as the adrenalin of deal-makers surged, businesses began to be purchased at prices so high that all free cash flow necessarily had to be allocated to the payment of interest. That left nothing for the paydown of debt. In effect, a Scarlett O'Hara "I'll think about it tomorrow" position in respect to principal payments was taken by borrowers and accepted by a new breed of lender, the buyer of original-issue junk bonds. Debt now became something to be refinanced rather than repaid. The change brings to mind a *New Yorker* cartoon in which the grateful borrower rises to shake the hand of the bank's lending officer and gushes: "I don't know how I'll ever repay you."

Soon borrowers found even the new, lax standards intolerably binding. To induce lenders to finance even sillier transactions, they introduced an abomination, EBDIT—Earnings Before Depreciation, Interest and Taxes—as the test of a company's ability to pay interest. Using this sawed-off yardstick, the borrower ignored depreciation as an expense on the theory that it did not require a current cash outlay.

Such an attitude is clearly delusional. At 95% of American businesses, capital expenditures that over time roughly approximate depreciation are a necessity and are every bit as real an expense as labor or utility costs. Even a high school dropout knows that to finance a car he must have income that covers not only interest and operating expenses, but also realistically-calculated depreciation. He would be laughed out of the bank if he started talking about EBDIT.

Capital outlays at a business can be skipped, of course, in any given month, just as a human can skip a day or even a week of eating. But if the skipping becomes routine and is not made up, the body weakens and eventually dies. Furthermore, a start and-stop feeding policy will over time produce a less healthy organism, human or corporate, than that produced by a steady diet. As businessmen, Charlie and I relish having competitors who are unable to fund capital expenditures.

You might think that waving away a major expense such as depreciation in an attempt to make a terrible deal look like a good one hits the limits of Wall Street's ingenuity. If so, you haven't been paying attention during the past few years. Promoters needed to find a way to justify even pricier acquisitions. Otherwise, they risked—heaven forbid—losing deals to other promoters with more "imagination."

So, stepping through the Looking Glass, promoters and their investment bankers proclaimed that EBDIT should now be measured against cash interest only, which meant that interest accruing on zero-coupon or PIK bonds could be ignored when the financial feasibility of a transaction was being assessed. This approach not only relegated depreciation expense to the let's-ignore-it corner, but gave similar treatment to what was usually a significant portion of interest expense. To their shame, many professional investment managers went along with this nonsense, though they usually were careful to do so only with clients' money, not their own. (Calling these managers "professionals" is actually too kind; they should be designated "promotees.")

Under this new standard, a business earning, say, $100 million pre-tax and having debt on which $90 million of interest must be paid currently, might use a zero-coupon of PIK issue to incur another $60 million of annual interest that would accrue and compound but not come due for some years. The rate on these issues would typically be very high, which means that the situation in year 2 might be $90 million cash interest plus $69 million accrued interest, and so on as the compounding proceeds. Such high-rate reborrowing schemes, which a few years ago were appropriately confined to the waterfront, soon became models of finance at virtually all major investment banking houses.

When they make these offerings, investment bankers display their humorous side: They dispense income and balance sheet projections extending five or more years into the future for companies they barely had heard of a few months earlier. If you are shown such schedules, I suggest that you join the fun: Ask the investment banker for the one-year budgets that his own firm prepared as the last few years began and then compare these with what actually happened.

Some time ago Ken Galbraith, in his witty and insightful *The Great Crash*, coined a new economic term: "the bezzle," defined as the current amount of undiscovered embezzlement. This financial creature has a magical quality: The embezzlers are richer by the amount of the bezzle, while the embezzlees do not yet feel poorer.

Professor Galbraith astutely pointed out that this sum should be added to the National Wealth so that we might know the Psychic National Wealth. Logically, a society that wanted to feel enormously prosperous would both encourage its citizens to embezzle and try not to detect the crime. By this means, "wealth" would balloon though not an erg of productive work had been done.

The satirical nonsense of the bezzle is dwarfed by the real-world nonsense of the zero-coupon bond. With zeros, one party to a contract can experience "income" without his opposite experiencing the pain of expenditure. In our illustration, a company capable of earning only $100 million dollars annually—and therefore capable of paying only that much in interest—magically creates "earnings" for bondholders of $150 million. As long as major investors willingly don their Peter Pan wings and repeatedly say "I believe," there is no limit to how much "income" can be created by the zero-coupon bond.

Wall Street welcomed this invention with the enthusiasm less-enlightened folk might reserve for the wheel or the plow. Here, finally, was an instrument that would let the Street make deals at prices no longer limited by actual earning power. The result, obviously, would be more transactions: Silly prices will always attract sellers. And, as Jesse Unruh might have put it, transactions are the mother's milk of finance.

The zero-coupon or PIK bond possesses an additional attraction for the promoter and investment banker, which is that the time elapsing between folly and failure can be stretched out. This is no small benefit. If the period before all costs must be faced is long, promoters can create a string of foolish deals—and take in lots of fees—before any chickens come home to roost from their earlier ventures.

But in the end, alchemy, whether it is metallurgical or financial, fails. A base business can not be transformed into a golden business by tricks of accounting or capital structure. The man claiming to be a financial alchemist may become rich. But gullible investors rather than business achievements will usually be the source of his wealth.

Whatever their weaknesses, we should add, many zero-coupon and PIK bonds will not default. We have in fact owned some and may buy more if their market becomes sufficiently distressed. (We've not, however, even considered buying a new issue from a weak credit.) No financial instrument is evil per se; it's just that some variations have far more potential for mischief than others.

The blue ribbon for mischief-making should go to the zero-coupon issuer unable to make its interest payments on a current basis. Our advice: Whenever an investment banker starts talking about EBDIT—or whenever someone creates a capital structure that does not allow all interest, both payable and accrued, to be comfortably met out of current cash flow net of ample capital expenditures—zip up your wallet. Turn the tables by suggesting that the promoter and his high-priced entourage accept zero-coupon fees, deferring their take until the zero-coupon bonds have been paid in full. See then how much enthusiasm for the deal endures.

Our comments about investment bankers may seem harsh. But Charlie and I—in our hopelessly old-fashioned way—believe that they should perform a gatekeeping role, guarding investors against the promoter's propensity to indulge in excess. Promoters, after all, have throughout time exercised the same judgment and restraint in accepting money that alcoholics have exercised in accepting liquor. At a minimum, therefore, the banker's conduct should rise to that of a responsible bartender who, when necessary, refuses the profit from the next drink to avoid sending a drunk out on the highway. In recent years, unfortunately, many leading investment firms have found bartender morality to be an intolerably restrictive standard. Lately, those who have traveled the high road in Wall Street have not encountered heavy traffic.

One distressing footnote: The cost of the zero-coupon folly will not be borne solely by the direct participants. Certain savings and loan associations were heavy buyers of such bonds, using cash that came from FSLIC-insured deposits. Straining to show splendid earnings, these buyers recorded—but did not receive—ultra-high interest income on these issues. Many of these associations are now in major trouble. Had their loans to shaky credits worked, the owners of the associations would have pocketed the profits. In the many cases in which the loans will fail, the taxpayer will pick up the bill. To paraphrase Jackie Mason, at these associations it was the managers who should have been wearing the ski masks.

## C.  *Preferred Stock*[29]

We only want to link up with people whom we like, admire, and trust.  John Gutfreund at Salomon, Colman Mockler, Jr. at Gillette, Ed Colodny at USAir, and Andy Sigler at Champion meet this test in spades.

They in turn have demonstrated some confidence in us, insisting in each case that our preferreds have unrestricted voting rights on a fully-converted basis, an arrangement that is far from standard in corporate finance.  In effect they are trusting us to be intelligent owners, thinking about tomorrow *instead* of today, just as we are trusting them to be intelligent managers, thinking about tomorrow *as well* as today.

The preferred-stock structures we have negotiated will provide a mediocre return for us if industry economics hinder the performance of our investees, but will produce reasonably attractive results for us if they can earn a return comparable to that of American industry in general.  We believe that Gillette, under Colman's management, will far exceed that return and believe that John, Ed, and Andy will reach it unless industry conditions are harsh.

Under almost any conditions, we expect these preferreds to return us our money plus dividends.  If that is all we get, though, the result will be disappointing, because we will have given up flexibility and consequently will have missed some significant opportunities that are bound to present themselves during the decade.  Under that scenario, we will have obtained only a preferred-stock yield during a period when the typical preferred stock will have held no appeal for us whatsoever.  The only way Berkshire can achieve satisfactory results from its four preferred issues is to have the common stocks of the investee companies do well.

Good management and at least tolerable industry conditions will be needed if that is to happen.  But we believe Berkshire's investment will also help and that the other shareholders of each investee will profit over the years ahead from our preferred-stock purchase.  The help will come from the fact that each company now has a major, stable, and interested shareholder whose Chairman and Vice Chairman have, through Berkshire's investments, indirectly committed a very large amount of their own money to these undertakings.  In dealing with our investees, Charlie and I will be supportive, analytical, and objective.  We recognize that we are working with experienced CEOs who are very much in command

---

[29] [Divided by hash lines: 1989; 1994; 1996; 1990; 1995; 1997.]

of their own business but who nevertheless, at certain moments, appreciate the chance to test their thinking on someone without ties to their industry or to decisions of the past.

As a group, these convertible preferreds will not produce the returns we can achieve when we find a business with wonderful economic prospects that is unappreciated by the market. Nor will the returns be as attractive as those produced when we make our favorite form of capital deployment, the acquisition of 80% or more of a fine business with a fine management. But both opportunities are rare, particularly in a size befitting our present and anticipated resources.

In summation, Charlie and I feel that our preferred stock investments should produce returns moderately above those achieved by most fixed-income portfolios and that we can play a minor but enjoyable and constructive role in the investee companies.

---

Mistakes occur at the time of decision. We can only make our mistake-*du-jour* award, however, when the foolishness of a decision becomes obvious. By this measure, 1994 was a vintage year with keen competition for the gold medal. Here, I would like to tell you that the mistakes I will describe originated with Charlie. But whenever I try to explain things that way, my nose begins to grow.

And the nominees are . . .

Late in 1993 I sold 10 million shares of Cap Cities at $63; at year-end 1994, the price was $85¼. (The difference is $222.5 million for those of you who wish to avoid the pain of calculating the damage yourself.) When we purchased the stock at $17.25 in 1986, I told you that I had previously sold our Cap Cities holdings at $4.30 per share during 1978-80, and added that I was at a loss to explain my earlier behavior.[30] Now I've become a repeat offender. Maybe it's time to get a guardian appointed.

Egregious as it is, the Cap Cities decision earns only a silver medal. Top honors go to a mistake I made five years ago that fully ripened in 1994: Our $358 million purchase of USAir preferred stock, on which the dividend was suspended in September. [T]his deal [w]as an "unforced error," meaning that I was neither pushed into the investment nor misled by anyone when making it. Rather,

---

[30] [*See* the essay "Value" Investing: A Redundancy in Part II.D. The per share figures in the two essays differ because of stock splits.]

this was a case of sloppy analysis, a lapse that may have been caused by the fact that we were buying a senior security or by hubris. Whatever the reason, the mistake was large.

Before this purchase, I simply failed to focus on the problems that would inevitably beset a carrier whose costs were both high and extremely difficult to lower. In earlier years, these life-threatening costs posed few problems. Airlines were then protected from competition by regulation, and carriers could absorb high costs because they could pass them along by way of fares that were also high.

When deregulation came along, it did not immediately change the picture: The capacity of low-cost carriers was so small that the high-cost lines could, in large part, maintain their existing fare structures. During this period, with the longer-term problems largely invisible but slowly metastasizing, the costs that were non-sustainable became further embedded.

As the seat capacity of the low-cost operators expanded, their fares began to force the old-line, high-cost airlines to cut their own. The day of reckoning for these airlines could be delayed by infusions of capital (such as ours into USAir), but eventually a fundamental rule of economics prevailed: In an unregulated commodity business, a company must lower its costs to competitive levels or face extinction. This principle should have been obvious to your Chairman, but I missed it.

Seth Schofield, [then] CEO of USAir, has worked diligently to correct the company's historical cost problems but, to date, has not managed to do so. In part, this is because he has had to deal with a moving target, the result of certain major carriers having obtained labor concessions and other carriers having benefitted from "fresh-start" costs that came out of bankruptcy proceedings. (As Herb Kelleher, CEO of Southwest Airlines, has said: "Bankruptcy court for airlines has become a health spa.") Additionally, it should be no surprise to anyone that those airline employees who contractually receive above-market salaries will resist any reduction in these as long as their checks continue to clear.

Despite this difficult situation, USAir may yet achieve the cost reductions it needs to maintain its viability long-term. But it is far from sure that will happen.

Accordingly, we wrote our USAir investment down to $89.5 million, or 25¢ on the dollar, at year end 1994. This valuation reflects both a possibility that our preferred will have its value fully or largely restored and an opposite possibility that the stock will eventually become worthless. Whatever the outcome, we will heed a prime rule of investing: You don't have to make it back the way that you lost it.

The accounting effects of our USAir writedown are compli-cated. On our balance sheet, we carry all stocks at estimated mar-ket value. Therefore, at the end of last year's third quarter, we were carrying our USAir preferred at $89.5 million, or 25% of cost. In other words, our net worth was at that time reflecting a value for USAir that was far below our $358 million cost.

But in the fourth quarter, we concluded that the decline in value was, in accounting terms, "other than temporary," and that judgment required us to send the writedown of $268.5 million through our income statement. The amount had no other fourth-quarter effect. That is, it did not reduce our net worth, because the diminution of value had already been reflected there.

Charlie and I will not stand for reelection to USAir's board at the upcoming annual meeting. Should Seth wish to consult with us, however, we will be pleased to be of any help that we can.

---

When Richard Branson, the wealthy owner of Virgin Atlantic Airways, was asked how to become a millionaire, he had a quick answer: "There's really nothing to it. Start as a billionaire and then buy an airline." Unwilling to accept Branson's proposition on faith, your Chairman decided in 1989 to test it by investing $358 million in a $9\frac{1}{4}$% preferred stock of USAir.

I liked and admired Ed Colodny, the company's then-CEO, and I still do. But my analysis of USAir's business was both super-ficial and wrong. I was so beguiled by the company's long history of profitable operations, and by the protection that ownership of a senior security seemingly offered me, that I overlooked the crucial point: USAir's revenues would increasingly feel the effects of an unregulated, fiercely competitive market whereas its cost structure was a holdover from the days when regulation protected profits. These costs, if left unchecked, portended disaster, however reassur-ing the airline's past record might be.

To rationalize its costs, however, USAir needed major im-provements in its labor contracts—and that's something most air-lines have found it extraordinarily difficult to get, short of credibly threatening, or actually entering, bankruptcy. USAir was to be no exception. Immediately after we purchased our preferred stock, the imbalance between the company's costs and revenues began to grow explosively. In the 1990-1994 period, USAir lost an aggregate of $2.4 billion, a performance that totally wiped out the book equity of its common stock.

For much of this period, the company paid us our preferred dividends, but in 1994 payment was suspended. A bit later, with the situation looking particularly gloomy, we wrote down our investment by 75%, to $89.5 million. Thereafter, during much of 1995, I offered to sell our shares at 50% of face value. Fortunately, I was unsuccessful.

Mixed in with my many mistakes at USAir was one thing I got right: Making our investment, we wrote into the preferred contract a somewhat unusual provision stipulating that "penalty dividends"—to run five percentage points over the prime rate—would be accrued on any arrearages. This meant that when our $9\frac{1}{4}\%$ dividend was omitted for two years, the unpaid amounts compounded at rates ranging between $13\frac{1}{4}\%$ and 14%.

Facing this penalty provision, USAir had every incentive to pay arrearages just as promptly as it could. And in the second half of 1996, when USAir turned profitable, it indeed began to pay, giving us $47.9 million. We owe Stephen Wolf, the company's CEO, a huge thank-you for extracting a performance from the airline that permitted this payment. Even so, USAir's performance has recently been helped significantly by an industry tailwind that may be cyclical in nature. The company still has basic cost problems that must be solved.

In any event, the prices of USAir's publicly-traded securities tell us that our preferred stock is now probably worth its par value of $358 million, give or take a little. In addition, we have over the years collected an aggregate of $240.5 million in dividends (including $30 million received in 1997).

Early in 1996, before any accrued dividends had been paid, I tried once more to unload our holdings—this time for about $335 million. You're lucky: I again failed in my attempt to snatch defeat from the jaws of victory.

In another context, a friend once asked me: "If you're so rich, why aren't you smart?" After reviewing my sorry performance with USAir, you may conclude he had a point.

---

In making the USAir purchase, your Chairman displayed exquisite timing: I plunged into the business at almost the exact moment that it ran into severe problems. (No one pushed me; in tennis parlance, I committed an "unforced error.") The company's troubles were brought on both by industry conditions and by the post-merger difficulties it encountered in integrating Piedmont, an affliction I should have expected since almost all airline mergers have been followed by operational turmoil.

In short order, Ed Colodny and Seth Schofield resolved the second problem: The airline now gets excellent marks for service. Industry-wide problems have proved to be far more serious. Since our purchase, the economics of the airline industry have deteriorated at an alarming pace, accelerated by the kamikaze pricing tactics of certain carriers. The trouble this pricing has produced for all carriers illustrates an important truth: In a business selling a commodity-type product, it's impossible to be a lot smarter than your dumbest competitor.

However, unless the industry is decimated during the next few years, our USAir investment should work out all right. Ed and Seth decisively addressed the current turbulence by making major changes in operations. Even so, our investment is now less secure than at the time I made it.

Our convertible preferred stocks are relatively simple securities, yet I should warn you that, if the past is any guide, you may from time to time read inaccurate or misleading statements about them. Last year, for example, several members of the press calculated the value of all our preferreds as equal to that of the common stock into which they are convertible. By their logic, that is, our Salomon preferred, convertible into common at $38, would be worth 60% of face value if Salomon common were selling at $22.80. But there is a small problem with this line of reasoning: Using it, one must conclude that all of the value of a convertible preferred resides in the conversion privilege and that value of a non-convertible preferred of Salomon would be zero, no matter what its coupon or terms for redemption.

The point you should keep in mind is that most of the value of our convertible preferreds is derived from their fixed-income characteristics. That means the securities cannot be worth less than the value they would possess as non-convertible preferreds and may be worth more because of their conversion options.

---

Berkshire made five private purchases of convertible preferred stocks during the 1987-91 period and the time seems right to discuss their status.

In each case we had the option of sticking with these preferreds as fixed-income securities or converting them into common stock. Initially, their value to us came primarily from their fixed-income characteristics. The option we had to convert was a kicker.

Our $300 million private purchase of American Express "Percs" was a modified form of common stock whose fixed-income characteristics contributed only a minor portion of its initial value. Three years after we bought them, the Percs automatically were converted to common stock. In contrast, [our other convertible preferred stocks] were set to become common stocks only if we wished them to—a crucial difference.

When we purchased our convertible securities, I told you that we expected to earn after-tax returns from them that "moderately" exceeded what we could earn from the medium-term fixed-income securities they replaced. We beat this expectation—but only because of the performance of a single issue. I also told you that these securities, as a group, would "not produce the returns we can achieve when we find a business with wonderful economic prospects." Unfortunately, that prediction was fulfilled. Finally, I said that "under almost any conditions, we expect these preferreds to return us our money plus dividends." That's one I would like to have back. Winston Churchill once said that "eating my words has never given me indigestion." My assertion, however, that it was almost impossible for us to lose money on our preferreds has caused me some well-deserved heartburn.

Our best holding has been Gillette, which we told you from the start was a superior business. Ironically, though, this is also the purchase in which I made my biggest mistake—of a kind, however, never recognized on financial statements.

We paid $600 million in 1989 for Gillette preferred shares that were convertible into 48 million (split-adjusted) common shares. Taking an alternative route with the $600 million, I probably could have purchased 60 million shares of common from the company. The market on the common was then about $10.50, and given that this would have been a huge private placement carrying important restrictions, I probably could have bought the stock at a discount of at least 5%. I can't be sure about this, but it's likely that Gillette's management would have been just as happy to have Berkshire opt for common.

But I was far too clever to do that. Instead, for less than two years, we received some extra dividend income (the difference between the preferred's yield and that of the common), at which point the company—quite properly—called the issue, moving to do that as quickly as was possible. If I had negotiated for common rather than preferred, we would have been better off at year end 1995 by $625 million, minus the "excess" dividends of about $70 million.

In the case of Champion, the ability of the company to call our preferred at 115% of cost forced a move out of us last August that we would rather have delayed. In this instance, we converted our shares just prior to the pending call and offered them to the company at a modest discount.

Charlie and I have never had a conviction about the paper industry—actually, I can't remember ever owning the common stock of a paper producer in my 54 years of investing—so our choice in August was whether to sell in the market or to the company. Our Champion capital gain was moderate—about 19% after tax from a six-year investment—but the preferred delivered us a good after-tax dividend yield throughout our holding period. (That said, many press accounts have overstated the after-tax yields earned by property-casualty insurance companies on dividends paid to them. What the press has failed to take into account is a change in the tax law that took effect in 1987 and that significantly reduced the dividends received credit applicable to insurers.)

Our First Empire preferred [was to] be called on March 31, 1996, the earliest date allowable. We are comfortable owning stock in well-run banks, and we will convert and keep our First Empire common shares. Bob Wilmers, CEO of the company, is an outstanding banker, and we love being associated with him.

Our other two preferreds have been disappointing, though the Salomon preferred has modestly outperformed the fixed-income securities for which it was a substitute. However, the amount of management time Charlie and I have devoted to this holding has been vastly greater than its economic significance to Berkshire. Certainly I never dreamed I would take a new job at age 60—Salomon interim chairman, that is—because of an earlier purchase of a fixed-income security.

Soon after our purchase of the Salomon preferred in 1987, I wrote that I had "no special insights regarding the direction or future profitability of investment banking." Even the most charitable commentator would conclude that I have since proved my point.

To date, our option to convert into Salomon common has not proven of value. Furthermore, the Dow Industrials have doubled since I committed to buy the preferred, and the brokerage group has performed equally as well. That means my decision to go with

Salomon because I saw value in the conversion option must be graded as very poor. Even so, the preferred has continued under some trying conditions to deliver as a fixed-income security, and the 9% dividend is currently quite attractive.

Unless the preferred is converted, its terms require redemption of 20% of the issue on October 31 of each year, 1995-99, and $140 million of our original $700 million was taken on schedule last year. (Some press reports labeled this a sale, but a senior security that matures is not "sold.") Though we did not elect to convert the preferred that matured last year, we have four more bites at the conversion apple, and I believe it quite likely that we will yet find value in our right to convert.

----

The common stocks of both Gillette and First Empire [into which Berkshire's preferreds had been converted] have risen substantially, in line with the companies' excellent performance. At year end, the $600 million we put into Gillette in 1989 had appreciated to $4.8 billion, and the $40 million we committed to First Empire in 1991 had risen to $236 million.

Our two laggards [USAir and Salomon], meanwhile, have come to life in a very major way. In a transaction that finally rewarded its long-suffering shareholders, Salomon recently merged into Travelers Group. All of Berkshire's shareholders–including me, very personally–owe a huge debt to Deryck Maughan and Bob Denham for, first, playing key roles in saving Salomon from extinction following its 1991 scandal and, second, restoring the vitality of the company to a level that made it an attractive acquisition for Travelers. I have often said that I wish to work with executives that I like, trust and admire. No two fit that description better than Deryck and Bob.

Berkshire's final results from its Salomon investment won't be tallied for some time, but it is safe to say that they will be far better than I anticipated two years ago. Looking back, I think of my Salomon experience as having been both fascinating and instructional, though for a time in 1991-92 [when serving as its chairman] I felt like the drama critic who wrote: "I would have enjoyed the play except that I had an unfortunate seat. It faced the stage."

The resuscitation of US Airways borders on the miraculous. Those who have watched my moves in this investment know that I have compiled a record that is unblemished by success. I was wrong in originally purchasing the stock, and I was wrong later, in repeatedly trying to unload our holdings at 50 cents on the dollar.

Two changes at the company coincided with its remarkable rebound: (1) Charlie and I left the board of directors and (2) Stephen Wolf became CEO. Fortunately for our egos, the second event was the key: Stephen Wolf's accomplishments at the airline have been phenomenal.

There still is much to do at US Airways, but survival is no longer an issue. Consequently, the company made up the dividend arrearages on our preferred during 1997, adding extra payments to compensate us for the delay we suffered. The company's common stock, furthermore, has risen from a low of $4 to a recent high of $73.

Our preferred has been called for redemption on March 15. But the rise in the company's stock has given our conversion rights, which we thought worthless not long ago, great value. It is now almost certain that our US Airways shares will produce a decent profit–that is, if my cost for Maalox is excluded–and the gain could even prove indecent.

Next time I make a big, dumb decision, Berkshire shareholders will know what to do: *Phone Mr. Wolf.*

\*     \*     \*     \*     \*

In addition to the convertible preferreds, we purchased one other private placement in 1991, $300 million of American Express Percs. This security was essentially a common stock that featured a tradeoff in its first three years: We received extra dividend payments during that period, but we were also capped in the price appreciation we could realize. Despite the cap, this holding has proved extraordinarily profitable thanks to a move by your Chairman that combined luck and skill–110% luck, the balance skill.

Our Percs were due to convert into common stock in August 1994, and in the month before I was mulling whether to sell upon conversion. One reason to hold was Amex's outstanding CEO, Harvey Golub, who seemed likely to maximize whatever potential the company had (a supposition that has since been proved–in spades). But the size of that potential was in question: Amex faced relentless competition from a multitude of card-issuers, led by Visa. Weighing the arguments, I leaned toward sale.

Here's where I got lucky. During that month of decision, I played golf at Prouts Neck, Maine with Frank Olson, CEO of Hertz. Frank is a brilliant manager, with intimate knowledge of the card business. So from the first tee on I was quizzing him about the industry. By the time we reached the second green, Frank had con-

vinced me that Amex's corporate card was a terrific franchise, and
I had decided not to sell.  On the back nine I turned buyer, and in a
few months Berkshire owned 10% of the company.

We now have a $3 billion gain in our Amex shares, and I natu-
rally feel very grateful to Frank.  But George Gillespie, our mutual
friend, says that I am confused about where my gratitude should
go.  After all, he points out, it was he who arranged the game and
assigned me to Frank's foursome.

### D.    *Unconventional Commitments*[31]

When we can't find our favorite commitment–a well-run and
sensibly-priced business with fine economics–we usually opt to put
new money into very short-term instruments of the highest quality.
Sometimes, however, we venture elsewhere.  Obviously we believe
that the alternative commitments we make are more likely to result
in profit than loss.  But we also realize that they do not offer the
certainty of profit that exists in a wonderful business secured at an
attractive price.  Finding that kind of opportunity, we *know* that we
are going to make money–the only question being when.  With alternative investments, we *think* that we are going to make money.
But we also recognize that we will sometimes realize losses, occasionally of substantial size.

We had three non-traditional positions at year end.  The first
was derivative contracts for 14.0 million barrels of oil, that being
what was then left of a 45.7 million barrel position we established
in 1994-95.  Contracts for 31.7 million barrels were settled in 1995-
97, and these supplied us with a pre-tax gain of about $61.9 million.
Our remaining contracts expire during 1998 and 1999.  In these, we
had an unrealized gain of $11.6 million at year end.  Accounting
rules require that commodity positions be carried at market value.
Therefore, both our annual and quarterly financial statements reflect any unrealized gain or loss in these contracts.  When we established our contracts, oil for future delivery seemed modestly
underpriced.  Today, though, we have no opinion as to its
attractiveness.

Our second non-traditional commitment is in silver.  Last year,
we purchased 111.2 million ounces.  Marked to market, that position produced a pre-tax gain of $97.4 million for us in 1997.  In a
way, this is a return to the past for me: Thirty years ago, I bought
silver because I anticipated its demonetization by the U.S. Gov-

---

[31] [1997.]

ernment. Ever since, I have followed the metal's fundamentals but not owned it. In recent years, bullion inventories have fallen materially, and last summer Charlie and I concluded that a higher price would be needed to establish equilibrium between supply and demand. Inflation expectations, it should be noted, play no part in our calculation of silver's value.

Finally, our largest non-traditional position at year end was $4.6 billion, at amortized cost, of long-term zero-coupon obligations of the U.S. Treasury. These securities pay no interest. Instead, they provide their holders a return by way of the discount at which they are purchased, a characteristic that makes their market prices move rapidly when interest rates change. If rates rise, you lose heavily with zeros, and if rates fall, you make outsized gains. Since rates fell in 1997, we ended the year with an unrealized pretax gain of $598.8 million in our zeros. Because we carry the securities at market value, that gain is reflected in year end book value.

In purchasing zeros, rather than staying with cash-equivalents, we risk looking very foolish: A macro-based commitment such as this never has anything close to a 100% probability of being successful. However, you pay Charlie and me to use our best judgment–not to avoid embarrassment–and we will occasionally make an unconventional move when we believe the odds favor it. Try to think kindly of us when we blow one. Along with President Clinton, we will be feeling your pain: The Munger family has more than 90% of its net worth in Berkshire and the Buffetts more than 99%.

## IV. COMMON STOCK

Occasional outbreaks of those two super-contagious diseases, fear and greed, will forever occur in the investment community. The timing of these epidemics will be unpredictable. And the market aberrations produced by them will be equally unpredictable, both as to duration and degree. Therefore, we never try to anticipate the arrival or departure of either disease. Our goal is more modest: we simply attempt to be fearful when others are greedy and to be greedy only when others are fearful.

As this is written, little fear is visible in Wall Street. Instead, euphoria prevails—and why not? What could be more exhilarating than to participate in a bull market in which the rewards to owners of businesses become gloriously uncoupled from the plodding performances of the businesses themselves. Unfortunately, however, stocks can't outperform businesses indefinitely.

Indeed, because of the heavy transaction and investment management costs they bear, stockholders as a whole and over the long term must inevitably underperform the companies they own. If American business, in aggregate, earns about 12% on equity annually, investors must end up earning significantly less. Bull markets can obscure mathematical laws, but they cannot repeal them.[32]

### A.  *The Bane of Trading: Transaction Costs*[33]

It is likely that in a few months Berkshire shares will be traded on the New York Stock Exchange. Our move there would be made possible by a new listing rule that the Exchange's Board of Governors has passed and asked the SEC to approve. If that approval is forthcoming, we expect to apply for a listing, which we believe will be granted.

Up to now, the Exchange has required newly-listed companies to have a minimum of 2,000 shareholders who each own 100 shares or more. The purpose of this rule is to insure that NYSE-listed companies enjoy the broad investor interest that facilitates an orderly market. The 100-share standard corresponds to the trading unit ("round lot") for all common stocks now listed on the Exchange.

Because [in 1988] Berkshire ha[d] relatively few shares outstanding (1,146,642), it [did] not have the number of 100-shares-or-more holders that the Exchange has required. A ten-share holding

---

32 [Introductory essay, 1986.]
33 [Letter dated August 5, 1988 sent to Berkshire shareholders and reprinted 1988.]

of Berkshire, however, represents a significant investment commitment. In fact, ten Berkshire shares have a value greater than that of 100 shares of any NYSE-listed stock. The Exchange, therefore, is willing to have Berkshire shares trade in *ten*-share "round lots."

The Exchange's proposed rule simply changes the 2,000 shareholder minimum from one measured by holders of 100 shares or more to one measured by holders of a round lot or more. Berkshire can easily meet this amended test.

Charlie Munger, Berkshire's Vice Chairman, and I are delighted at the prospect of listing, since we believe this move will benefit our shareholders. We have two criteria by which we judge what marketplace would be best for Berkshire stock. First, we hope for the stock to consistently trade at a price rationally related to its intrinsic business value. If it does, the investment result achieved by each shareholder will approximate Berkshire's business result during his period of ownership.

Such an outcome is far from automatic. Many stocks swing between levels of severe undervaluation and overvaluation. When this happens, owners are rewarded or penalized in a manner wildly at variance with how the business has performed during their period of ownership. We want to avoid such capricious results. Our goal is to have our shareholder-partners profit from the achievements of the business rather than from the foolish behavior of their co-owners.

Consistently rational prices are produced by rational owners, both current and prospective. All of our policies and communications are designed to attract the business-oriented long-term owner and to filter out possible buyers whose focus is short-term and market-oriented. To date we have been successful in this attempt, and Berkshire shares have consistently sold in an unusually narrow range around intrinsic business value. We do not believe that a NYSE listing will improve or diminish Berkshire's prospects for consistently selling at an appropriate price; the quality of our shareholders will produce a good result whatever the marketplace.

But we do believe that the listing will reduce transaction costs for Berkshire's shareholders—and that is important. Though we want to attract shareholders who will stay around for a long time, we also want to minimize the costs incurred by shareholders when they enter or exit. In the long run, the aggregate pre-tax rewards to our owners will equal the business gains achieved by the company less the transaction costs imposed by the marketplace—that is, commissions charged by brokers plus the net realized spreads of market-makers. Overall, we believe these transaction costs will be reduced materially by a NYSE listing.

[T]ransaction costs are very heavy for active stocks, often amounting to 10% or more of the earnings of a public company. In effect, these costs act as a hefty tax on owners, albeit one based on individual decisions to "change chairs" and one that is paid to the financial community rather than to Washington. Our policies and your investment attitude have reduced this "tax" on Berkshire owners to what we believe is the lowest level among large public companies. A NYSE listing should further reduce this cost for Berkshire's owners by narrowing the market-maker's spread.

Under NYSE rules we must have at least two independent directors. Among the Board of Directors you elected in May, only Malcolm Chace, Jr. meets their test of independence.

But from this deficiency comes a good result. Charlie and I are pleased to inform you that Walter Scott, Jr., CEO of the Peter Kiewit Sons', Inc. has joined the Berkshire board. PKS is one of the remarkable business stories of our time. The company, which is employee-owned, has a long-term financial record so good that I'm not going to recite it for fear of stirring unrest among our shareholders. Throughout his lifetime, Pete Kiewit ran the company as a strict meritocracy and it was in this tradition that he picked Walter to succeed him upon his death. Walter instinctively thinks like an owner and he will feel at home on the Berkshire board.

One final comment: *You should clearly understand that we are not seeking a NYSE listing for the purpose of achieving a higher valuation on Berkshire shares. Berkshire should sell, and we hope will sell, on the NYSE at prices similar to those it would have commanded in the over-the-counter market, given similar economic circumstances.* The NYSE listing should not induce you to buy or sell; it simply should cut your costs somewhat should you decide to do either.

### B. *Attracting the Right Sort of Investor*[34]

Berkshire's shares were listed on the [NYSE] on November 29, 1988. Let me clarify one point not dealt with in the letter [set forth above]: Though our round lot for trading on the NYSE is ten shares, any number of shares from one on up can be bought or sold.

---

[34] [1988.]

As the [foregoing] letter explains, our primary goal in listing was to reduce transaction costs, and we believe this goal is being achieved. Generally, the spread between the bid and asked price on the NYSE has been well below the spread that prevailed in the over-the-counter market.

Henderson Brothers, Inc., the specialist in our shares, is the oldest continuing specialist firm on the Exchange; its progenitor, William Thomas Henderson, bought his seat for $500 on September 8, 1861. (Recently, seats were selling for about $625,000.) Among the 54 firms acting as specialists, HBI ranks second in number of stocks assigned, with 83. We were pleased when Berkshire was allocated to HBI, and have been delighted with the firm's performance. Jim Maguire, Chairman of HBI, personally manages the trading in Berkshire, and we could not be in better hands.

In two respects our goals probably differ somewhat from those of most listed companies. First, we do not want to maximize the price at which Berkshire shares trade. We wish instead for them to trade in a narrow range centered at intrinsic business value (which we hope increases at a reasonable—or, better yet, unreasonable—rate). Charlie and I are bothered as much by significant overvaluation as significant undervaluation. Both extremes will inevitably produce results for many shareholders that will differ sharply from Berkshire's business results. If our stock price instead consistently mirrors business value, each of our shareholders will receive an investment result that roughly parallels the business results of Berkshire during his holding period.

Second, we wish for very little trading activity. If we ran a private business with a few passive partners, we would be disappointed if those partners, and their replacements, frequently wanted to leave the partnership. Running a public company, we feel the same way.

Our goal is to attract long-term owners who, at the time of purchase, have no timetable or price target for sale but plan instead to stay with us indefinitely. We don't understand the CEO who wants lots of stock activity, for that can be achieved only if many of his owners are constantly exiting. At what other organization—school, club, church, etc.—do leaders cheer when members leave? (However if there were a broker whose livelihood depended upon the membership turnover in such organizations, you could be sure that there would be at least one proponent of activity, as in: "There hasn't been much going on in Christianity for a while; maybe we should switch to Buddhism next week.")

Of course, some Berkshire owners will need or want to sell from time to time, and we wish for good replacements who will pay them a fair price. Therefore we try, through our policies, performance, and communications, to attract new shareholders who understand our operations, share our time horizons, and measure us as we measure ourselves. If we can continue to attract this sort of shareholder—and, just as important, can continue to be uninteresting to those with short-term or unrealistic expectations—Berkshire shares should consistently sell at prices reasonably related to business value.[35]

## C.  *Dividend Policy and Share Repurchases*[36]

Dividend policy is often reported to shareholders, but seldom explained. A company will say something like, "Our goal is to pay out 40% to 50% of earnings and to increase dividends at a rate at least equal to the rise in the CPI". And that's it—no analysis will be supplied as to why that particular policy is best for the owners of the business. Yet, allocation of capital is crucial to business and investment management. Because it is, we believe managers and owners should think hard about the circumstances under which earnings should be retained and under which they should be distributed.

The first point to understand is that all earnings are not created equal. In many businesses—particularly those that have high asset/profit ratios—inflation causes some or all of the reported earnings to become ersatz. The ersatz portion—let's call these earnings "restricted"—cannot, if the business is to retain its economic position, be distributed as dividends. Were these earnings to be paid out, the business would lose ground in one or more of the following areas: its ability to maintain its unit volume of sales, its long-term competitive position, its financial strength. No matter how conservative its payout ratio, a company that consistently dis-

---

[35] [The following is from 1989:]

With more than a year behind him of trading Berkshire's stock on the New York Stock Exchange, our specialist, Jim Maguire of [HBI] continues his outstanding performance. Before we listed, dealer spreads often were 3% or more of market price. Jim has maintained the spread at 50 points or less, which at current prices is well under 1%. Shareholders who buy or sell benefit significantly from this reduction in transaction costs.

Because we are delighted by our experience with Jim, HBI and the NYSE, I said as much in ads that have been run in a series placed by the NYSE. Normally I shun testimonials, but I was pleased in this instance to publicly compliment the Exchange.

[36] [Divided by hash lines: 1984; 1984; 1999.]

tributes restricted earnings is destined for oblivion unless equity capital is otherwise infused.

Restricted earnings are seldom valueless to owners, but they often must be discounted heavily. In effect, they are conscripted by the business, no matter how poor its economic potential. (This retention-no-matter-how-unattractive-the-return situation was communicated unwittingly in a marvelously ironic way by Consolidated Edison a decade ago. At the time, a punitive regulatory policy was a major factor causing the company's stock to sell as low as one-fourth of book value: i.e., every time a dollar of earnings was retained for reinvestment in the business, that dollar was transformed into only 25¢ of market value. But, despite this gold-into-lead process, most earnings were reinvested in the business rather than paid to owners. Meanwhile, at construction and maintenance sites throughout New York, signs proudly proclaimed the corporate slogan, "Dig We Must".)

Restricted earnings need not concern us further in this dividend discussion. Let's turn to the much-more-valued unrestricted variety. These earnings may, with equal feasibility, be retained or distributed. In our opinion, management should choose whichever course makes greater sense for the owners of the business.

This principle is not universally accepted. For a number of reasons managers like to withhold unrestricted, readily distributable earnings from shareholders—to expand the corporate empire over which the managers rule, to operate from a position of exceptional financial comfort, etc. But we believe there is only one valid reason for retention. Unrestricted earnings should be retained only when there is a reasonable prospect—backed preferably by historical evidence or, when appropriate, by a thoughtful analysis of the future—that *for every dollar retained by the corporation, at least one dollar of market value will be created for owners.* This will happen only if the capital retained produces incremental earnings equal to, or above, those generally available to investors.

To illustrate, let's assume that an investor owns a risk-free 10% perpetual bond with one very unusual feature. Each year the investor can elect either to take his 10% coupon in cash, or to reinvest the coupon in more 10% bonds with identical terms: i.e., a perpetual life and coupons offering the same cash-or-reinvest options. If, in any given year, the prevailing interest rate on long-term, risk-free bonds is 5%, it would be foolish for the investor to take his coupon in cash since the 10% bonds he could instead choose would be worth considerably more than 100¢ on the dollar.

Under these circumstances, the investor wanting to get his hands on cash should take his coupon in additional bonds and then immediately sell them. By doing that, he would realize more cash than if he had taken his coupon directly in cash. Assuming all bonds were held by rational investors, no one would opt for cash in an era of 5% interest, not even those bondholders needing cash for living purposes.

If, however, interest rates were 15%, no rational investor would want his money invested for him at 10%. Instead, the investor would choose to take his coupon in cash, even if his personal cash needs were nil. The opposite course—reinvestment of the coupon—would give an investor additional bonds with market value far less than the cash he could have elected. If he should want 10% bonds, he can simply take the cash received and buy them in the market, where they will be available at a large discount.

An analysis similar to that made by our hypothetical bond-holder is appropriate for owners in thinking about whether a company's unrestricted earnings should be retained or paid out. Of course, the analysis is much more difficult and subject to error because the rate earned on reinvested earnings is not a contractual figure, as in our bond case, but rather a fluctuating figure. Owners must guess as to what the rate will average over the intermediate future. However, once an informed guess is made, the rest of the analysis is simple: you should wish your earnings to be reinvested if they can be expected to earn high returns, and you should wish them paid to you if low returns are the likely outcome of reinvestment.

Many corporate managers reason very much along these lines in determining whether subsidiaries should distribute earnings to their parent company. At that level, the managers have no trouble thinking like intelligent owners. But payout decisions at the parent company level often are a different story. Here managers frequently have trouble putting themselves in the shoes of their share-holder-owners.

With this schizoid approach, the CEO of a multi-divisional company will instruct Subsidiary A, whose earnings on incremental capital may be expected to average 5%, to distribute all available earnings in order that they may be invested in Subsidiary B, whose earnings on incremental capital are expected to be 15%. The CEO's business school oath will allow no lesser behavior. But if his own long-term record with incremental capital is 5%—and market rates are 10%—he is likely to impose a dividend policy on shareholders of the parent company that merely follows some historical or industry-wide payout pattern. Furthermore, he will expect managers of subsidiaries to give him a full account as to why it makes sense for earnings to be retained in their operations rather than distributed to the parent-owner. But seldom will he supply *his* owners with a similar analysis pertaining to the whole company.

In judging whether managers should retain earnings, shareholders should not simply compare total incremental earnings in recent years to total incremental capital because that relationship may be distorted by what is going on in a core business. During an inflationary period, companies with a core business characterized by extraordinary economics can use small amounts of incremental capital in that business at very high rates of return (as was discussed in last year's section on Goodwill).[37] But, unless they are experiencing tremendous unit growth, outstanding businesses by definition generate large amounts of excess cash. If a company sinks most of this money in other businesses that earn low returns, the company's overall return on retained capital may nevertheless appear excellent because of the extraordinary returns being earned by the portion of earnings incrementally invested in the core business. The situation is analogous to a Pro-Am golf event: even if all of the amateurs are hopeless duffers, the team's best-ball score will be respectable because of the dominating skills of the professional.

Many corporations that consistently show good returns both on equity and on overall incremental capital have, indeed, employed a large portion of their retained earnings on an economically unattractive, even disastrous, basis. Their marvelous core businesses, however, whose earnings grow year after year, camouflage repeated failures in capital allocation elsewhere (usually involving high-priced acquisition of businesses that have inherently mediocre economics). The managers at fault periodically report on the lesson they have learned from the latest disappointment. They then usually seek out future lessons. (Failure seems to go to their heads.)

In such cases, shareholders would be far better off if earnings were retained only to expand the high-return business, with the balance paid in dividends or used to repurchase stock (an action that increases the owners' interest in the exceptional business while sparing them participation in subpar businesses). Managers of

---

[37] [*See* the essay Economic Goodwill Versus Accounting Goodwill in Part VI.C.]

high-return businesses who consistently employ much of the cash thrown off by those businesses in other ventures with low returns should be held to account for those allocation decisions, regardless of how profitable the overall enterprise is.

Nothing in this discussion is intended to argue for dividends that bounce around from quarter to quarter with each wiggle in earnings or in investment opportunities. Shareholders of public corporations understandably prefer that dividends be consistent and predictable. Payments, therefore, should reflect long-term expectations for both earnings and returns on incremental capital. Since the long-term corporate outlook changes only infrequently, dividend patterns should change no more often. But over time distributable earnings that have been withheld by managers should earn their keep. If earnings have been unwisely retained, it is likely that managers, too, have been unwisely retained.

---

The companies in which we have our largest investments have all engaged in significant stock repurchases at times when wide discrepancies existed between price and value. As shareholders, we find this encouraging and rewarding for two important reasons— one that is obvious, and one that is subtle and not always understood. The obvious point involves basic arithmetic: major repurchases at prices well below per-share intrinsic business value immediately increase, in a highly significant way, that value. When companies purchase their own stock, they often find it easy to get $2 of present value for $1. Corporate acquisition programs almost never do as well and, in a discouragingly large number of cases, fail to get anything close to $1 of value for each $1 expended.

The other benefit of repurchases is less subject to precise measurement but can be fully as important over time. By making repurchases when a company's market value is well below its business value, management clearly demonstrates that it is given to actions that enhance the wealth of shareholders, rather than to actions that expand management's domain but that do nothing for (or even harm) shareholders. Seeing this, shareholders and potential shareholders increase their estimates of future returns from the business. This upward revision, in turn, produces market prices more in line with intrinsic business value. These prices are entirely rational. Investors should pay more for a business that is lodged in the hands of a manager with demonstrated pro-shareholder leanings than for one in the hands of a self-interested manager marching to a different drummer. (To make the point extreme, how much would you pay to be a minority shareholder of a company controlled by Robert Vesco?)

The key word is "demonstrated". A manager who consistently turns his back on repurchases, when these clearly are in the interests of owners, reveals more than he knows of his motivations. No matter how often or how eloquently he mouths some public relations-inspired phrase such as "maximizing shareholder wealth" (this season's favorite), the market correctly discounts assets lodged with him. His heart is not listening to his mouth—and, after a while, neither will the market.

---

[A] number of shareholders have suggested to us that Berkshire repurchase its shares. Usually the requests were rationally based, but a few leaned on spurious logic.

There is only one combination of facts that makes it advisable for a company to repurchase its shares: First, the company has available funds–cash plus sensible borrowing capacity–beyond the near-term needs of the business and, second, finds its stock selling in the market below its intrinsic value, conservatively-calculated. To this we add a caveat: Shareholders should have been supplied all the information they need for estimating that value. Otherwise, insiders could take advantage of their uninformed partners and buy out their interests at a fraction of true worth. We have, on rare occasions, seen that happen. Usually, of course, chicanery is employed to drive stock prices up, not down.

The business "needs" that I speak of are of two kinds: First, expenditures that a company must make to maintain its competitive position (*e.g.*, the remodeling of stores at Helzberg's) and, second, optional outlays, aimed at business growth, that management expects will produce more than a dollar of value for each dollar spent (R. C. Willey's expansion into Idaho).

When available funds exceed needs of those kinds, a company with a growth-oriented shareholder population can buy new businesses or repurchase shares. If a company's stock is selling well below intrinsic value, repurchases usually make the most sense. In the mid-1970s, the wisdom of making these was virtually screaming at managements, but few responded. In most cases, those that did made their owners much wealthier than if alternative courses of action had been pursued. Indeed, during the 1970s (and, spasmodically, for some years thereafter) we searched for companies that were large repurchasers of their shares. This often was a tipoff that the company was both undervalued and run by a shareholder-oriented management.

That day is past. Now, repurchases are all the rage, but are all too often made for an unstated and, in our view, ignoble reason: to pump or support the stock price. The shareholder who chooses to sell today, of course, is benefitted by any buyer, whatever his origin or motives. But the *continuing* shareholder is penalized by repurchases above intrinsic value. Buying dollar bills for $1.10 is not good business for those who stick around.

Charlie and I admit that we feel confident in estimating intrinsic value for only a portion of traded equities and then only when we employ a range of values, rather than some pseudo-precise figure. Nevertheless, it appears to us that many companies now making repurchases are overpaying departing shareholders at the expense of those who stay. In defense of those companies, I would say that it is natural for CEOs to be optimistic about their own businesses. They also know a whole lot more about them than I do. However, I can't help but feel that too often today's repurchases are dictated by management's desire to "show confidence" or be in fashion rather than by a desire to enhance per-share value.

Sometimes, too, companies say they are repurchasing shares to offset the shares issued when stock options granted at much lower prices are exercised. This "buy high, sell low" strategy is one many unfortunate investors have employed–but never intentionally! Managements, however, seem to follow this perverse activity very cheerfully.

Of course, both option grants and repurchases may make sense–but if that's the case, it's not because the two activities are logically related. Rationally, a company's decision to repurchase shares or to issue them should stand on its own feet. Just because stock has been issued to satisfy options–or for any other reason–does not mean that stock should be repurchased at a price above intrinsic value. Correspondingly, a stock that sells well below intrinsic value should be repurchased whether or not stock has previously been issued (or may be because of outstanding options).

You should be aware that, at certain times in the past, I have erred in *not* making repurchases. My appraisal of Berkshire's value was then too conservative or I was too enthused about some alternative use of funds. We have therefore missed some opportunities–though Berkshire's trading volume at these points was too light for us to have done much buying, which means that the gain in our per-share value would have been minimal. (A repurchase of, say, 2% of a company's shares at a 25% discount from per-share intrinsic value produces only a ½% gain in that value at most–and even less if the funds could alternatively have been deployed in value-building moves.)

Some of the letters we've received clearly imply that the writer is unconcerned about intrinsic value considerations but instead wants us to trumpet an intention to repurchase so that the stock will rise (or quit going down). If the writer wants to sell tomorrow, his thinking makes sense–for him!–but if he intends to hold, he should instead hope the stock falls and trades in enough volume for us to buy a lot of it. That's the only way a repurchase program can have any real benefit for a continuing shareholder.

We will not repurchase shares unless we believe Berkshire stock is selling well below intrinsic value, conservatively calculated. Nor will we attempt to talk the stock up or down. (Neither publicly or privately have I ever told anyone to buy or sell Berkshire shares.) Instead we will give all shareholders–and potential shareholders–the same valuation-related information we would wish to have if our positions were reversed.

Recently, when the A shares fell below $45,000, we considered making repurchases. We decided, however, to delay buying, if indeed we elect to do *any*, until shareholders have had the chance to review this report. If we do find that repurchases make sense, we will only rarely place bids on the New York Stock Exchange ("NYSE"). Instead, we will respond to offers made directly to us at or below the NYSE bid. If you wish to offer stock, have your broker call Mark Millard at 402-346-1400. When a trade occurs, the broker can either record it in the "third market" or on the NYSE. We will favor purchase of the B shares if they are selling at more than a 2% discount to the A. We will not engage in transactions involving fewer than 10 shares of A or 50 shares of B.

Please be clear about one point: We will *never* make purchases with the intention of stemming a decline in Berkshire's price. Rather we will make them if and when we believe that they represent an attractive use of the Company's money. At best, repurchases are likely to have only a very minor effect on the future rate of gain in our stock's intrinsic value.

D.  *Stock Splits and Trading Activity*[38]

We often are asked why Berkshire does not split its stock. The assumption behind this question usually appears to be that a split would be a pro-shareholder action. We disagree. Let me tell you why.

One of our goals is to have Berkshire Hathaway stock sell at a price rationally related to its intrinsic business value. (But note "rationally related," not "identical": if well-regarded companies are generally selling in the market at large discounts from value, Berkshire might well be priced similarly.) The key to a rational stock price is rational shareholders, both current and prospective.

If the holders of a company's stock and/or the prospective buyers attracted to it are prone to make irrational or emotion-based decisions, some pretty silly stock prices are going to appear periodically. Manic-depressive personalities produce manic-depressive valuations. Such aberrations may help us in buying and selling the stocks of other companies. But we think it is in both your interest and ours to minimize their occurrence in the market for Berkshire.

To obtain only high quality shareholders is no cinch. Mrs. Astor could select her 400, but anyone can buy any stock. Entering members of a shareholder "club" cannot be screened for intellectual capacity, emotional stability, moral sensitivity or acceptable dress. Shareholder eugenics, therefore, might appear to be a hopeless undertaking.

In large part, however, we feel that high quality ownership can be attracted and maintained if we consistently communicate our business and ownership philosophy—*along with no other conflicting messages*—and then let self selection follow its course. For example, self selection will draw a far different crowd to a musical event advertised as an opera than one advertised as a rock concert—even though anyone can buy a ticket to either.

Through our policies and communications—our "advertisements"—we try to attract investors who will understand our operations, attitudes and expectations. (And, fully as important, we try to dissuade those who won't.) We want those who think of themselves as business owners and invest in companies with the intention of staying a long time. And, we want those who keep their eyes focused on business results, not market prices.

---

[38] [1983.]

Investors possessing those characteristics are in a small minority, but we have an exceptional collection of them. I believe well over 90%—probably over 95%—of our shares are held by those who were shareholders of Berkshire or Blue Chip five years ago. And I would guess that over 95% of our shares are held by investors for whom the holding is at least double the size of their next largest. Among companies with at least several thousand public shareholders and more than $1 billion of market value, we are almost certainly the leader in the degree to which our shareholders think and act like owners. Upgrading a shareholder group that possesses these characteristics is not easy.

Were we to split the stock or take other actions focusing on stock price rather than business value, we would attract an entering class of buyers inferior to the exiting class of sellers. At $1300, there are very few investors who can't afford a Berkshire share. Would a potential one-share purchaser be better off if we split 100 for 1 so he could buy 100 shares? Those who think so and who would buy the stock because of the split or in anticipation of one would definitely downgrade the quality of our present shareholder group. (Could we really improve our shareholder group by trading some of our present clear-thinking members for impressionable new ones who, preferring paper to value, feel wealthier with nine $10 bills than with one $100 bill?) People who buy for non-value reasons are likely to sell for non-value reasons. Their presence in the picture will accentuate erratic price swings unrelated to underlying business developments.

We will try to avoid policies that attract buyers with a short-term focus on our stock price and try to allow policies that attract informed long-term investors focusing on business values. Just as you purchased your Berkshire shares in a market populated by rational informed investors, you deserve a chance to sell—should you ever want to—in the same kind of market. We will work to keep it in existence.

One of the ironies of the stock market is the emphasis on activity. Brokers, using terms such as "marketability" and "liquidity", sing the praises of companies with high share turnover (those who cannot fill your pocket will confidently fill your ear). But investors should understand that what is good for the croupier is not good for the customer. A hyperactive stock market is the pickpocket of enterprise.

For example, consider a typical company earning, say, 12% on equity. Assume a very high turnover rate in its shares of 100% per year. If a purchase and sale of the stock trades at book value, the owners of our hypothetical company will pay, in aggregate, 2% of the company's net worth annually for the privilege of transferring ownership. This activity does nothing for the earnings of the business, and means that 1/6 of them are lost to the owners through the "frictional" cost of transfer. (And this calculation does not count option trading, which would increase frictional costs still further.)

All that makes for a rather expensive game of musical chairs. Can you imagine the agonized cry that would arise if a governmental unit were to impose a new 16⅔% tax on earnings of corporations or investors? By market activity, investors can impose upon themselves the equivalent of such a tax.

(We are aware of the pie-expanding argument that says that such activities improve the rationality of the capital allocation process. We think that this argument is specious and that, on balance, hyperactive equity markets subvert rational capital allocation and act as pie shrinkers. Adam Smith felt that all noncollusive acts in a free market were guided by an invisible hand that led an economy to maximum progress; our view is that casino-type markets and hair-trigger investment management act as an invisible foot that trips up and slows down a forward-moving economy.)

E. *Shareholder Strategies*[39]

Late last year Berkshire's stock price crossed $10,000. Several shareholders have mentioned to me that the high price causes them problems: They like to give shares away each year and find themselves impeded by the tax rule that draws a distinction between annual gifts of $10,000 or under to a single individual and those above $10,000. That is, those gifts no greater than $10,000 are completely tax-free; those above $10,000 require the donor to use up a portion of his or her lifetime exemption from gift and estate taxes, or, if that exemption has been exhausted, to pay gift taxes.

I can suggest three ways to address this problem. The first would be useful to a married shareholder, who can give up to $20,000 annually to a single recipient, as long as the donor files a gift tax return containing his or her spouse's written consent to gifts made during the year.

Secondly, a shareholder, married or not, can make a bargain sale. Imagine, for example, that Berkshire is selling for $12,000 and that one wishes to make only a $10,000 gift. In that case, sell

---

[39] [1992.]

the stock to the giftee for $2,000. (Caution: You will be taxed on the amount, if any, by which the sales price to your giftee exceeds your tax basis.)

Finally, you can establish a partnership with people to whom you are making gifts, fund it with Berkshire shares, and simply give percentage interests in the partnership away each year. These interests can be for any value that you select. If the value is $10,000 or less, the gift will be tax-free.

We issue the customary warning: Consult with your own tax advisor before taking action on any of the more esoteric methods of gift-making.

We hold to the view about stock splits that we set forth in the [preceding essay]. Overall, we believe our owner-related policies—including the no-split policy—have helped us assemble a body of shareholders that is the best associated with any widely-held American corporation. Our shareholders think and behave like rational long-term owners and view the business much as Charlie and I do. Consequently, our stock consistently trades in a price range that is sensibly related to intrinsic value.

Additionally, we believe that our shares turn over far less actively than do the shares of any other widely-held company. The frictional costs of trading—which act as a major "tax" on the owners of many companies—are virtually non-existent at Berkshire. (The market-making skills of Jim Maguire, our New York Stock Exchange specialist, definitely help to keep these costs low.) Obviously a split would not change this situation dramatically. Nonetheless, there is no way that our shareholder group would be upgraded by the new shareholders enticed by a split. Instead we believe that modest degradation would occur.

### F.  *Berkshire's Recapitalization*[40]

At the Annual Meeting you will be asked to approve a recapitalization of Berkshire, creating two classes of stock. If the plan is adopted, our existing common stock will be designated as Class A Common Stock and a new Class B Common Stock will be authorized.

Each share of the "B" will have the rights of 1/30th of an "A" share with these exceptions: First, a B share will have 1/200th of the vote of an A share (rather than 1/30th of the vote). Second, the B

---

[40] [Divided by hash lines: 1995; 1996.]

will not be eligible to participate in Berkshire's shareholder-designated charitable contributions program.

When the recapitalization is complete, each share of A will become convertible, at the holder's option and at any time, into 30 shares of B. This conversion privilege will not extend in the opposite direction. That is, holders of B shares will not be able to convert them into A shares.

We expect to list the B shares on the New York Stock Exchange, where they will trade alongside the A stock. To create the shareholder base necessary for a listing—and to ensure a liquid market in the B stock—Berkshire expects to make a public offering for cash of at least $100 million of new B shares. The offering will be made only by means of a prospectus.

The market will ultimately determine the price of the B shares. Their price, though, should be in the neighborhood of 1/30th of the price of the A shares.

Class A shareholders who wish to give gifts may find it convenient to convert a share or two of their stock into Class B shares. Additionally, arbitrage-related conversions will occur if demand for the B is strong enough to push its price to slightly above 1/30th of the price of A.

However, because the Class A stock will entitle its holders to full voting rights and access to Berkshire's contributions program, these shares will be superior to the Class B shares and we would expect most shareholders to remain holders of the Class A—which is precisely what the Buffett and Munger families plan to do, except in those instances when we ourselves might convert a few shares to facilitate gifts. The prospect that most shareholders will stick to the A stock suggests that it will enjoy a somewhat more liquid market than the B.

There are tradeoffs for Berkshire in this recapitalization. But they do not arise from the proceeds of the offering—we will find constructive uses for the money—nor in any degree from the price at which we will sell the B shares. As I write this—with Berkshire stock at $36,000—Charlie and I do not believe it undervalued. Therefore, the offering we propose will not diminish the per-share intrinsic value of our existing stock. Let me also put our thoughts about valuation more baldly: Berkshire is selling at a price at which Charlie and I would not consider buying it.

What Berkshire will incur by way of the B stock are certain added costs, including those involving the mechanics of handling a larger number of shareholders. On the other hand, the stock should be a convenience for people wishing to make gifts. And those of you who have hoped for a split have gained a do-it-yourself method of bringing one about.

We are making this move, though, for other reasons—having to do with the appearance of expense-laden unit trusts purporting to be low-priced "clones" of Berkshire and sure to be aggressively marketed. The idea behind these vehicles is not new: In recent years, a number of people have told me about their wish to create an "all-Berkshire" investment fund to be sold at a low dollar price. But until recently, the promoters of these investments heard out my objections and backed off.

I did not discourage these people because I prefer large investors over small. Were it possible, Charlie and I would love to turn $1,000 into $3,000 for multitudes of people who would find that gain an important answer to their immediate problems.

In order to quickly triple small stakes, however, we would have to just as quickly turn our present market capitalization of $43 billion into $129 billion (roughly the market cap of General Electric, America's most highly valued company). *We can't come close to doing that*. The very best we hope for is—on average—to double Berkshire's per-share intrinsic value every five years, and we may well fall far short of that goal.

In the end, Charlie and I do not care whether our shareholders own Berkshire in large or small amounts. What we wish for are shareholders of any size who are knowledgeable about our operations, share our objectives and long-term perspective, and are aware of our limitations, most particularly those imposed by our large capital base.

The unit trusts that have recently surfaced fly in the face of these goals. They would be sold by brokers working for big commissions, would impose other burdensome costs on their shareholders, and would be marketed *en masse* to unsophisticated buyers, apt to be seduced by our past record and beguiled by the publicity Berkshire and I have received in recent years. The sure outcome: a multitude of investors destined to be disappointed.

Through our creation of the B stock—a low-denomination product far superior to Berkshire-only trusts—we hope to make the clones unmerchandisable.

But both present and prospective Berkshire shareholders should pay special attention to one point: Though the per-share intrinsic value of our stock has grown at an excellent rate during the past five years, its market price has grown still faster. The stock, in other words, has outperformed the business.

That kind of market overperformance cannot persist indefinitely, neither for Berkshire nor any other stock. *Inevitably, there will be periods of underperformance as well.* The price volatility that results, though endemic to public markets, is not to our liking. What we would prefer instead is to have the market price of Berkshire precisely track its intrinsic value. Were the stock to do that, every shareholder would benefit during his period of ownership in exact proportion to the progress Berkshire itself made in the period.

Obviously, the market behavior of Berkshire's stock will never conform to this ideal. But we will come closer to this goal than we would otherwise if our present and prospective shareholders are informed, business-oriented and not exposed to high-commission salesmanship when making their investment decisions. To that end, we are better off if we can blunt the merchandising efforts of the unit trust—and that is the reason we are creating the B stock.

---

[W]e made two good-sized offerings through Salomon [during 1996], both with interesting aspects. The first was our sale in May of 517,500 shares of Class B Common, which generated net proceeds of $565 million. As I have told you before, we made this sale in response to the threatened creation of unit trusts that would have marketed themselves as Berkshire look-alikes. In the process, they would have used our past, and definitely nonrepeatable, record to entice naive small investors and would have charged these innocents high fees and commissions.

I think it would have been quite easy for such trusts to have sold many billions of dollars worth of units, and I also believe that early marketing successes by these trusts would have led to the formation of others. (In the securities business, whatever can be sold will be sold.) The trusts would have meanwhile indiscriminately poured the proceeds of their offerings into a supply of Berkshire shares that is fixed and limited. The likely result: a speculative bubble in our stock. For at least a time, the price jump would have been self-validating, in that it would have pulled new waves of naive and impressionable investors into the trusts and set off still more buying of Berkshire shares.

Some Berkshire shareholders choosing to exit might have found that outcome ideal, since they could have profited at the expense of the buyers entering with false hopes. Continuing shareholders, however, would have suffered once reality set in, for at that point Berkshire would have been burdened with both hundreds of thousands of unhappy, indirect owners (trustholders, that is) and a stained reputation.

Our issuance of the B shares not only arrested the sale of the trusts, but provided a low-cost way for people to invest in Berkshire if they still wished to after hearing the warnings we issued. To blunt the enthusiasm that brokers normally have for pushing new issues—because that's where the money is—we arranged for our offering to carry a commission of only 1½%, the lowest payoff that we have ever seen in common stock underwriting. Additionally, we made the amount of the offering open-ended, thereby repelling the typical IPO buyer who looks for a short-term price spurt arising from a combination of hype and scarcity.

Overall, we tried to make sure that the B stock would be purchased only by investors with a long-term perspective. Those efforts were generally successful: Trading volume in the B shares immediately following the offering—a rough index of "flipping"—was far below the norm for a new issue. In the end we added about 40,000 shareholders, most of whom we believe both understand what they own and share our time horizons.

Salomon could not have performed better in the handling of this unusual transaction. Its investment bankers understood perfectly what we were trying to achieve and tailored every aspect of the offering to meet these objectives. The firm would have made far more money—perhaps ten times as much—if our offering had been standard in its make-up. But the investment bankers involved made no attempt to tweak the specifics in that direction. Instead they came up with ideas that were counter to Salomon's financial interest but that made it much more certain Berkshire's goals would be reached. Terry Fitzgerald captained this effort, and we thank him for the job that he did.

Given that background, it won't surprise you to learn that we again went to Terry when we decided late in the year to sell an issue of Berkshire notes that can be exchanged for a portion of the Salomon shares that we hold. In this instance, once again, Salomon did an absolutely first-class job, selling $500 million principal amount of five-year notes for $447.1 million. Each $1,000 note is exchangeable into 17.65 shares and is callable in three years at accreted value. Counting the original issue discount and a 1% coupon, the securities will provide a yield of 3% to maturity for holders who do not exchange them for Salomon stock. But it seems quite likely that the notes will be exchanged before their maturity. If that happens, our interest cost will be about 1.1% for the period prior to exchange.

In recent years, it has been written that Charlie and I are unhappy about all investment-banking fees. That's dead wrong. We have paid a great many fees over the last 30 years—beginning with the check we wrote to Charlie Heider upon our purchase of National Indemnity in 1967—and we are delighted to make payments that are commensurate with performance. In the case of the 1996 transactions at Salomon Brothers we more than got our money's worth.

## V. Mergers and Acquisitions

Of all our activities at Berkshire, the most exhilarating for Charlie and me is the acquisition of a business with excellent economic characteristics and a management that we like, trust and admire. Such acquisitions are not easy to make but we look for them constantly. In the search, we adopt the same attitude one might find appropriate in looking for a spouse: It pays to be active, interested, and open-minded, but it does not pay to be in a hurry.

In the past, I've observed that many acquisition-hungry managers were apparently mesmerized by their childhood reading of the story about the frog-kissing princess. Remembering her success, they pay dearly for the right to kiss corporate toads, expecting wondrous transfigurations. Initially, disappointing results only deepen their desire to round up new toads. ("Fanaticism," said [Santayana], "consists of redoubling your effort when you've forgotten your aim.") Ultimately, even the most optimistic manager must face reality. Standing knee-deep in unresponsive toads, he then announces an enormous "restructuring" charge. In this corporate equivalent of a Head Start program, the CEO receives the education but the stockholders pay the tuition.

In my early days as a manager I, too, dated a few toads. They were cheap dates—I've never been much of a sport—but my results matched those of acquirers who courted higher-priced toads. I kissed and they croaked.

After several failures of this type, I finally remembered some useful advice I once got from a golf pro (who, like all pros who have had anything to do with my game, wishes to remain anonymous). Said the pro: "Practice doesn't make perfect; practice makes permanent." And thereafter I revised my strategy and tried to buy good businesses at fair prices rather than fair businesses at good prices.[41]

### A. Bad Motives and High Prices[42]

As our history indicates, we are comfortable both with total ownership of businesses and with marketable securities representing small portions of businesses. We continually look for ways to employ large sums in each area. (But we try to avoid small commitments—"If something's not worth doing at all, it's not worth

---

[41] [Introductory essay, 1992.]
[42] [Divided by hash lines: 1981; 1982; 1997; 1994.]

doing well".) Indeed, the liquidity requirements of our insurance businesses mandate major investments in marketable securities.

Our acquisition decisions will be aimed at maximizing real economic benefits, not at maximizing either managerial domain or reported numbers for accounting purposes. (In the long run, managements stressing accounting appearance over economic substance usually achieve little of either.)

Regardless of the impact upon immediately reportable earnings, we would rather buy 10% of Wonderful Business T at X per share than 100% of T at 2X per share. Most corporate managers prefer just the reverse, and have no shortage of stated rationales for their behavior.

However, we suspect three motivations—usually unspoken—to be, singly or in combination, the important ones in most high-premium takeovers:

(1) Leaders, business or otherwise, seldom are deficient in animal spirits and often relish increased activity and challenge. At Berkshire, the corporate pulse never beats faster than when an acquisition is in prospect.

(2) Most organizations, business or otherwise, measure themselves, are measured by others, and compensate their managers far more by the yardstick of size than by any other yardstick. (Ask a Fortune 500 manager where his corporation stands on that famous list and, invariably, the number responded will be from the list ranked by size of sales; he may well not even know where his corporation places on the list *Fortune* just as faithfully compiles ranking the same 500 corporations by profitability.)

(3) Many managements apparently were overexposed in impressionable childhood years to the story in which the imprisoned handsome prince is released from a toad's body by a kiss from a beautiful princess. Consequently, they are certain their managerial kiss will do wonders for the profitability of Company T(arget).

Such optimism is essential. Absent that rosy view, why else should the shareholders of Company A(cquisitor) want to own an interest in T at the 2X takeover cost rather than at the X market price they would pay if they made direct purchases on their own?

In other words, investors can always buy toads at the going price for toads. If investors instead bankroll princesses who wish to pay double for the right to kiss the toad, those kisses had better pack some real dynamite. We've observed many kisses but very few miracles. Nevertheless, many managerial princesses remain serenely confident about the future potency of their kisses—even after their corporate backyards are knee-deep in unresponsive toads. In fairness, we should acknowledge that some acquisition records have been dazzling. Two major categories stand out.

The first involves companies that, through design or accident, have purchased only businesses that are particularly well adapted to an inflationary environment. Such favored business must have two characteristics: (1) an ability to increase prices rather easily (even when product demand is flat and capacity is not fully utilized) without fear of significant loss of either market share or unit volume, and (2) an ability to accommodate large dollar volume increases in business (often produced more by inflation than by real growth) with only minor additional investment of capital. Managers of ordinary ability, focusing solely on acquisition possibilities meeting these tests, have achieved excellent results in recent decades. However, very few enterprises possess both characteristics, and competition to buy those that do has now become fierce to the point of being self-defeating.

The second category involves the managerial superstars—men who can recognize that rare prince who is disguised as a toad, and who have managerial abilities that enable them to peel away the disguise. We salute such managers as Ben Heineman at Northwest Industries, Henry Singleton at Teledyne, Erwin Zaban at National Service Industries, and especially Tom Murphy at Capital Cities Communications (a real managerial "twofer", whose acquisition efforts have been properly focused in Category 1 and whose operating talents also make him a leader of Category 2). From both direct and vicarious experience, we recognize the difficulty and rarity of these executives' achievements. (So do they; these champs have made very few deals in recent years, and often have found repurchase of their own shares to be the most sensible employment of corporate capital.)

Your Chairman, unfortunately, does not qualify for Category 2. And, despite a reasonably good understanding of the economic factors compelling concentration in Category 1, our actual acquisition activity in that category has been sporadic and inadequate. Our preaching was better than our performance. (We neglected the Noah principle: predicting rain doesn't count, building arks does.)

We have tried occasionally to buy toads at bargain prices with results that have been chronicled in past reports. Clearly our kisses fell flat. We have done well with a couple of princes—but they were princes when purchased. At least our kisses didn't turn them into toads. And, finally, we have occasionally been quite successful in purchasing fractional interests in easily-identifiable princes at toad-like prices.

———————

Berkshire and Blue Chip are considering merger in 1983. If it takes place, it will involve an exchange of stock based upon an identical valuation method applied to both companies. The one other significant issuance of shares by Berkshire or its affiliated companies that occurred during present management's tenure was in the 1978 merger of Berkshire with Diversified Retailing Company.

Our share issuances follow a simple basic rule: we will not issue shares unless we receive as much intrinsic business value as we give. Such a policy might seem axiomatic. Why, you might ask, would anyone issue dollar bills in exchange for fifty-cent pieces? Unfortunately, many corporate managers have been willing to do just that.

The first choice of these managers in making acquisitions may be to use cash or debt. But frequently the CEO's cravings outpace cash and credit resources (certainly mine always have). Frequently, also, these cravings occur when his own stock is selling far below intrinsic business value. This state of affairs produces a moment of truth. At that point, as Yogi Berra has said, "You can observe a lot just by watching." For shareholders then will find which objective the management truly prefers—expansion of domain or maintenance of owners' wealth.

The need to choose between these objectives occurs for some simple reasons. Companies often sell in the stock market below their intrinsic business value. But when a company wishes to sell out completely, in a negotiated transaction, it inevitably wants to—and usually can—receive full business value in whatever kind of currency the value is to be delivered. If cash is to be used in payment, the seller's calculation of value received couldn't be easier. If stock of the buyer is to be the currency, the seller's calculation is still relatively easy: just figure the market value in cash of what is to be received in stock.

Meanwhile, the buyer wishing to use his own stock as currency for the purchase has no problems if the stock is selling in the market at full intrinsic value.

But suppose it is selling at only half intrinsic value. In that case, the buyer is faced with the unhappy prospect of using a substantially undervalued currency to make its purchase.

Ironically, were the buyer to instead be a seller of its *entire* business, it too could negotiate for, and probably get, full intrinsic business value. But when the buyer makes a partial sale of itself— *and that is what the issuance of shares to make an acquisition amounts to*—it can customarily get no higher value set on its shares than the market chooses to grant it.

The acquirer who nevertheless barges ahead ends up using an undervalued (market value) currency to pay for a fully valued (negotiated value) property. In effect, the acquirer must give up $2 of value to receive $1 of value. Under such circumstances, a marvelous business purchased at a fair sales price becomes a terrible buy. For gold valued as gold cannot be purchased intelligently through the utilization of gold—or even silver—valued as lead.

If, however, the thirst for size and action is strong enough, the acquirer's manager will find ample rationalizations for such a value-destroying issuance of stock. Friendly investment bankers will reassure him as to the soundness of his actions. (Don't ask the barber whether you need a haircut.)

A few favorite rationalizations employed by stock-issuing managements follow:

(a) "The company we're buying is going to be worth a lot more in the future." (Presumably so is the interest in the old business that is being traded away; future prospects are implicit in the business valuation process. If 2X is issued for X, the imbalance still exists when both parts double in business value.)

(b) "We have to grow." (Who, it might be asked, is the "we"? For present shareholders, the reality is that all existing businesses shrink when shares are issued. Were Berkshire to issue shares tomorrow for an acquisition, Berkshire would own everything that it now owns plus the new business, but *your* interest in such hard-to-match businesses as See's Candy Shops, National Indemnity, etc. would automatically be reduced. If (1) your family owns a 120-acre farm and (2) you invite a neighbor with 60 acres of comparable land to merge his farm into an equal partnership— with you to be managing partner, then (3) your managerial domain will have grown to 180 acres but you will have permanently shrunk by 25% your family's ownership interest in both acreage and crops. Managers who want to expand their domain at the expense of owners might better consider a career in government.)

(c) "Our stock is undervalued and we've minimized its use in this deal—but we need to give the selling shareholder 51% in stock and 49% in cash so that certain of those shareholders can get the tax-free exchange they want." (This argument acknowledges that it is beneficial to the acquirer to hold down the issuance of shares, and we like that. But if it hurts old owners to utilize shares on a 100% basis, it very likely hurts on a 51% basis. After all, a man is not charmed if a spaniel defaces his lawn, just because it's a spaniel and not a St. Bernard. And the wishes of sellers can't be the determinant of the best interests of the buyer—what would happen if, heaven forbid, the seller insisted that as a condition of merger the CEO of the acquirer be replaced?)

There are three ways to avoid destruction of value for old owners when shares are issued for acquisitions. One is to have a true business-value-for-business-value merger, such as the Berkshire-Blue Chip combination is intended to be. Such a merger attempts to be fair to shareholders of *both* parties, with each receiving just as much as it gives in terms of intrinsic business value. The Dart Industries-Kraft and Nabisco-Standard Brands mergers appeared to be of this type, but they are the exceptions. It's not that acquirers wish to avoid such deals; it's just that they are very hard to do.

The second route presents itself when the acquirer's stock sells at or above its intrinsic business value. In that situation, the use of stock as currency actually may enhance the wealth of the acquiring company's owners. Many mergers were accomplished on this basis in the 1965-69 period. The results were the converse of most of the activity since 1970: the shareholders of the *acquired* company received very inflated currency (frequently pumped up by dubious accounting and promotional techniques) and were the losers of wealth through such transactions.

During recent years the second solution has been available to very few large companies. The exceptions have primarily been those companies in glamorous or promotional businesses to which the market temporarily attaches valuations at or above intrinsic business valuation.

The third solution is for the acquirer to go ahead with the acquisition, but then subsequently repurchase a quantity of shares equal to the number issued in the merger. In this manner, what originally was a stock-for-stock merger can be converted, effectively, into a cash-for-stock acquisition. Repurchases of this kind are damage-repair moves. Regular readers will correctly guess that we much prefer repurchases that directly enhance the wealth of owners instead of repurchases that merely repair previous damage. Scoring touchdowns is more exhilarating than recovering one's fumbles. But, when a fumble has occurred, recovery is important and we heartily recommend damage-repair repurchases that turn a bad stock deal into a fair cash deal.

The language utilized in mergers tends to confuse the issues and encourage irrational actions by managers. For example, "dilution" is usually carefully calculated on a pro forma basis for both book value and current earnings per share. Particular emphasis is given to the latter item. When that calculation is negative (dilutive) from the acquiring company's standpoint, a justifying explanation will be made (internally, if not elsewhere) that the lines will cross favorably at some point in the future. (While deals often fail in practice, they never fail in projections—if the CEO is visibly panting over a prospective acquisition, subordinates and consultants will supply the requisite projections to rationalize any price.) Should the calculation produce numbers that are immediately positive—that is, anti-dilutive—for the acquirer, no comment is thought to be necessary.

The attention given this form of dilution is overdone: current earnings per share (or even earnings per share of the next few years) are an important variable in most business valuations, but far from all-powerful.

There have been plenty of mergers, non-dilutive in this limited sense, that were instantly value-destroying for the acquirer. And some mergers that have diluted current and near-term earnings per share have in fact been value-enhancing. What really counts is whether a merger is dilutive or anti-dilutive in terms of intrinsic business value (a judgment involving consideration of many variables). We believe calculation of dilution from this viewpoint to be all-important (and too seldom made).

A second language problem relates to the equation of exchange. If Company A announces that it will issue shares to merge with Company B, the process is customarily described as "Company A to Acquire Company B", or "B Sells to A". Clearer thinking about the matter would result if a more awkward but more accurate description were used: "Part of A sold to acquire B", or "Owners of B to receive part of A in exchange for their properties". In a trade, what you are giving is just as important as what you are getting. This remains true even when the final tally on what is being given is delayed. Subsequent sales of common stock or convertible issues, either to complete the financing for a deal or to restore balance sheet strength, must be fully counted in evaluating the fundamental mathematics of the original acquisition. (If corporate pregnancy is going to be the consequence of corporate mating, the time to face that fact is before the moment of ecstasy.)

Managers and directors might sharpen their thinking by asking themselves if they would sell 100% of their business on the same basis they are being asked to sell part of it. And if it isn't smart to sell all on such a basis, they should ask themselves why it is smart to sell a portion. A cumulation of small managerial stupidities will produce a major stupidity—not a major triumph. (Las Vegas has been built upon the wealth transfers that occur when people engage in seemingly-small disadvantageous capital transactions.)

The "giving versus getting" factor can most easily be calculated in the case of registered investment companies. Assume Investment Company X, selling at 50% of asset value, wishes to merge with Investment Company Y. Assume, also, that Company X therefore decides to issue shares equal in market value to 100% of Y's asset value.

Such a share exchange would leave X trading $2 of its previous intrinsic value for $1 of Y's intrinsic value. Protests would promptly come forth from both X's shareholders and the SEC, which rules on the fairness of registered investment company mergers. Such a transaction simply would not be allowed.

In the case of manufacturing, service, financial companies, etc., values are not normally as precisely calculable as in the case of investment companies. But we have seen mergers in these industries that just as dramatically destroyed value for the owners of the acquiring company as was the case in the hypothetical illustration above. This destruction could not happen if management and directors would assess the fairness of any transaction by using the same yardstick in the measurement of both businesses.

Finally, a word should be said about the "double whammy" effect upon owners of the acquiring company when value-diluting stock issuances occur. Under such circumstances, the first blow is the loss of intrinsic business value that occurs through the merger itself. The second is the downward revision in market valuation that, quite rationally, is given to that now-diluted business value. For current and prospective owners understandably will not pay as much for assets lodged in the hands of a management that has a record of wealth-destruction through unintelligent share issuances as they will pay for assets entrusted to a management with precisely equal operating talents, but a known distaste for anti-owner actions. Once management shows itself insensitive to the interests of owners, shareholders will suffer a long time from the price/value ratio afforded their stock (relative to other stocks), no matter what assurances management gives that the value-diluting action taken was a one-of-a-kind event.

Those assurances are treated by the market much as one-bug-in-the-salad explanations are treated at restaurants. Such explanations, even when accompanied by a new waiter, do not eliminate a drop in the demand (and hence market value) for salads, both on the part of the offended customer and his neighbors pondering what to order. Other things being equal, the highest stock market prices relative to intrinsic business value are given to companies whose managers have demonstrated their unwillingness to issue shares at any time on terms unfavorable to the owners of the business.

---

I've mentioned that we strongly prefer to use cash rather than Berkshire stock in acquisitions. A study of the record will tell you why: If you aggregate all of our stock-only mergers (excluding those we did with two affiliated companies, Diversified Retailing and Blue Chip Stamps), you will find that our shareholders are slightly worse off than they would have been had I not done the transactions. Though it hurts me to say it, when I've issued stock, I've cost you money.

Be clear about one thing: This cost has *not* occurred because we were misled in any way by sellers or because they thereafter failed to manage with diligence and skill. On the contrary, the sellers were completely candid when we were negotiating our deals and have been energetic and effective ever since.

Instead, our problem has been that we own a truly marvelous collection of businesses, which means that trading away a portion of them for something new almost never makes sense. When we issue shares in a merger, we reduce your ownership in all of our businesses–partly-owned companies such as Coca-Cola, Gillette and American Express, and all of our terrific operating companies as well. An example from sports will illustrate the difficulty we face: For a baseball team, acquiring a player who can be expected to bat .350 is almost always a wonderful event–*except* when the team must trade a .380 hitter to make the deal.

Because our roster is filled with .380 hitters, we have tried to pay cash for acquisitions, and here our record has been far better. Starting with National Indemnity in 1967, and continuing with, among others, See's, Buffalo News, Scott Fetzer and GEICO, we have acquired–for cash–a number of large businesses that have performed incredibly well since we bought them. These acquisitions have delivered Berkshire tremendous value–indeed, far more than I anticipated when we made our purchases.

We believe that it is almost impossible for us to "trade up" from our present businesses and managements. Our situation is the opposite of Camelot's Mordred, of whom Guenevere commented, "The one thing I can say for him is that he is bound to marry well. Everybody is above him." Marrying well is extremely difficult for Berkshire.

––––––––––

[I]n contemplating business mergers and acquisitions, many managers tend to focus on whether the transaction is immediately dilutive or anti-dilutive to earnings per share (or, at financial institutions, to per-share book value). An emphasis of this sort carries great dangers. [I]magine that a 25-year-old first-year MBA student is considering merging his future economic interests with those of a 25-year-old day laborer. The MBA student, a non-earner, would find that a "share-for-share" merger of his equity interest in himself with that of the day laborer would enhance his near-term earnings (in a big way!). But what could be sillier for the student than a deal of this kind?

In corporate transactions, it's equally silly for the would-be purchaser to focus on current earnings when the prospective acquiree has either different prospects, a different mix of operating and non-operating assets, or a different capital structure. At Berkshire, we have rejected many merger and purchase opportunities that would have boosted current and near-term earnings but that would have reduced per-share intrinsic value. Our approach, rather, has been to follow Wayne Gretzky's advice: "Go to where the puck is going to be, not to where it is." As a result, our shareholders are now many billions of dollars richer than they would have been if we had used the standard catechism.

The sad fact is that most major acquisitions display an egregious imbalance: They are a bonanza for the shareholders of the acquiree; they increase the income and status of the acquirer's management; and they are a honey pot for the investment bankers and other professionals on both sides. But, alas, they usually reduce the wealth of the acquirer's shareholders, often to a substantial extent. That happens because the acquirer typically gives up more intrinsic value than it receives. Do that enough, says John Medlin, the retired head of Wachovia Corp., and "you are running a chain letter in reverse."

Over time, the skill with which a company's managers allocate capital has an enormous impact on the enterprise's value. Almost by definition, a really good business generates far more money (at least after its early years) than it can use internally. The company could, of course, distribute the money to shareholders by way of dividends or share repurchases. But often the CEO asks a strategic planning staff, consultants or investment bankers whether an acquisition or two might make sense. That's like asking your interior decorator whether you need a $50,000 rug.

The acquisition problem is often compounded by a biological bias: Many CEOs attain their positions in part because they possess an abundance of animal spirits and ego. If an executive is heavily endowed with these qualities—which, it should be acknowledged, sometimes have their advantages—they won't disappear when he reaches the top. When such a CEO is encouraged by his advisors to make deals, he responds much as would a teenage boy who is encouraged by his father to have a normal sex life. It's not a push he needs.

Some years back, a CEO friend of mine—in jest, it must be said—unintentionally described the pathology of many big deals. This friend, who ran a property-casualty insurer, was explaining to his directors why he wanted to acquire a certain life insurance company. After droning rather unpersuasively through the economics and strategic rationale for the acquisition, he abruptly abandoned the script. With an impish look, he simply said: "Aw, fellas, all the other kids have one."

At Berkshire, our managers will continue to earn extraordinary returns from what appear to be ordinary businesses. As a first step, these managers will look for ways to deploy their earnings advantageously in their businesses. What's left, they will send to Charlie and me. We then will try to use those funds in ways that build per-share intrinsic value. Our goal will be to acquire either part or all of businesses that we believe we understand, that have good, sustainable underlying economics, and that are run by managers whom we like, admire and trust.

### B.   *Sensible Share Repurchases Versus Greenmail*[43]

Our endorsement of repurchases is limited to those dictated by price/value relationships and does not extend to the "greenmail" repurchase—a practice we find odious and repugnant. In these transactions, two parties achieve their personal ends by exploitation of an innocent and unconsulted third party. The players are: (1) the "shareholder" extortionist who, even before the ink on his stock certificate dries, delivers his "your-money-or-your-life" message to managers; (2) the corporate insiders who quickly seek peace at any price—as long as the price is paid by someone else; and (3) the shareholders whose money is used by (2) to make (1) go away. As the dust settles, the mugging, transient shareholder gives his speech on "free enterprise", the muggee management gives its speech on "the best interests of the company", and the innocent shareholder standing by mutely funds the payoff.

### C.   *Leveraged Buyouts*[44]

If successful corporate business acquisition is so hard, how does one explain the widespread recent success of most of the leveraged-buy-out ("LBO") operators who have purchased corporations? A huge part of the answer comes from income-tax effects and other simple effects. When, in a typical LBO, the typical mostly equity corporate capitalization was replaced by 90% debt plus a new 10%-of-capitalization common stock position:

   (1) the combined market value of all the new common stock plus all the new debt became much higher than the previous market value of all the older common stock, because the existing stream of pre-tax earnings was no longer shared with corporate income tax collectors who, in many cases, had previously received more cash each year than shareholders; and

   (2) even after the value-enhancing effect of the corporate tax reduction was shared with former shareholders by paying them extra-high prices to leave, a retained residue of value-enhancing tax effect made the new common stock

---

[43] [1984.]

[44] [1989 Wesco Financial Corporation Letter to Shareholders, by Charles T. Munger. Reprinted with permission.]

(which now became much like a speculative warrant with good terms) worth considerably more than cost as the ink dried on acquisition papers; and

(3) the new "owners" then resorted to strategies, difficult neither to conceive nor implement, including the following:

   (a) they eliminated many of the easily removable costs (largely personnel costs) and sub-par segments which in some mix (i) bedevil successful corporations (including ours) with sloth and folly and (ii) create their humane grace and, through present sacrifice, good long-term prospects, justifying sacrifice endured; and

   (b) they sold off a few operations at super-high prices, sometimes exercising the easiest microeconomic insight by selling to a direct competitor and sometimes selling to a surprisingly easy-to-find non-competitive corporate buyer, not owned by its managers, willing to pay almost as high a price as a competitor would; and

(4) the new "owners" then profited, in due course, not only from the tax effect and other simple reshuffling activities described above, but also from the wonderful upside effects of extreme financial leverage during a long business boom accompanied by a rising stock market.

Whether the country wants a large number (or even any) of its large corporations to have extremely leveraged capitalizations, except through occasional adversity, presents interesting social questions. Is one social function of corporations to be financially strong so that they act as shock absorbers, protecting dependent employees, suppliers and customers from part of the volatility implicit in capitalism? Was Ben Franklin right when he included the following folk wisdom in *Poor Richard's Almanac*: "It is hard for an empty sack to stand upright." Is a weak corporation, borrowed to the hilt, the social equivalent of a bridge with an inadequate reserve of structural strength? Granting that leveraged buy outs have some favorable effects (as well as unfavorable effects) on long term efficiency, how many thousands of able people do we wish to attract into promotional corporate recapitalization activity which (1) reduces corporate income taxes, (2) often tests the limits of antitrust law, and (3) focuses business attention on short-term cash generation to pay down oppressive levels of debt? Finally, as Columbia Law School's Professor Lou Lowenstein puts it (more or less): "Do we really want entire corporate businesses, as important social institutions, continuously traded like pork belly contracts?"

However the social questions are answered, three aspects of the present situation are clear. First, the corporate tax effect is so large in LBO transactions that easy success in such transactions does not imply that success is easy in ordinary corporate acquisitions. Second, the hordes of leveraged-buy-out operators now with us raise the general level of acquisition prices to the detriment of other would-be acquirers, including Wesco, which are not willing to maximize tax benefits through maximized borrowing. And, third, the LBO operator will not go away so long as present permissive laws last. The operators have a real advantage under such laws, not just a fig leaf aiding promotion. Even though failure and disgrace will reduce their number, and prices paid in leveraged-buy-out transactions will fall, the capitalized value of reducing the corporate income tax will remain. Therefore, plenty of rational incentive will remain for transactions. The LBO genie will encounter reverses, but he is not going back in the bottle unless ordered to do so by new laws.

It should also be noted that the LBO operators' incentives to bid high do not end with real advantages derived from tax law and willingness to reshuffle businesses with much speed and few scruples. Additional incentives for high bids come from typical structures in which general partners of LBO partnerships risk little of their own money (often less than none after fees are taken into account), yet share significantly in gains. Such arrangements are similar to the system of the race track tout. And who has ever seen a tout who didn't want his backer to make a lot of bets?

To Wesco, as a non-LBO operator, the good-corporate-acquisition game was always tough. And that game in each recent year has become more like fishing for muskies at Leech Lake, in Minnesota, where the writer's earliest business partner, Ed Hoskins, had the following conversation with his Indian guide:

"Are any muskies caught in this lake?"

"More muskies are caught in this lake than in any other lake in Minnesota. This lake is famous for muskies."

"How long have you been fishing here?"

"19 years."

"And how many muskies have you caught?"

"None."

When a management has our point of view, infrequency of business acquisition may safely be predicted. Whether this happens, as we like to believe, because the game is hard for almost everyone, or merely because the game is hard for us, the result for Wesco shareholders is the same: less worthwhile activity than we all would like. But there may be one consolation: A series of big, incorrectable acquisition troubles, with no meaningful salvage, is seldom caused by people who think the acquisition game is like fishing for muskies at Leech Lake.

### D. *Sound Acquisition Policies*[45]

It may seem strange that we exult over a year in which we made three acquisitions, given that we have regularly used these pages to question the acquisition activities of most managers. Rest assured, Charlie and I haven't lost our skepticism: We believe most deals do damage to the shareholders of the acquiring company. Too often, the words from *HMS Pinafore* apply: "Things are seldom what they seem, skim milk masquerades as cream." Specifically, sellers and their representatives invariably present financial projections having more entertainment value than educational value. In the production of rosy scenarios, Wall Street can hold its own against Washington.

In any case, why potential buyers even look at projections prepared by sellers baffles me. Charlie and I never give them a glance, but instead keep in mind the story of the man with an ailing horse. Visiting the vet, he said: "Can you help me? Sometimes my horse walks just fine and sometimes he limps." The vet's reply was pointed: "No problem—when he's walking fine, sell him." In the world of mergers and acquisitions, that horse would be peddled as Secretariat.

At Berkshire, we have all the difficulties in perceiving the future that other acquisition-minded companies do. Like [them] also, we face the inherent problem that the seller of a business practically always knows far more about it than the buyer and also picks the time of sale—a time when the business is likely to be walking "just fine."

Even so, we do have a few advantages, perhaps the greatest being that we *don't* have a strategic plan. Thus we feel no need to proceed in an ordained direction (a course leading almost invariably to silly purchase prices) but can instead simply decide what makes sense for our owners. In doing that, we always mentally

---

[45] [Divided by hash lines: 1995; 1991 (the latter with similar versions beginning in 1982 and continuing thereafter).]

compare any move we are contemplating with dozens of other opportunities open to us, including the purchase of small pieces of the
best businesses in the world via the stock market. Our practice of
making this comparison—acquisitions against passive investments—is a discipline that managers focused simply on expansion
seldom use.

Talking to *Time* magazine a few years back, Peter Drucker got
to the heart of things: "I will tell you a secret: Dealmaking beats
working. Dealmaking is exciting and fun, and working is grubby.
Running anything is primarily an enormous amount of grubby detail work . . . dealmaking is romantic, sexy. That's why you have
deals that make no sense."

In making acquisitions, we have a further advantage: As payment, we can offer sellers a stock backed by an extraordinary collection of outstanding businesses. An individual or a family
wishing to dispose of a single fine business, but also wishing to defer personal taxes indefinitely, is apt to find Berkshire stock a particularly comfortable holding. I believe, in fact, that this calculus
played an important part in the two acquisitions for which we paid
shares in 1995.

Beyond that, sellers sometimes care about placing their companies in a corporate home that will both endure and provide
pleasant, productive working conditions for their managers. Here
again, Berkshire offers something special. Our managers operate
with extraordinary autonomy. Additionally, our ownership structure enables sellers to know that when I say we are buying to keep,
the promise means something. For our part, we like dealing with
owners who care what happens to their companies and people. A
buyer is likely to find fewer unpleasant surprises dealing with that
type of seller than with one simply auctioning off his business.

In addition to the foregoing being an explanation of our acquisition style, it is, of course, a not-so-subtle sales pitch. If you own
or represent a business earning $[50] million or more before tax,
and it fits the criteria [set forth below], just give me a call. Our
discussion will be confidential. And if you aren't interested now,
file our proposition in the back of your mind: We are never going
to lose our appetite for buying companies with good economics
and excellent management.

Concluding this little dissertation on acquisitions, I can't resist
repeating a tale told me last year by a corporate executive. The
business he grew up in was a fine one, with a long-time record of
leadership in its industry. Its main product, however, was distress-

ingly glamorless. So several decades ago, the company hired a management consultant who—naturally—advised diversification, the then-current fad. ("Focus" was not yet in style.) Before long, the company acquired a number of businesses, each after the consulting firm had gone through a long—and expensive—acquisition study. And the outcome? Said the executive sadly, "When we started, we were getting 100% of our earnings from the original business. After ten years, we were getting 150%."

---

It's discouraging to note that though we have on four occasions made major purchases of companies whose sellers were represented by prominent investment banks, we were in only one of these instances contacted by the investment bank. In the other three cases, I myself or a friend initiated the transaction at some point after the investment bank had solicited its own list of prospects. We would love to see an intermediary earn its fee by thinking of us—and therefore repeat here what we're looking for:

(1) Large purchases (at least $[50] million of before-tax earnings),

(2) Demonstrated consistent earning power (future projections are of little interest to us, nor are "turnaround" situations),

(3) Businesses earning good returns on equity while employing little or no debt,

(4) Management in place (we can't supply it),

(5) Simple businesses (if there's lots of technology, we won't understand it),

(6) An offering price (we don't want to waste our time or that of the seller by talking, even preliminarily, about a transaction when price is unknown).

We will not engage in unfriendly takeovers. We can promise complete confidentiality and a very fast answer—customarily within five minutes—as to whether we're interested. (With [H.H.] Brown, we didn't even need to take five.) We prefer to buy for cash, but will consider issuing stock when we receive as much in intrinsic business value as we give.

Our favorite form of purchase is one [in which] the company's owner-managers wish to generate significant amounts of cash, sometimes for themselves, but often for their families or inactive shareholders. At the same time, these managers wish to remain significant owners who continue to run their companies just as they have in the past. We think we offer a particularly good fit for owners with such objectives, and we invite potential sellers to check us out by contacting people with whom we have done business in the past.

Charlie and I frequently get approached about acquisitions that don't come close to meeting our tests: We've found that if you advertise an interest in buying collies, a lot of people will call hoping to sell you their cocker spaniels. A line from a country song expresses our feeling about new ventures, turnarounds, or auction-like sales: "When the phone don't ring, you'll know it's me."[46]

Besides being interested in the purchase of businesses as described above, we are also interested in the negotiated purchase of large, but not controlling, blocks of stock comparable to those we hold in Capital Cities, Salomon, Gillette, USAir, Champion, and American Express. We are not interested, however, in receiving suggestions about purchases we might make in the general stock market.[47]

### E.   *On Selling One's Business*[48]

Most business owners spend the better part of their lifetimes building their businesses. By experience built upon endless repetition, they sharpen their skills in merchandising, purchasing, personnel selection, etc. It's a learning process, and mistakes made in one year often contribute to competence and success in succeeding years.

In contrast, owner-managers sell their business only once— frequently in an emotionally-charged atmosphere with a multitude of pressures coming from different directions. Often, much of the pressure comes from brokers whose compensation is contingent upon consummation of a sale, regardless of its consequences for both buyer and seller. The fact that the decision is so important, both financially and personally, to the owner can make the process more, rather than less, prone to error. And, mistakes made in the once-in-a-lifetime sale of a business are not reversible.

Price is very important, but often is not the most critical aspect of the sale. You and your family have an extraordinary business— one of a kind in your field—and any buyer is going to recognize

---

46 [In 1988 and 1989, the last sentence read: "Our interest in new ventures, turn-arounds, or auction-like sales can best be expressed by the Goldwynism: 'Please include me out.'"]

47 [Later letters include the following sentence: "The larger the company, the greater will be our interest: We would like to make an acquisition in the $5-20 billion range."]

48 [Divided by hash lines: 1990 Appendix B—form of letter sent to potential sellers of businesses; 1999.]

that. It's also a business that is going to get more valuable as the years go by. So if you decide not to sell now, you are very likely to realize more money later on. With that knowledge you can deal from strength and take the time required to select the buyer you want.

If you should decide to sell, I think Berkshire Hathaway offers some advantages that most other buyers do not. Practically all of these buyers will fall into one of two categories:

(1) A company located elsewhere but operating in your business or in a business somewhat akin to yours. Such a buyer—no matter what promises are made—will usually have managers who feel they know how to run your business operations and, sooner or later, will want to apply some hands-on "help." If the acquiring company is much larger, it often will have squads of managers, recruited over the years in part by promises that they will get to run future acquisitions. They will have their own way of doing things and, even though your business record undoubtedly will be far better than theirs, human nature will at some point cause them to believe that their methods of operating are superior. You and your family probably have friends who have sold their businesses to larger companies, and I suspect that their experiences will confirm the tendency of parent companies to take over the running of their subsidiaries, particularly when the parent knows the industry, or thinks it does.

(2) A financial maneuverer, invariably operating with large amounts of borrowed money, who plans to resell either to the public or to another corporation as soon as the time is favorable. Frequently, this buyer's major contribution will be to change accounting methods so that earnings can be presented in the most favorable light just prior to his bailing out. [T]his sort of transaction is becoming much more frequent because of a rising stock market and the great supply of funds available for such transactions.

If the sole motive of the present owners is to cash their chips and put the business behind them—and plenty of sellers fall in this category—either type of buyer that I've just described is satisfactory. But if the sellers' business represents the creative work of a lifetime and forms an integral part of their personality and sense of being, buyers of either type have serious flaws.

Berkshire is another kind of buyer—a rather unusual one. We buy to keep, but we don't have, and don't expect to have, operating people in our parent organization. All of the businesses we own are run autonomously to an extraordinary degree. In most cases, the managers of important businesses we have owned for many years have not been to Omaha or even met each other. When we buy a business, the sellers go on running it just as they did before the sale; we adapt to their methods rather than vice versa.

We have no one—family, recently recruited MBAs, etc.—to whom we have promised a chance to run businesses we have bought from owner-managers. And we won't have.

You know of some of our past purchases. I'm enclosing a list of everyone from whom we have ever bought a business, and I invite you to check with them as to our performance versus our promises. You should be particularly interested in checking with the few whose businesses did not do well in order to ascertain how we behaved under difficult conditions.

Any buyer will tell you that he needs you personally—and if he has any brains, he most certainly does need you. But a great many buyers, for the reasons mentioned above, don't match their subsequent actions to their earlier words. We will behave exactly as promised, both because we have so promised, and because we need to in order to achieve the best business results.

This need explains why we would want the operating members of your family to retain a 20% interest in the business. We need 80% to consolidate earnings for tax purposes, which is a step important to us. It is equally important to us that the family members who run the business remain as owners. Very simply, we would not want to buy unless we felt key members of present management would stay on as our partners. Contracts cannot guarantee your continued interest; we would simply rely on your word.

The areas I get involved in are capital allocation and selection and compensation of the top man. Other personnel decisions, operating strategies, etc. are his bailiwick. Some Berkshire managers talk over some of their decisions with me; some don't. It depends upon their personalities and, to an extent, upon their own personal relationship with me.

If you should decide to do business with Berkshire, we would pay in cash. Your business would not be used as collateral for any loan by Berkshire. There would be no brokers involved.

Furthermore, there would be no chance that a deal would be announced and that the buyer would then back off or start suggesting adjustments (with apologies, of course, and with an explanation that banks, lawyers, boards of directors, etc. were to be blamed). And finally, you would know exactly with whom you are dealing. You would not have one executive negotiate the deal only to have someone else in charge a few years later, or have the president regretfully tell you that his board of directors required this change or that (or possibly required sale of your business to finance some new interest of the parent's).

It's only fair to tell you that you would be no richer after the sale than now. The ownership of your business already makes you wealthy and soundly invested. A sale would change the form of your wealth, but it wouldn't change its amount. If you sell, you will have exchanged a 100%-owned valuable asset that you understand for another valuable asset—cash—that will probably be invested in small pieces (stocks) of other businesses that you understand less well. There is often a sound reason to sell but, if the transaction is a fair one, the reason is not so that the seller can become wealthier.

I will not pester you; if you have any possible interest in selling, I would appreciate your call. I would be extraordinarily proud to have Berkshire, along with the key members of your family, own _____; I believe we would do very well financially; and I believe you would have just as much fun running the business over the next 20 years as you have had during the past 20.

Sincerely,

/s/ Warren E. Buffett

---

Our acquisitions usually develop [as referrals from other managers who have sold to us in the past]. At other companies, executives may devote themselves to pursuing acquisition possibilities with investment bankers, utilizing an auction process that has become standardized. In this exercise the bankers prepare a "book" that makes me think of the Superman comics of my youth. In the Wall Street version, a formerly mild-mannered company emerges from the investment banker's phone booth able to leap over competitors in a single bound and with earnings moving faster than a speeding bullet. Titillated by the book's description of the acquiree's powers, acquisition-hungry CEOs–Lois Lanes all, beneath their cool exteriors–promptly swoon.

What's particularly entertaining in these books is the precision with which earnings are projected for many years ahead. If you ask the author-banker, however, what his own firm will earn *next month*, he will go into a protective crouch and tell you that business and markets are far too uncertain for him to venture a forecast.

Here's one story I can't resist relating: In 1985, a major investment banking house undertook to sell Scott Fetzer, offering it widely–but with no success. Upon reading of this strikeout, I wrote Ralph Schey, then and now Scott Fetzer's CEO, expressing an interest in buying the business. I had never met Ralph, but within a week we had a deal. Unfortunately, Scott Fetzer's letter of engagement with the banking firm provided it a $2.5 million fee upon sale, even if it had nothing to do with finding the buyer. I guess the lead banker felt he should do something for his payment, so he graciously offered us a copy of the book on Scott Fetzer that his firm had prepared. With his customary tact, Charlie responded: "I'll pay $2.5 million *not* to read it."

At Berkshire, our carefully-crafted acquisition strategy is simply to wait for the phone to ring. Happily, it sometimes does so, usually because a manager who sold to us earlier has recommended to a friend that he think about following suit.

## F.   *Advantages in Acquisitions*[49]

Two economic factors probably contributed to the rush of acquisition activity we experienced last year. First, many managers and owners foresaw near-term slowdowns in their businesses—and, in fact, we purchased several companies whose earnings will almost certainly decline this year from peaks they reached in 1999 or 2000. The declines make no difference to us, given that we expect all of our businesses to now and then have ups and downs. (Only in the sales presentations of investment banks do earnings move forever upward.) We don't care about the bumps; what matters are the overall results. But the decisions of other people are sometimes affected by the near-term outlook, which can both spur sellers and temper the enthusiasm of purchasers who might otherwise compete with us.

A second factor that helped us in 2000 was that the market for junk bonds dried up as the year progressed. In the two preceding years, junk bond purchasers had relaxed their standards, buying the obligations of ever-weaker issuers at inappropriate prices. The effects of this laxity were felt last year in a ballooning of defaults. In this environment, "financial" buyers of businesses—those who wish to buy using only a sliver of equity—became unable to borrow all they thought they needed. What they could still borrow, moreover, came at a high price. Consequently, LBO operators became

---

[49] [2000.]

less aggressive in their bidding when businesses came up for sale last year. Because we analyze purchases on an all-equity basis, our evaluations did not change, which means we became considerably more competitive.

Aside from the economic factors that benefited us, we now enjoy a major and growing advantage in making acquisitions in that we are often the buyer of choice for the seller. That fact, of course, doesn't assure a deal—sellers have to like our price, and we have to like their business and management—but it does help.

We find it meaningful when an owner *cares* about whom he sells to. We like to do business with someone who loves his company, not just the money that a sale will bring him (though we certainly understand why he likes that as well). When this emotional attachment exists, it signals that important qualities will likely be found within the business: honest accounting, pride of product, respect for customers, and a loyal group of associates having a strong sense of direction. The reverse is apt to be true, also. When an owner auctions off his business, exhibiting a total lack of interest in what follows, you will frequently find that it has been dressed up for sale, particularly when the seller is a "financial owner." And if owners behave with little regard for their business and its people, their conduct will often contaminate attitudes and practices throughout the company.

When a business masterpiece has been created by a lifetime—or several lifetimes—of unstinting care and exceptional talent, it should be important to the owner what corporation is entrusted to carry on its history. Charlie and I believe Berkshire provides an almost unique home. We take our obligations to the people who created a business very seriously, and Berkshire's ownership structure ensures that we can fulfill our promises. When we tell John Justin that his business (Justin Industries) will remain headquartered in Fort Worth, or assure the Bridge family that its operation (Ben Bridge Jeweler) will not be merged with another jeweler, these sellers can take those promises to the bank.

How much better it is for the "painter" of a business Rembrandt to personally select its permanent home than to have a trust officer or uninterested heirs auction it off. Throughout the years we have had great experiences with those who recognize that truth and apply it to their business creations. We'll leave the auctions to others.

## VI. ACCOUNTING AND VALUATION

To those of you who are uninterested in accounting, I apologize for this dissertation. I realize that many of you do not pore over our figures, but instead hold Berkshire primarily because you know that: (1) Charlie and I have the bulk of our money in Berkshire; (2) we intend to run things so that your gains or losses are in direct proportion to ours; (3) the record has so far been satisfactory. There is nothing necessarily wrong with this kind of "faith" approach to investing. Other shareholders, however, prefer an "analysis" approach and we want to supply the information they need. In our own investing, we search for situations in which both approaches give us the same answer.[50]

### A. *A Satire on Accounting Shenanigans*[51]

### *U.S. STEEL ANNOUNCES SWEEPING MODERNIZATION SCHEME\**

Myron C. Taylor, Chairman of U.S. Steel Corporation, today announced the long awaited plan for completely modernizing the world's largest industrial enterprise. Contrary to expectations, no changes will be made in the company's manufacturing or selling policies. Instead, the bookkeeping system is to be entirely revamped. By adopting and further improving a number of modern accounting and financial devices the corporation's earning power will be amazingly transformed. Even under the subnormal conditions of 1935, it is estimated that the new bookkeeping methods would have yielded a reported profit of close to $50 per share on the common stock. The scheme of improvement is the result of a comprehensive survey made by Messrs. Price, Bacon, Guthrie & Colpitts; it includes the following six points:
1. Writing down of Plant Account to Minus $1,000,000,000.
2. Par Value of Common Stock to be reduced to 1¢.
3. Payment of all wages and salaries in option warrants.
4. Inventories to be carried at $1.
5. Preferred Stock to be replaced by non-interest bearing bonds redeemable at 50% discount.
6. A $1,000,000,000 Contingency Reserve to be established.

---

[50] [Introductory essay, 1988.]
[51] [1990 Appendix A.]
\* An unpublished satire by Ben Graham, written in 1936 and given by the author to Warren Buffett in 1954.

173

The official statement of this extraordinary Modernization Plan follows in full:

The Board of Directors of U.S. Steel Corporation is pleased to announce that after intensive study of the problems arising from changed conditions in the industry, it has approved a comprehensive plan for remodeling the Corporation's accounting methods. A survey by a Special Committee, aided and abetted by Messrs. Price, Bacon, Guthrie & Colpitts, revealed that our company has lagged somewhat behind other American business enterprises in utilizing certain advanced bookkeeping methods, by means of which the earning power may be phenomenally enhanced without requiring any cash outlay or any changes in operating or sales conditions. It has been decided not only to adopt these newer methods, but to develop them to a still higher stage of perfection. The changes adopted by the Board may be summarized under six heads, as follows:

1.   Fixed Assets to be written down to *Minus $1,000,000,000.*

Many representative companies have relieved their income accounts of all charges for depreciation by writing down their plant account to $1. The Special Committee points out that if their plants are worth only $1, the fixed assets of U.S. Steel Corporation are worth a good deal less than that sum. It is now a well-recognized fact that many plants are in reality a liability rather than an asset, entailing not only depreciation charges, but taxes, maintenance, and other expenditures. Accordingly, the Board has decided to extend the write-down policy initiated in the 1935 report, and to mark down the Fixed Assets from $1,338,522,858.96 to a round *Minus $1,000,000,000.*

The advantages of this move should be evident. As the plant wears out, the liability becomes correspondingly reduced. Hence, instead of the present depreciation charge of some $47,000,000 yearly there will be an annual *appreciation credit* of 5%, or $50,000,000. This will increase earnings by no less than $97,000,000 per annum.

2.   Reduction of Par Value of Common Stock to 1¢, and

3.   Payment of Salaries and Wages in Option Warrants.

Many corporations have been able to reduce their overhead expenses substantially by paying a large part of their executive salaries in the form of options to buy stock, which carry no charge against earnings. The full possibilities of this modern device have apparently not been adequately realized. The Board of Directors have adopted the following advanced form of this idea:

The entire personnel of the Corporation are to receive their compensation in the form of rights to buy common stock at $50 per share, at the rate of one purchase right for each $50 of salary and/ or wages in their present amounts. The par value of the common stock is to be reduced to 1¢.

The almost incredible advantages of this new plan are evident from the following:

A. The payroll of the Corporation will be entirely eliminated, a saving of $250,000,000 per annum, based on 1935 operations.

B. At the same time, the effective compensation of all our employees will be increased severalfold. Because of the large earnings per share to be shown on our common stock under the new methods, it is certain that the shares will command a price in the market far above the option level of $50 per share, making the readily realizable value of these option warrants greatly in excess of the present cash wages that they will replace.

C. The Corporation will realize an additional large annual profit through the exercise of these warrants. Since the par value of the common stock will be fixed at 1¢, there will be a gain of $49.99 on each share subscribed for. In the interest of conservative accounting, however, this profit will not be included in the income account, but will be shown separately as a credit to Capital Surplus.

D. The Corporation's cash position will be enormously strengthened. In place of the present annual cash *outgo* of $250,000,000 for wages (1935 basis), there will be annual cash *inflow* of $250,000,000 through exercise of the subscription warrants for 5,000,000 shares of common stock. The Company's large earnings and strong cash position will permit the payment of a liberal dividend which, in turn, will result in the exercise of these option warrants immediately after issuance which, in turn, will further improve the cash position which, in turn, will permit a higher dividend rate—and so on, indefinitely.

4. Inventories to be carried at $1.

Serious losses have been taken during the depression due to the necessity of adjusting inventory value to market. Various enterprises—notably in the metal and cotton-textile fields—have successfully dealt with this problem by carrying all or part of their inventories at extremely low unit prices. The U.S. Steel Corporation has decided to adopt a still more progressive policy, and to carry its entire inventory at $1. This will be effected by an appropriate write-down at the end of each year, the amount of said write-down to be charged to the Contingency Reserve hereinafter referred to.

The benefits to be derived from this new method are very great. Not only will it obviate all possibility of inventory depreciation, but it will substantially enhance the annual earnings of the Corporation. The inventory on hand at the beginning of the year, valued at $1, will be sold during the year at an excellent profit. It is estimated that our income will be increased by means of this method to the extent of at least $150,000,000 per annum which, by a coincidence, will about equal the amount of the write-down to be made each year against Contingency Reserve.

A minority report of the Special Committee recommends that Accounts Receivable and Cash also be written down to $1, in the interest of consistency and to gain additional advantages similar to those just discussed. This proposal has been rejected for the time being because our auditors still require that any recoveries of receivables and cash so charged off be credited to surplus instead of to the year's income. It is expected, however, that this auditing rule—which is rather reminiscent of the horse-and-buggy days—will soon be changed in line with modern tendencies. Should this occur, the minority report will be given further and favorable consideration.

5.   Replacement of Preferred Stock by Non-Interest Bearing Bonds Redeemable at 50% Discount.

During the recent depression many companies have been able to offset their operating losses by including in income profits arising from repurchases of their own bonds at a substantial discount from par. Unfortunately the credit of U.S. Steel Corporation has always stood so high that this lucrative source of revenue has not hitherto been available to it. The Modernization Scheme will remedy this condition.

It is proposed that each share of preferred stock be exchanged for $300 face value of non-interest-bearing sinking-fund notes, redeemable by lot at 50% of face value in 10 equal annual installments. This will require the issuance of $1,080,000,000 of new notes, of which $108,000,000 will be retired each year at a cost to the Corporation of only $54,000,000, thus creating an annual profit of the same amount.

Like the wage-and/or-salary plan described under 3. above, this arrangement will benefit both the Corporation and its preferred stockholders. The latter are assured payment for their present shares at 150% of par value over an average period of five years. Since short-term securities yield practically no return at present, the non-interest-bearing feature is of no real importance. The Corporation will convert its present annual *charge* of $25,000,000 for preferred dividends into an annual bond-retirement *profit* of $54,000,000—an aggregate yearly gain of $79,000,000.

6.   Establishment of a Contingency Reserve of $1,000,000,000.

The Directors are confident that the improvements hereinbefore described will assure the Corporation of a satisfactory earning power under all conditions in the future. Under modern accounting methods, however, it is unnecessary to incur the slightest risk of loss through adverse business developments of any sort, since all these may be provided for in advance by means of a Contingency Reserve.

The Special Committee has recommended that the Corporation create such a Contingency Reserve in the fairly substantial amount of $1,000,000,000. As previously set forth, the annual write-down of inventory of $1 will be absorbed by this reserve. To prevent eventual exhaustion of the Contingency Reserve, it has been further decided that it be replenished each year by transfer of an appropriate sum from Capital Surplus. Since the latter is expected to increase each year by not less than $250,000,000 through the exercise of the Stock Option Warrants (see 3. above), it will readily make good any drains on the Contingency Reserve.

In setting up this arrangement, the Board of Directors must confess regretfully that they have been unable to improve upon the devices already employed by important corporations in transferring large sums between Capital, Capital Surplus, Contingency Reserves and other Balance Sheet Accounts. In fact, it must be admitted that our entries will be somewhat too simple, and will lack that element of extreme mystification that characterizes the most advanced procedure in this field. The Board of Directors, however, have insisted upon clarity and simplicity in framing their Modernization Plan, even at the sacrifice of possible advantage to the Corporation's earning power.

In order to show the combined effect of the new proposals upon the Corporation's earning power, we submit herewith a condensed Income Account for 1935 on two bases, viz:

|  | A. As Reported | B. Pro-Forma Giving Effect to Changes Proposed Herewith |
|---|---|---|
| Gross Receipts from all Sources (Including Inter Company) ............... | $765,000,000 | $765,000,000 |
| Salaries and Wages ...................... | 251,000,000 | — |
| Other Operating Expenses and Taxes ...... | 461,000,000 | 311,000,000 |
| Depreciation ........................... | 47,000,000 | (50,000,000) |
| Interest ................................ | 5,000,000 | 5,000,000 |
| Discount on Bonds Retired................ | — | (54,000,000) |
| Preferred Dividends...................... | 25,000,000 | — |
| Balance for Common ..................... | (24,000,000) | 553,000,000 |
| Average Shares Outstanding............... | 8,703,252 | 11,203,252 |
| Earned Per Share........................ | ($2.76) | $49.80 |

In accordance with a somewhat antiquated custom there is appended herewith a condensed pro-forma Balance Sheet of the U.S. Steel Corporation as of December 31, 1935, after giving effect to proposed changes in asset and liability accounts.

## ASSETS

| | |
|---|---|
| Fixed Assets, net .............................. | ($1,000,000,000) |
| Cash Assets ................................... | 142,000,000 |
| Receivables.................................... | 56,000,000 |
| Inventory...................................... | 1 |
| Miscellaneous Assets .......................... | 27,000,000 |
| Total ..................................... | ($774,999,999) |

## LIABILITIES

| | |
|---|---|
| Common Stock Par 1¢ (Par Value $87,032.52) Stated Value* ............................ | ($3,500,000,000) |
| Subsidiaries' Bonds and Stocks .................. | 113,000,000 |
| New Sinking Fund Notes ...................... | 1,080,000,000 |
| Current Liabilities ............................. | 69,000,000 |
| Contingency Reserve .......................... | 1,000,000,000 |
| Other Reserves................................. | 74,000,000 |
| Initial Surplus ................................ | 389,000,001 |
| Total ..................................... | ($774,999,999) |

*Given a Stated Value differing from Par Value, in accordance with the laws of the State of Virginia, where the company will be re-incorporated.

It is perhaps unnecessary to point out to our stockholders that modern accounting methods give rise to balance sheets differing somewhat in appearance from those of a less advanced period. In view of the very large earning power that will result from these changes in the Corporation's Balance Sheet, it is not expected that undue attention will be paid to the details of assets and liabilities.

In conclusion, the Board desires to point out that the combined procedure, whereby plant will be carried at a minus figure, our wage bill will be eliminated, and inventory will stand on our books at virtually nothing, will give U.S. Steel Corporation an enormous competitive advantage in the industry. We shall be able to sell our products at exceedingly low prices and still show a handsome margin of profit. It is the considered view of the Board of Directors that under the Modernization Scheme we shall be able to undersell all competitors to such a point that the anti-trust laws will constitute the only barrier to 100% domination of the industry.

In making this statement, the Board is not unmindful of the possibility that some of our competitors may seek to offset our new advantages by adopting similar accounting improvements. We are confident, however, that U.S. Steel will be able to retain the loyalty of its customers, old and new, through the unique prestige that will accrue to it as the originator and pioneer in these new fields of service to the user of steel. Should necessity arise, moreover, we believe we shall be able to maintain our deserved superiority by introducing still more advanced bookkeeping methods, which are even now under development in our Experimental Accounting Laboratory.

## B.    *Look-Through Earnings*[52]

When one company owns part of another company, appropriate accounting procedures pertaining to that ownership interest must be selected from one of three major categories. The percentage of voting stock that is owned, in large part, determines which category of accounting principles should be utilized.

Generally accepted accounting principles require (subject to exceptions, naturally . . . ) full consolidation of sales, expenses, taxes, and earnings of business holdings more than 50% owned. Blue Chip Stamps, 60% owned by Berkshire Hathaway Inc., falls into this category. Therefore, all Blue Chip income and expense items are included in full in Berkshire's Consolidated Statement of Earnings, with the 40% ownership interest of others in Blue Chip's net earnings reflected in the Statement as a deduction for "minority interest".

---

[52] [Divided by hash lines: 1980; 1990; 1982; 1991, 1979.]

Full inclusion of underlying earnings from another class of holdings, companies owned 20% to 50% (usually called "investees"), also normally occurs. Earnings from such companies—for example, Wesco Financial, controlled by Berkshire but only 48% owned—are included via a one-line entry in the owner's Statement of Earnings. Unlike the over-50% category, all items of revenue and expense are omitted; just the proportional share of net income is included. Thus, if Corporation A owns one-third of Corporation B, one-third of B's earnings, whether or not distributed by B, will end up in A's earnings. There are some modifications, both in this and the over-50% category, for intercorporate taxes and purchase price adjustments, the explanation of which we will save for a later day. (We know you can hardly wait.)

Finally come holdings representing less than 20% ownership of another corporation's voting securities. In these cases, accounting rules dictate that the owning companies include in their earnings only dividends received from such holdings. Undistributed earnings are ignored. Thus, should we own 10% of Corporation X with earnings of $10 million in 1980, we would report in our earnings (ignoring relatively minor taxes on intercorporate dividends) either (a) $1 million if X declared the full $10 million in dividends; (b) $500,000 if X paid out 50%, or $5 million, in dividends; or (c) zero if X reinvested all earnings.

We impose this short—and over-simplified—course in accounting upon you because Berkshire's concentration of resources in the insurance field produces a corresponding concentration of its assets in companies in that third (less than 20% owned) category. Many of these companies pay out relatively small proportions of their earnings in dividends. This means that only a small proportion of their current earning power is recorded in our own current operating earnings. But, while our reported operating earnings reflect only the dividends received from such companies, our economic well-being is determined by their earnings, not their dividends.

Our holdings in this third category of companies have increased dramatically in recent years as our insurance business has prospered and as securities markets have presented particularly attractive opportunities in the common stock area. The large increase in such holdings, plus the growth of earnings experienced by those partially-owned companies, has produced an unusual result; the part of "our" earnings that these companies retained last year (the part not paid to us in dividends) exceeded the total reported annual operating earnings of Berkshire Hathaway. Thus, conventional accounting only allows less than half of our earnings "iceberg" to appear above the surface, in plain view. Within the corporate world such a result is quite rare; in our case it is likely to be recurring.

Our own analysis of earnings reality differs somewhat from generally accepted accounting principles, particularly when those principles must be applied in a world of high and uncertain rates of inflation. (But it's much easier to criticize than to improve such accounting rules. The inherent problems are monumental.) We have owned 100% of businesses whose reported earnings were not worth close to 100 cents on the dollar to us even though, in an accounting sense, we totally controlled their disposition. (The "control" was theoretical. Unless we reinvested all earnings, massive deterioration in the value of assets already in place would occur. But those reinvested earnings had no prospect of earning anything close to a market return on capital.) We have also owned small fractions of businesses with extraordinary reinvestment possibilities whose retained earnings had an economic value to us far in excess of 100 cents on the dollar.

*The value to Berkshire Hathaway of retained earnings is not determined by whether we own 100%, 50%, 20% or 1% of the businesses in which they reside. Rather, the value of those retained earnings is determined by the use to which they are put and the subsequent level of earnings produced by that usage.* This is true whether we determine the usage, or whether managers we did not hire—but did elect to join—determine that usage. (It's the act that counts, not the actors.) And the value is in no way affected by the inclusion or non-inclusion of those retained earnings in our own reported operating earnings. If a tree grows in a forest partially owned by us, but we don't record the growth in our financial statements, we still own part of the tree.

Our view, we warn you, is non-conventional. But we would rather have earnings for which we did not get accounting credit put to good use in a 10%-owned company by a management we did not personally hire, than have earnings for which we did get credit put into projects of more dubious potential by another management—even if we are that management.

---

The term "earnings" has a precise ring to it. And when an earnings figure is accompanied by an unqualified auditor's certificate, a naive reader might think it comparable in certitude to π, calculated to dozens of decimal places.

In reality, however, earnings can be as pliable as putty when a charlatan heads the company reporting them. Eventually truth will surface, but in the meantime a lot of money can change hands. Indeed, some important American fortunes have been created by the monetization of accounting mirages.

Berkshire's own reported earnings are misleading in a different, but important, way: We have huge investments in companies ("investees") whose earnings far exceed their dividends and in which we record our share of earnings only to the extent of the dividends we receive. The extreme case is Capital Cities/ABC, Inc. Our 17% share of the company's earnings amounted to more than $83 million last year. Yet only about $530,000 ($600,000 of dividends it paid us less some $70,000 of tax) is counted in Berkshire's GAAP earnings. The residual $82 million-plus stayed with Cap Cities as retained earnings, which work for our benefit but go unrecorded on our books.

Our perspective on such "forgotten-but-not-gone" earnings is simple: The way they are accounted for is of no importance, but their ownership and subsequent utilization is all-important. We care not whether the auditors hear a tree fall in the forest; we do care who owns the tree and what's next done with it.

When Coca-Cola uses retained earnings to repurchase its shares, the company increases our percentage ownership in what I regard to be the most valuable franchise in the world. (Coke also, of course, uses retained earnings in many other value-enhancing ways.) Instead of repurchasing stock, Coca-Cola could pay those funds to us in dividends, which we could then use to purchase more Coke shares. That would be a less efficient scenario: Because of taxes we would pay on dividend income, we would not be able to increase our proportionate ownership to the degree that Coke can, acting for us. If this less efficient procedure were followed, however, Berkshire would report far greater "earnings."

I believe the best way to think about our earnings is in terms of "look-through" results, calculated as follows: Take $250 million, which is roughly our share of the 1990 operating earnings retained by our investees; subtract $30 million, for the incremental taxes we would have owed had that $250 million been paid to us in dividends; and add the remainder, $220 million, to our reported operating earnings of $371 million. Thus our 1990 "look-through" earnings" were about $590 million.

In our view, the value to all owners of the retained earnings of a business enterprise is determined by the effectiveness with which those earnings are used—and not by the size of one's ownership percentage. If you have owned .01 of 1% of Berkshire during the past decade, you have benefited economically in full measure from your share of our retained earnings, no matter what your accounting system. Proportionately, you have done just as well as if you had owned the magic 20%. But if you have owned 100% of a great many capital-intensive businesses during the decade, retained earnings that were credited fully and with painstaking precision to you under standard accounting methods have resulted in minor or zero economic value. This is not a criticism of accounting procedures. We would not like to have the job of designing a better system. It's simply to say that managers and investors alike must understand that accounting numbers are the beginning, not the end, of business valuation.

In most corporations, less-than-20% ownership positions are unimportant (perhaps, in part, because they prevent maximization of cherished reported earnings) and the distinction between accounting and economic results we have just discussed matters little. But in our own case, such positions are of very large and growing importance. Their magnitude, we believe, is what makes our reported operating earnings figure of limited significance.

---

Within [the] gigantic auction arena [composed of the entire array of major American corporations], it is our job to select businesses with economic characteristics allowing each dollar of retained earnings to be translated eventually into at least a dollar of market value. Despite a lot of mistakes, we have so far achieved this goal. In doing so, we have been greatly assisted by Arthur Okun's patron saint for economists—St. Offset. In some cases, that is, retained earnings attributable to our ownership position have had insignificant or even negative impact on market value, while in other major positions a dollar retained by an investee corporation has been translated into two or more dollars of market value. To date, our corporate over-achievers have more than offset the laggards. If we can continue this record, it will validate our efforts to maximize "economic" earnings, regardless of the impact upon "accounting" earnings.

We also believe that investors can benefit by focusing on their own look-through earnings. To calculate these, they should determine the underlying earnings attributable to the shares they hold in their portfolio and total these. The goal of each investor should be to create a portfolio (in effect, a "company") that will deliver him or her the highest possible look-through earnings a decade or so from now.

An approach of this kind will force the investor to think about long-term business prospects rather than short-term stock market prospects, a perspective likely to improve results. It's true, of course, that, in the long run, the scoreboard for investment decisions is market price. But prices will be determined by future earnings. In investing, just as in baseball, to put runs on the scoreboard one must watch the playing field, not the scoreboard.

---

The primary test of managerial economic performance is the achievement of a high earnings rate on equity capital employed (without undue leverage, accounting gimmickry, etc.) and not the achievement of consistent gains in earnings per share. In our view, many businesses would be better understood by their shareholder owners, as well as the general public, if managements and financial analysts modified the primary emphasis they place upon earnings per share, and upon yearly changes in that figure.

### C.  *Economic Goodwill Versus Accounting Goodwill*[53]

[O]ur intrinsic business value considerably exceeds book value. There are two major reasons:

(1) Standard accounting principles require that common stocks held by our insurance subsidiaries be stated on our books at market value, but that other stocks we own be carried at the lower of aggregate cost or market. At the end of 1983, the market value of this latter group exceeded carrying value by $70 million pre-tax, or about $50 million after tax. This excess belongs in our intrinsic business value, but is not included in the calculation of book value;

(2) More important, we own several businesses that possess economic Goodwill (which is properly includable in intrinsic business value) far larger than the accounting Goodwill that is carried on our balance sheet and reflected in book value.

---

53 [Divided by hash lines: 1983; 1983 Appendix; 1996 Owner's Manual.]

You can live a full and rewarding life without ever thinking about Goodwill and its amortization. But students of investment and management should understand the nuances of the subject. My own thinking has changed drastically from 35 years ago when I was taught to favor tangible assets and to shun businesses whose value depended largely upon economic Goodwill. This bias caused me to make many important business mistakes of omission, although relatively few of commission.

Keynes identified my problem: "The difficulty lies not in the new ideas but in escaping from the old ones." My escape was long delayed, in part because most of what I had been taught by the same teacher had been (and continues to be) so extraordinarily valuable. Ultimately, business experience, direct and vicarious, produced my present strong preference for businesses that possess large amounts of enduring Goodwill and that utilize a minimum of tangible assets.

I recommend the [following essay] to those who are comfortable with accounting terminology and who have an interest in understanding the business aspects of Goodwill. Whether or not you wish to tackle the [essay] you should be aware that Charlie and I believe that Berkshire possesses very significant economic Goodwill value above that reflected in our book value.

---

[The following discussion] deals only with economic and accounting Goodwill—not the goodwill of everyday usage. For example, a business may be well liked, even loved, by most of its customers but possess no economic goodwill. (AT&T, before the breakup, was generally well thought of, but possessed not a dime of economic Goodwill.) And, regrettably, a business may be disliked by its customers but possess substantial, and growing economic Goodwill. So, just for the moment, forget emotions and focus only on economics and accounting.

When a business is purchased, accounting principles require that the purchase price first be assigned to the fair value of the identifiable assets that are acquired. Frequently the sum of the fair values put on the assets (after the deduction of liabilities) is less than the total purchase price of the business. In that case, the difference is assigned to an asset entitled "excess of cost over equity in net assets acquired". To avoid constant repetition of this mouthful, we will substitute "Goodwill."

Accounting Goodwill arising from businesses purchased before November 1970 has a special standing. Except under rare circumstances, it can remain an asset on the balance sheet as long as the business bought is retained. That means no amortization charges to gradually extinguish that asset need be made against earnings.

The case is different, however, with purchases made from November 1970 on. When these create Goodwill, it must be amortized over not more than 40 years through charges—of equal amount in every year—to the earnings account. Since 40 years is the maximum period allowed, 40 years is what managements (including us) usually elect.

That's how accounting Goodwill works. To see how it differs from economic reality, let's look at an example close at hand. We'll round some figures, and greatly oversimplify, to make the example easier to follow. We'll also mention some implications for investor and manager.

Blue Chip Stamps bought See's early in 1972 for $25 million, at which time See's had about $8 million of net tangible assets. (Throughout this discussion, accounts receivable will be classified as tangible assets, a definition proper for business analysis.) This level of tangible assets was adequate to conduct the business without use of debt, except for short periods seasonally. See's was earning about $2 million after tax at the time, and such earnings seemed conservatively representative of future earning power in constant 1972 dollars.

Thus our first lesson: businesses logically are worth far more than net tangible assets when they can be expected to produce earnings on such assets considerably in excess of market rates of return. The capitalized value of this excess return is economic Goodwill.

In 1972 (and now) relatively few businesses could be expected to consistently earn the 25% after tax on net tangible assets that was earned by See's—doing it, furthermore, with conservative accounting and no financial leverage. It was not the fair market value of the inventories, receivables or fixed assets that produced the premium rates of return. Rather it was a combination of intangible assets, particularly a pervasive favorable reputation with consumers based upon countless pleasant experiences they have had with both product and personnel.

Such a reputation creates a consumer franchise that allows the value of the product to the purchaser, rather than its production cost, to be the major determinant of selling price. Consumer franchises are a prime source of economic Goodwill. Other sources include governmental franchises not subject to profit regulation, such as television stations, and an enduring position as the low cost producer in an industry.

Let's return to the accounting in the See's example. Blue Chip's purchase of See's at $17 million over net tangible assets required that a Goodwill account of this amount be established as an asset on Blue Chip's books and that $425,000 be charged to income annually for 40 years to amortize that asset. By 1983, after 11 years of such charges, the $17 million had been reduced to about $12.5 million. Berkshire, meanwhile, owned 60% of Blue Chip and, therefore, also 60% of See's. This ownership meant that Berkshire's balance sheet reflected 60% of See's Goodwill, or about $7.5 million.

In 1983 Berkshire acquired the rest of Blue Chip in a merger that required purchase accounting as contrasted to the "pooling" treatment allowed for some mergers. Under purchase accounting, the "fair value" of the shares we gave to (or "paid") Blue Chip holders had to be spread over the net assets acquired from Blue Chip. This "fair value" was measured, as it almost always is when public companies use their shares to make acquisitions, by the market value of the shares given up.

The assets "purchased" consisted of 40% of everything owned by Blue Chip (as noted, Berkshire already owned the other 60%). What Berkshire "paid" was more than the net identifiable assets we received by $51.7 million, and was assigned to two pieces of Goodwill: $28.4 million to See's and $23.3 million to Buffalo Evening News.

After the merger, therefore, Berkshire was left with a Goodwill asset for See's that had two components: the $7.5 million remaining from the 1971 purchase, and $28.4 million newly created by the 40% "purchased" in 1983. Our amortization charge now will be about $1.0 million for the next 28 years, and $.7 million for the following 12 years, 2002 through 2013.

In other words, different purchase dates and prices have given us vastly different asset values and amortization charges for two pieces of the same asset. (We repeat our usual disclaimer: we have no better accounting system to suggest. The problems to be dealt with are mind boggling and require arbitrary rules.)

But what are the economic realities? One reality is that the amortization charges that have been deducted as costs in the earnings statement each year since acquisition of See's were not true economic costs. We know that because See's last year earned $13 million after taxes on about $20 million of net tangible assets—a performance indicating the existence of economic Goodwill far larger than the total original cost of our accounting Goodwill. In other words, while accounting Goodwill regularly decreased from the moment of purchase, economic Goodwill increased in irregular but very substantial fashion.

Another reality is that annual amortization charges in the future will not correspond to economic costs. It is possible, of course, that See's economic Goodwill will disappear. But it won't shrink in even decrements or anything remotely resembling them. What is more likely is that the Goodwill will increase—in current, if not in constant, dollars—because of inflation.

That probability exists because true economic Goodwill tends to rise in nominal value proportionally with inflation. To illustrate how this works, let's contrast a See's kind of business with a more mundane business. When we purchased See's in 1972, it will be recalled, it was earning about $2 million on $8 million of net tangible assets. Let us assume that our hypothetical mundane business then had $2 million of earnings also, but needed $18 million in net tangible assets for normal operations. Earning only 11% on required tangible assets, that mundane business would possess little or no economic Goodwill.

A business like that, therefore, might well have sold for the value of its net tangible assets, or for $18 million. In contrast, we paid $25 million for See's, even though it had no more in earnings and less than half as much in "honest-to-God" assets. Could less really have been more, as our purchase price implied? The answer is "yes"—*even if both businesses were expected to have flat unit volume*—as long as you anticipated, as we did in 1972, a world of continuous inflation.

To understand why, imagine the effect that a doubling of the price level would subsequently have on the two businesses. Both would need to double their nominal earnings to $4 million to keep themselves even with inflation. This would seem to be no great trick: just sell the same number of units at double earlier prices and, assuming profit margins remain unchanged, profits also must double.

But, crucially, to bring that about, both businesses probably would have to double their nominal investment in net tangible assets, since that is the kind of economic requirement that inflation usually imposes on businesses, both good and bad. A doubling of dollar sales means correspondingly more dollars must be employed immediately in receivables and inventories. Dollars employed in fixed assets will respond more slowly to inflation, but probably just as surely. And all of this inflation-required investment will produce no improvement in rate of return. The motivation for this investment is the survival of the business, not the prosperity of the owner.

Remember, however, that See's had net tangible assets of only $8 million. So it would only have had to commit an additional $8 million to finance the capital needs imposed by inflation. The mundane business, meanwhile, had a burden over twice as large—a need for $18 million of additional capital.

After the dust had settled, the mundane business, now earning $4 million annually, might still be worth the value of its tangible assets, or $36 million. That means its owners would have gained only a dollar of nominal value for every new dollar invested. (This is the same dollar-for-dollar result they would have achieved if they had added money to a savings account.)

See's, however, also earning $4 million, might be worth $50 million if valued (as it logically would be) on the same basis as it was at the time of our purchase. So it would have gained $25 million in nominal value while the owners were putting up only $8 million in additional capital—over $3 of nominal value gained for each $1 invested.

Remember, even so, that the owners of the See's kind of business were forced by inflation to ante up $8 million in additional capital just to stay even in real profits. Any unleveraged business that requires some net tangible assets to operate (and almost all do) is hurt by inflation. Businesses needing little in the way of tangible assets simply are hurt the least.

And that fact, of course, has been hard for many people to grasp. For years the traditional wisdom—long on tradition, short on wisdom—held that inflation protection was best provided by businesses laden with natural resources, plants and machinery, or other tangible assets ("In Goods We Trust"). It doesn't work that way. Asset-heavy businesses generally earn low rates of return—rates that often barely provide enough capital to fund the inflationary needs of the existing business, with nothing left over for real growth, for distribution to owners, or for acquisition of new businesses.

In contrast, a disproportionate number of the great business fortunes built up during the inflationary years arose from ownership of operations that combined intangibles of lasting value with relatively minor requirements for tangible assets. In such cases earnings have bounded upward in nominal dollars, and these dollars have been largely available for the acquisition of additional businesses. This phenomenon has been particularly evident in the communications business. That business has required little in the way of tangible investment—yet its franchises have endured. During inflation, Goodwill is the gift that keeps giving.

But that statement applies, naturally, only to true economic Goodwill. Spurious accounting Goodwill—and there is plenty of it around—is another matter. When an overexcited management purchases a business at a silly price, the same accounting niceties described earlier are observed. Because it can't go anywhere else, the silliness ends up in the Goodwill account. Considering the lack of managerial discipline that created the account, under such circumstances it might better be labeled "No-Will". Whatever the term, the 40-year ritual typically is observed and the adrenalin so capitalized remains on the books as an "asset" just as if the acquisition had been a sensible one.

\*   \*   \*   \*   \*

If you cling to any belief that accounting treatment of Goodwill is the best measure of economic reality, I suggest one final item to ponder.

Assume a company with $20 per share of net worth, all tangible assets. Further assume the company has internally developed some magnificent consumer franchise, or that it was fortunate enough to obtain some important television stations by original FCC grant. Therefore, it earns a great deal on tangible assets, say $5 per share, or 25%.

With such economics, it might sell for $100 per share or more, and it might well also bring that price in a negotiated sale of the entire business.

Assume an investor buys the stock at $100 per share, paying in effect $80 per share for Goodwill (just as would a corporate purchaser buying the whole company). Should the investor impute a $2 per share amortization charge annually ($80 divided by 40 years) to calculate "true" earnings per share? And, if so, should the new "true" earnings of $3 per share cause him to rethink his purchase price?

\* \* \* \* \*

We believe managers and investors alike should view intangible assets from two perspectives:

(1) In analysis of operating results—that is, in evaluating the underlying economics of a business unit—amortization charges should be ignored. What a business can be expected to earn on unleveraged net tangible assets, excluding any charges against earnings for amortization of Goodwill, is the best guide to the economic attractiveness of the operation. It is also the best guide to the current value of the operation's economic Goodwill.

(2) In evaluating the wisdom of business acquisitions, amortization charges should be ignored also. They should be deducted neither from earnings nor from the cost of the business. This means forever viewing purchased Goodwill at its full cost, before any amortization. Furthermore, cost should be defined as including the full intrinsic business value—not just the recorded accounting value—of all consideration given, irrespective of market prices of the securities involved at the time of merger and irrespective of whether pooling treatment was allowed. For example, what we truly paid in the Blue Chip merger for 40% of the Goodwill of See's and the News was considerably more than the $51.7 million entered on our books. This disparity exists because the market value of the Berkshire shares given up in the merger was less than their intrinsic business value, which is the value that defines the true cost to us.

Operations that appear to be winners based upon perspective (1) may pale when viewed from perspective (2). A good business is not always a good purchase—although it's a good place to look for one.

---

When Berkshire buys a business for a premium over the GAAP net worth of the acquiree—as will usually be the case, since most companies we'd want to buy don't come at a discount—that premium has to be entered on the asset side of our balance sheet. There are loads of rules about just how a company should record the premium. But to simplify this discussion, we will focus on "Goodwill," the asset item to which almost all of Berkshire's acquisition premiums have been allocated. For example, when we recently acquired the half of GEICO we didn't previously own, we recorded goodwill of about $1.6 billion.

GAAP requires Goodwill to be amortized—that is, written off—over a period no longer than 40 years. Therefore, to extinguish our $1.6 billion in GEICO Goodwill, we will annually take charges of about $40 million against our earnings.

In an accounting sense, consequently, our GEICO Goodwill will disappear gradually in even-sized bites. But the one thing I can guarantee you is that the *economic* Goodwill we have purchased at GEICO will not decline in the same measured way. In fact, my best guess is that the economic goodwill assignable to GEICO will not decline at all, but rather will increase—and probably in a very substantial way.

I made a similar statement in our 1983 Annual Report about the Goodwill attributed to See's Candy, when I used that company as an example in a discussion of Goodwill accounting. At that time, our balance sheet carried about $36 million of See's Goodwill. We have since been charging about $1 million against earnings every year in order to amortize the asset, and the See's Goodwill on our balance sheet is now down to about $23 million. In other words, from an accounting standpoint, See's is now presented as having lost a good deal of goodwill since 1983.

The economic facts could not be more different. In 1983, See's earned about $27 million pre-tax on $11 million of net operating assets; in 1995 it earned $50 million on only $5 million of net operating assets. Clearly See's economic Goodwill has increased dramatically during the interval rather than decreased. Just as clearly, See's is worth many hundreds of millions of dollars more than its stated value on our books.

We could, of course, be wrong, but we expect GEICO's gradual loss of accounting value to be paired with increases in its economic value. Certainly that has been the pattern at most of our subsidiaries, not just See's. That is why we regularly present our operating earnings in a way that allows you to ignore all purchase-accounting adjustments.

In the future, also, we will adopt a similar policy for look-through earnings, moving to a form of presentation that rids these earnings of the major purchase-accounting adjustments of investees. We will not apply this policy to companies that have only small amounts of goodwill on their books, such as Coca-Cola or Gillette. We will extend it, however, to Wells Fargo and Disney, which have both recently made huge acquisitions and are conse-quently dealing with exceptionally large goodwill charges.

Before leaving this subject, we should issue an important warning: Investors are often led astray by CEOs and Wall Street analysts who equate depreciation charges with the amortization charges we have just discussed. In no way are the two the same: With rare exceptions, depreciation is an economic cost every bit as real as wages, materials, or taxes. Certainly that is true at Berk-shire and at virtually all the other businesses we have studied. Fur-thermore, we do *not* think so-called EBITDA (earnings before interest, taxes, depreciation and amortization) is a meaningful measure of performance. Managements that dismiss the impor-tance of depreciation—and emphasize "cash flow" or EBITDA—are apt to make faulty decisions, and you should keep that in mind as you make your own investment decisions.

### D.  *Owner Earnings and the Cash Flow Fallacy*[54]

[Many business acquisitions require] major purchase-price ac-counting adjustments, as prescribed by generally accepted account-ing principles (GAAP). The GAAP figures, of course, are the ones used in our consolidated financial statements. But, in our view, the GAAP figures are not necessarily the most useful ones for inves-tors or managers. Therefore, the figures shown for specific operat-ing units are earnings before purchase-price adjustments are taken into account. In effect, these are the earnings that would have been reported by the businesses if we had not purchased them.

A discussion of our reasons for preferring this form of presen-tation [follows. It] will never substitute for a steamy novel and def-initely is not required reading. However, I know that among our 6,000 shareholders there are those who are thrilled by my essays on accounting—and I hope that both of you enjoy [it].

---

First a short quiz: below are abbreviated 1986 statements of earnings for two companies. Which business is the more valuable?

---

[54] [Divided by hash lines: 1986; 1986 Appendix]

| | Company O | (000s Omitted) | Company N |
|---|---|---|---|
| Revenues........................ | | $677,240 | $677,240 |
| Cost of Goods Sold: | | | |
| Historical costs, excluding depreciation........... | $341,170 | $341,170 | |
| Special non-cash inventory costs......................... | | 4,979[1] | |
| Depreciation of plant and equipment.................. | 8,301 | 13,355[2] | |
| | | 349,471 | 359,504 |
| Gross Profit ...................... | | $327,769 | $317,736 |
| Selling & Admin. Expense .......... | $260,286 | $260,286 | |
| Amortization of Goodwill........... | | 595[3] | |
| | | 260,286 | 260,881 |
| Operating Profit ................... | | $ 67,483 | $ 56,855 |
| Other Income, Net ................. | | 4,135 | 4,135 |
| Pre-Tax Income ................... | | $ 71,618 | $ 60,990 |
| Applicable Income Tax: | | | |
| Historical deferred and current tax............................ | $ 31,387 | $ 31,387 | |
| Non-Cash Inter-period Allocation Adjustment........... | | 998[4] | |
| | | 31,387 | 32,385 |
| Net Income....................... | | $ 40,231 | $ 28,605 |

*(Numbers (1) through (4) designate items discussed later in this section.)*

As you've probably guessed, Companies O and N are the same business—Scott Fetzer. In the "O" (for "old") column we have shown what the company's 1986 GAAP earnings would have been if we had not purchased it; in the "N" (for "new") column we have shown Scott Fetzer's GAAP earnings as actually reported by Berkshire.

It should be emphasized that the two columns depict identical economics—i.e., the same sales, wages, taxes, etc. And both "companies" generate the same amount of cash for owners. Only the accounting is different.

So, fellow philosophers, which column presents truth? Upon which set of numbers should managers and investors focus?

Before we tackle those questions, let's look at what produces the disparity between O and N. We will simplify our discussion in some respects, but the simplification should not produce any inaccuracies in analysis or conclusions.

The contrast between O and N comes about because we paid an amount for Scott Fetzer that was different from its stated net worth. Under GAAP, such differences—such premiums or discounts—must be accounted for by "purchase-price adjustments." In Scott Fetzer's case, we paid $315 million for net assets that were carried on its books at $172.4 million. So we paid a premium of $142.6 million.

The first step in accounting for any premium paid is to adjust the carrying value of current assets to current values. In practice, this requirement usually does not affect receivables, which are routinely carried at current value, but often affects inventories. Because of a $22.9 million LIFO reserve and other accounting intricacies,[55] Scott Fetzer's inventory account was carried at a $37.3 million discount from current value. So, making our first accounting move, we used $37.3 million of our $142.6 million premium to increase the carrying value of the inventory.

Assuming any premium is left after current assets are adjusted, the next step is to adjust fixed assets to current value. In our case, this adjustment also required a few accounting acrobatics relating to deferred taxes. Since this has been billed as a simplified discussion, I will skip the details and give you the bottom line: $68.0 million was added to fixed assets and $13.0 million was eliminated from deferred tax liabilities. After making this $81.0 million adjustment, we were left with $24.3 million of premium to allocate.

Had our situation called for them, two steps would next have been required: the adjustment of intangible assets other than Goodwill to current fair values, and the restatement of liabilities to current fair values, a requirement that typically affects only long-term debt and unfunded pension liabilities. In Scott Fetzer's case, however, neither of these steps was necessary.

The final accounting adjustment we needed to make, after recording fair market values for all assets and liabilities, was the assignment of the residual premium to Goodwill (technically known as "excess of cost over the fair value of net assets acquired"). This residual amounted to $24.3 million. Thus, the balance sheet of Scott Fetzer immediately before the acquisition, which is summarized below in column O, was transformed by the purchase into the balance sheet shown in column N. In real terms, both balance sheets depict the same assets and liabilities—but, as you can see, certain figures differ significantly.

---

[55] [A LIFO reserve is the difference between the current cost to replace inventory and the amount shown as the cost of inventory on a balance sheet. This difference can grow significantly, especially during inflationary periods.]

|  | Company O | Company N |
|---|---|---|
|  | *(000s Omitted)* | |
| **Assets** | | |
| Cash and Cash Equivalents........... | $ 3,593 | $ 3,593 |
| Receivables, net ..................... | 90,919 | 90,919 |
| Inventories ......................... | 77,489 | 114,764 |
| Other ............................... | 5,954 | 5,954 |
| Total Current Assets ................. | 177,955 | 215,230 |
| Property, Plant, and Equipment, net .. | 80,967 | 148,960 |
| Investments in the Advances to Unconsolidated Subsidiaries and Joint Ventures ......................... | 93,589 | 93,589 |
| Other Assets, including Goodwill ..... | 9,836 | 34,210 |
|  | $362,347 | $491,989 |
| **Liabilities** | | |
| Notes Payable and Current Portion of Long-term Debt ................... | $ 4,650 | $ 4,650 |
| Accounts Payable.................... | 39,003 | 39,003 |
| Accrued Liabilities.................. | 84,939 | 84,939 |
| Total Current Liabilities ............. | 128,592 | 128,592 |
| Long-term Debt and Capitalized Leases ........................... | 34,669 | 34,669 |
| Deferred Income Taxes .............. | 17,052 | 4,075 |
| Other Deferred Credits .............. | 9,657 | 9,657 |
| Total Liabilities ..................... | 189,970 | 176,993 |
| Shareholder's Equity ................ | 172,377 | 314,996 |
|  | $362,347 | $491,989 |

The higher balance sheet figures shown in column N produce the lower income figures shown in column N of the earnings statement presented earlier. This is the result of the asset write-ups and of the fact that some of the written-up assets must be depreciated or amortized. The higher the asset figure, the higher the annual depreciation or amortization charge to earnings must be. The charges that flowed to the earnings statement because of the balance sheet write-ups were numbered in the statement of earnings shown earlier:

1.  $4,979,000 for non-cash inventory costs resulting, primarily, from reductions that Scott Fetzer made in its inventories during 1986; charges of this kind are apt to be small or non-existent in future years.
2.  $5,054,000 for extra depreciation attributable to the write-up of fixed assets; a charge approximating this amount will probably be made annually for 12 more years.
3.  $595,000 for amortization of Goodwill; this charge will be made annually for 39 more years in a slightly larger amount

because our purchase was made on January 6 and, therefore, the 1986 figure applies to only 98% of the year.

4.   $998,000 for deferred-tax acrobatics that are beyond my ability to explain briefly (or perhaps even non-briefly); a charge approximating this amount will probably be made annually for 12 more years.

By the end of 1986 the difference between the net worth of the "old" and "new" Scott Fetzer had been reduced from $142.6 million to $131.0 million by means of the extra $11.6 million that was charged to earnings of the new entity. As the years go by, similar charges to earnings will cause most of the premium to disappear, and the two balance sheets will converge. However, the higher land values and most of the higher inventory values that were established on the new balance sheet will remain unless land is disposed of or inventory levels are further reduced.

* * * * *

What does all this mean for owners? Did the shareholders of Berkshire buy a business that earned $40.2 million in 1986 or did they buy one earning $28.6 million? Were those $11.6 million of new charges a real economic cost to us? Should investors pay more for the stock of Company O than of Company N? And, if a business is worth some given multiple of earnings, was Scott Fetzer worth considerably more the day before we bought it than it was worth the following day?

If we think through these questions, we can gain some insights about what may be called "owner earnings." These represent (a) reported earnings plus (b) depreciation, depletion, amortization, and certain other non-cash charges such as Company N's items (1) and (4) less (c) the average annual amount of capitalized expenditures for plant and equipment, etc. that the business requires to fully maintain its long-term competitive position and its unit volume. (If the business requires additional working capital to maintain its competitive position and unit volume, the increment also should be included in (c). However, businesses following the LIFO inventory method usually do not require additional working capital if unit volume does not change.)

Our owner-earnings equation does not yield the deceptively precise figures provided by GAAP, since (c) must be a guess—and one sometimes very difficult to make. Despite this problem, we consider the owner earnings figure, not the GAAP figure, to be the relevant item for valuation purposes—both for investors in buying stocks and for managers in buying entire businesses.

The approach we have outlined produces "owner earnings" for Company O and Company N that are identical, which means valuations are also identical, just as common sense would tell you should be the case. This result is reached because the sum of (a) and (b) is the same in both columns O and N, and because (c) is necessarily the same in both cases.

And what do Charlie and I, as owners and managers, believe is the correct figure for the owner earnings of Scott Fetzer? Under current circumstances, we believe (c) is very close to the "old" company's (b) number of $8.3 million and much below the "new" company's (b) number of $19.9 million. Therefore, we believe that owner earnings are far better depicted by the reported earnings in the O column than by those in the N column. In other words, we feel owner earnings of Scott Fetzer are considerably larger than the GAAP figures that we report.

That is obviously a happy state of affairs. But calculations of this sort usually do not provide such pleasant news. Most managers probably will acknowledge that they need to spend something more than (b) on their businesses over the longer term just to hold their ground in terms of both unit volume and competitive position. When this imperative exists—that is, when (c) exceeds (b)—GAAP earnings overstate owner earnings. Frequently this overstatement is substantial. The oil industry has in recent years provided a conspicuous example of this phenomenon. Had most major oil companies spent only (b) each year, they would have guaranteed their shrinkage in real terms.

All of this points up the absurdity of the "cash flow" numbers that are often set forth in Wall Street reports. These numbers routinely include (a) plus (b)—but do not subtract (c). Most sales brochures of investment bankers also feature deceptive presentations of this kind. These imply that the business being offered is the commercial counterpart of the Pyramids—forever state-of-the-art, never needing to be replaced, improved or refurbished. Indeed, if all U.S. corporations were to be offered simultaneously for sale through our leading investment bankers—and if the sales brochures describing them were to be believed—governmental projections of national plant and equipment spending would have to be slashed by 90%.

"Cash Flow," true, may serve as a shorthand of some utility in descriptions of certain real estate businesses or other enterprises that make huge initial outlays and only tiny outlays thereafter. A company whose only holding is a bridge or an extremely long-lived gas field would be an example. But "cash flow" is meaningless in such businesses as manufacturing, retailing, extractive companies, and utilities because, for them, (c) is always significant. To be sure, businesses of this kind may in a given year be able to defer capital spending. But over a five- or ten-year period, they must make the investment—or the business decays.

Why, then, are "cash flow" numbers so popular today? In answer, we confess our cynicism: we believe these numbers are frequently used by marketers of businesses and securities in attempts to justify the unjustifiable (and thereby to sell what should be the unsaleable). When (a)—that is, GAAP earnings—looks by itself inadequate to service debt of a junk bond or justify a foolish stock price, how convenient it becomes for salesmen to focus on (a) + (b). But you shouldn't add (b) without subtracting (c): though dentists correctly claim that if you ignore your teeth they'll go away, the same is not true for (c). The company or investor believing that the debt-servicing ability or the equity valuation of an enterprise can be measured by totalling (a) and (b) while ignoring (c) is headed for certain trouble.

\*   \*   \*   \*   \*

To sum up: in the case of both Scott Fetzer and our other businesses, we feel that (b) on an historical-cost basis—i.e., with both amortization of intangibles and other purchase-price adjustments excluded—is quite close in amount to (c). (The two items are not identical, of course. For example, at See's we annually make capitalized expenditures that exceed depreciation by $500,000 to $1 million, simply to hold our ground competitively.) Our conviction about this point is the reason we show our amortization and other purchase-price adjustment items separately . . . and is also our reason for viewing the earnings of the individual businesses . . . as much more closely approximating owner earnings than the GAAP figures.

Questioning GAAP figures may seem impious to some. After all, what are we paying the accountants for if it is not to deliver us the "truth" about our business. But the accountants' job is to record, not to evaluate. The evaluation job falls to investors and managers.

Accounting numbers of course, are the language of business and as such are of enormous help to anyone evaluating the worth of a business and tracking its progress. Charlie and I would be lost without these numbers: they invariably are the starting point for us in evaluating our own businesses and those of others. Managers and owners need to remember, however, that accounting is but an aid to business thinking, never a substitute for it.

### E. *Intrinsic Value, Book Value, and Market Price*[56]

[Intrinsic value is] an all-important concept that offers the only logical approach to evaluating the relative attractiveness of investments and businesses. Intrinsic value can be defined simply: It is the discounted value of the cash that can be taken out of a business during its remaining life.

The calculation of intrinsic value, though, is not so simple. As our definition suggests, intrinsic value is an estimate rather than a precise figure, and it is additionally an estimate that must be changed if interest rates move or forecasts of future cash flows are revised. Two people looking at the same set of facts, moreover—and this would apply even to Charlie and me—will almost inevitably come up with at least slightly different intrinsic value figures. That is one reason we never give you our estimates of intrinsic value. What our annual reports do supply, though, are the facts that we ourselves use to calculate this value.

Meanwhile, we regularly report our per-share book value, an easily calculable number, though one of limited use. The limitations do not arise from our holdings of marketable securities, which are carried on our books at their current prices. Rather the inadequacies of book value have to do with the companies we control, whose values as stated on our books may be far different from their intrinsic values.

The disparity can go in either direction. For example, in 1964 we could state with certitude that Berkshire's per-share book value was $19.46. However, that figure considerably overstated the company's intrinsic value, since all of the company's resources were tied up in a sub-profitable textile business. Our textile assets had neither going-concern nor liquidation values equal to their carrying values. Today, however, Berkshire's situation is reversed: Our March 31, 1996 book value of $15,180 *far* understates Berkshire's intrinsic value, a point true because many of the businesses we control are worth much more than their carrying value.

---

[56] [Divided by hash lines: 1996 Owner's Manual; 1987; 1985; 1996.]

Inadequate though they are in telling the story, we give you Berkshire's book-value figures because they today serve as a rough, albeit significantly understated, tracking measure for Berkshire's intrinsic value. In other words, the percentage change in book value in any given year is likely to be reasonably close to that year's change in intrinsic value.

You can gain some insight into the differences between book value and intrinsic value by looking at one form of investment, a college education. Think of the education's cost as its "book value." If this cost is to be accurate, it should include the earnings that were foregone by the student because he chose college rather than a job.

For this exercise, we will ignore the important non-economic benefits of an education and focus strictly on its economic value. First, we must estimate the earnings that the graduate will receive over his lifetime and subtract from that figure an estimate of what he would have earned had he lacked his education. That gives us an excess earnings figure, which must then be discounted, at an appropriate interest rate, back to graduation day. The dollar result equals the intrinsic economic value of the education.

Some graduates will find that the book value of their education exceeds its intrinsic value, which means that whoever paid for the education didn't get his money's worth. In other cases, the intrinsic value of an education will far exceed its book value, a result that proves capital was wisely deployed. In all cases, what is clear is that book value is meaningless as an indicator of intrinsic value.

---

An interesting accounting irony overlays a comparison of the reported financial results of our controlled companies with those of the permanent minority holdings. [These holdings] have a market value of over $2 billion. Yet they produced only $11 million in reported after-tax earnings for Berkshire in 1987.

Accounting rules dictate that we take into income only the dividends these companies pay us—which are little more than nominal—rather than our share of their earnings, which in 1987 amounted to well over $100 million. On the other hand, accounting rules provide that the carrying value of these three holdings—owned, as they are, by insurance companies—must be recorded on our balance sheet at current market prices. The result: GAAP accounting lets us reflect in our net worth the up-to-date underlying values of the businesses we partially own, but does not let us reflect their underlying earnings in our income account.

In the case of our controlled companies, just the opposite is true. Here, we show full earnings in our income account but never change asset values on our balance sheet, no matter how much the value of a business might have increased since we purchased it.

Our mental approach to this accounting schizophrenia is to ignore GAAP figures and to focus solely on the future earning power of both our controlled and non-controlled businesses. Using this approach, we establish our own ideas of business value, keeping these independent from both the accounting values shown on our books for controlled companies and the values placed by a sometimes foolish market on our partially-owned companies. It is this business value that we hope to increase at a reasonable (or, preferably, unreasonable) rate in the years ahead.

––––––––––––

Historically, Berkshire shares have sold modestly below intrinsic business value. With the price there, purchasers could be certain (as long as they did not experience a widening of this discount) that their personal investment experience would at least equal the financial experience of the business. But recently the discount has disappeared, and occasionally a modest premium has prevailed.

The elimination of the discount means that Berkshire's market value increased even faster than business value (which, itself, grew at a pleasing pace). That was good news for any owner holding while that move took place, but it is bad news for the new or prospective owner. If the financial experience of new owners of Berkshire is merely to match the future financial experience of the company, any premium of market value over intrinsic business value that they pay must be maintained.

Over the long term there has been a more consistent relationship between Berkshire's market value and business value than has existed for any other publicly-traded equity with which I am familiar. This is a tribute to you. Because you have been rational, interested, and investment-oriented, the market price for Berkshire stock has almost always been sensible. This unusual result has been achieved by a shareholder group with unusual demographics: virtually all of our shareholders are individuals, not institutions. No other public company our size can claim the same.

Ben Graham told a story 40 years ago that illustrates why investment professionals behave as they do: An oil prospector, moving to his heavenly reward, was met by St. Peter with bad news. "You're qualified for residence", said St. Peter, "but, as you can see, the compound reserved for oil men is packed. There's no way to squeeze you in." After thinking a moment, the prospector asked if he might say just four words to the present occupants. That seemed harmless to St. Peter, so the prospector cupped his hands and yelled, "Oil discovered in hell." Immediately the gate to the compound opened and all of the oil men marched out to head for the nether regions. Impressed, St. Peter invited the prospector to move in and make himself comfortable. The prospector paused. "No," he said, "I think I'll go along with the rest of the boys. There might be some truth to that rumor after all."

---

In [the 1995] letter, with Berkshire shares selling at $36,000, I told you: (1) Berkshire's gain in market value in recent years had outstripped its gain in intrinsic value, even though the latter gain had been highly satisfactory; (2) that kind of overperformance could not continue indefinitely; (3) Charlie and I did not at that moment consider Berkshire to be undervalued.

Since I set down those cautions, Berkshire's intrinsic value has increased very significantly while the market price of our shares has changed little. This, of course, means that in 1996 Berkshire's stock underperformed the business. Consequently, today's price/value relationship is both much different from what it was a year ago and, as Charlie and I see it, more appropriate.

Over time, the aggregate gains made by Berkshire shareholders must of necessity match the business gains of the company. When the stock temporarily overperforms or underperforms the business, a limited number of shareholders—either sellers or buyers—receive outsized benefits at the expense of those they trade with. Generally, the sophisticated have an edge over the innocents in this game.

Though our primary goal is to maximize the amount that our shareholders, in total, reap from their ownership of Berkshire, we wish also to minimize the benefits going to some shareholders at the expense of others. These are goals we would have were we managing a family partnership, and we believe they make equal sense for the manager of a public company. In a partnership, fairness requires that partnership interests be valued equitably when partners enter or exit; in a public company, fairness prevails when market price and intrinsic value are in sync. Obviously, they won't always meet that ideal, but a manager—by his policies and communications—can do much to foster equity.

Of course, the longer a shareholder holds his shares, the more bearing Berkshire's business results will have on his financial experience—and the less it will matter what premium or discount to intrinsic value prevails when he buys and sells his stock. That's one reason we hope to attract owners with long-term horizons. Overall, I think we have succeeded in that pursuit. Berkshire probably ranks number one among large American corporations in the percentage of its shares held by owners with a long-term view.

### F.   *Aesop and Inefficient Bush Theory*[57]

The formula for valuing *all* assets that are purchased for financial gain has been unchanged since it was first laid out by a very smart man in about 600 B.C. (though he wasn't smart enough to know it was 600 B.C.).

The oracle was Aesop and his enduring, though somehwat incomplete, investment insight was "a bird in the hand is worth two in the bush." To flesh out this principle, you must answer only three questions. How certain are you that there are indeed birds in the bush? When will they emerge and how many will there be? What is the risk-free interest rate (which we consider to be the yield on long-term U.S. bonds)? If you can answer these three questions, you will know the maximum value of the bush—and the maximum number of the birds you now possess that should be offered for it. And, of course, don't literally think birds. Think dollars.

Aesop's investment axiom, thus expanded and converted into dollars, is immutable. It applies to outlays for farms, oil royalties, bonds, stocks, lottery tickets, and manufacturing plants. And neither the advent of the steam engine, the harnessing of electricity nor the creation of the automobile changed the formula one iota— nor will the Internet. Just insert the correct numbers, and you can rank the attractiveness of all possible uses of capital throughout the universe.

Common yardsticks such as dividend yield, the ratio of price to earnings or to book value, and even growth rates have *nothing* to do with valuation except to the extent they provide clues to the amount and timing of cash flows into and from the business. Indeed, growth can destroy value if it requires cash inputs in the early years of a project or enterprise that exceed the discounted value of the cash that those assets will generate in later years. Market commentators and investment managers who glibly refer to "growth" and "value" styles as contrasting approaches to investment are dis-

---

[57] [2000.]

playing their ignorance, not their sophistication. Growth is simply a component—usually a plus, sometimes a minus—in the value equation.

Alas, though Aesop's proposition and the third variable—that is, interest rates—are simple, plugging in numbers for the other two variables is a difficult task. Using precise numbers is, in fact, foolish; working with a range of possibilities is the better approach.

Usually, the range must be so wide that no useful conclusion can be reached. Occasionally, though, even very conservative estimates about the future emergence of birds reveal that the price quoted is startlingly low in relation to value. (Let's call this phenomenon the IBT—Inefficient Bush Theory.) To be sure, an investor needs some general understanding of business economics as well as the ability to think independently to reach a well-founded positive conclusion. But the investor does not need brilliance nor blinding insights.

At the other extreme, there are many times when the *most* brilliant of investors can't muster a conviction about the birds to emerge, not even when a very broad range of estimates is employed. This kind of uncertainty frequently occurs when new businesses and rapidly changing industries are under examination. In cases of this sort, any capital commitment must be labeled speculative.

Now, speculation—in which the focus is not on what an asset will produce but rather on what the next fellow will pay for it—is neither illegal, immoral nor un-American. But it is not a game in which Charlie and I wish to play. We bring nothing to the party, so why should we expect to take anything home?

The line separating investment and speculation, which is never bright and clear, becomes blurred still further when most market participants have recently enjoyed triumphs. Nothing sedates rationality like large doses of effortless money. After a heady experience of that kind, normally sensible people drift into behavior akin to that of Cinderella at the ball. They know that overstaying the festivities—that is, continuing to speculate in companies that have gigantic valuations relative to the cash they are likely to generate in the future—will eventually bring on pumpkins and mice. But they nevertheless hate to miss a single minute of what is one helluva party. Therefore, the giddy participants all plan to leave just seconds before midnight. There's a problem, though: They are dancing in a room in which the clocks have no hands.

Last year, we commented on the exuberance—and, yes, it was irrational—that prevailed, noting that investor expectations had grown to be several multiples of probable returns. One piece of evidence came from a Paine Webber-Gallup survey of investors conducted in December 1999, in which the participants were asked their opinion about the annual returns investors could expect to realize over the decade ahead. Their answers averaged 19%. That, for sure, was an irrational expectation: For American business as a whole, there couldn't possibly be enough birds in the 2009 bush to deliver such a return.

Far more irrational still were the huge valuations that market participants were then putting on businesses almost certain to end up being of modest or no value. Yet investors, mesmerized by soaring stock prices and ignoring all else, piled into these enterprises. It was as if some virus, racing wildly among investment professionals as well as amateurs, induced hallucinations in which the values of stocks in certain sectors became decoupled from the values of the businesses that underlay them.

This surreal scene was accompanied by much loose talk about "value creation." We readily acknowledge that there has been a huge amount of true value created in the past decade by new or young businesses, and that there is much more to come. But value is destroyed, not created, by any business that loses money over its lifetime, no matter how high its interim valuation may get.

What actually occurs in these cases is wealth *transfer*, often on a massive scale. By shamelessly merchandising birdless bushes, promoters have in recent years moved billions of dollars from the pockets of the public to their own purses (and to those of their friends and associates). The fact is that a bubble market has allowed the creation of bubble companies, entities designed more with an eye to making money *off* investors rather than *for* them. Too often, an IPO, not profits, was the primary goal of a company's promoters. At bottom, the "business model" for these companies has been the old-fashioned chain letter, for which many fee-hungry investment bankers acted as eager postmen.

But a pin lies in wait for every bubble. And when the two eventually meet, a new wave of investors learns some very old lessons: First, many in Wall Street—a community in which quality control is not prized—will sell investors anything they will buy. Second, speculation is most dangerous when it looks easiest.

At Berkshire, we make *no* attempt to pick the few winners that will emerge from an ocean of unproven enterprises. We're not smart enough to do that, and we know it. Instead, we try to apply Aesop's 2,600-year-old equation to opportunities in which we have reasonable confidence as to how many birds are in the bush and when they will emerge (a formulation that my grandsons would probably update to "A girl in a convertible is worth five in the phonebook."). Obviously, we can never precisely predict the timing of cash flows in and out of a business or their exact amount. We try, therefore, to keep our estimates conservative and to focus on industries where business surprises are unlikely to wreak havoc on owners. Even so, we make many mistakes: I'm the fellow, remember, who thought he understood the future economics of trading stamps, textiles, shoes and second-tier department stores.

Lately, the most promising "bushes" have been negotiated transactions for entire businesses, and that pleases us. You should clearly understand, however, that these acquisitions will at best provide us only reasonable returns. Really juicy results from negotiated deals can be anticipated only when capital markets are severly constrained and the whole business world is pessimistic. We are 180 degrees from that point.

## VII.   Accounting Policy and Tax Matters

Despite the shortcomings of generally accepted accounting principles (GAAP), I would hate to have the job of devising a better set of rules. The limitations of the existing set, however, need not be inhibiting: CEOs are free to treat GAAP statements as a beginning rather than an end to their obligation to inform owners and creditors—and indeed they should. After all, any manager of a subsidiary company would find himself in hot water if he reported barebones GAAP numbers that omitted key information needed by his boss, the parent corporation's CEO. Why, then, should the CEO himself withhold information vitally useful to *his* bosses—the shareholder-owners of the corporation?

What needs to be reported is data—whether GAAP, non-GAAP, or extra-GAAP—that helps financially-literate readers answer three key questions: (1) Approximately how much is this company worth? (2) What is the likelihood that it can meet its future obligations? and (3) How good a job are its managers doing, given the hand they have been dealt?

In most cases, answers to one or more of these questions are somewhere between difficult and impossible to glean from the minimum GAAP presentation. The business world is simply too complex for a single set of rules to effectively describe economic reality for all enterprises, particularly those operating in a wide variety of businesses, such as Berkshire.

Further complicating the problem is the fact that many managements view GAAP not as a standard to be met, but as an obstacle to overcome. Too often their accountants willingly assist them. ("How much," says the client, "is two plus two?" Replies the cooperative accountant, "What number did you have in mind?") Even honest and well-intentioned managements sometimes stretch GAAP a bit in order to present figures they think will more appropriately describe their performance. Both the smoothing of earnings and the "big bath" quarter are "white lie" techniques employed by otherwise upright managements.

Then there are managers who actively use GAAP to deceive and defraud. They know that many investors and creditors accept GAAP results as gospel. So these charlatans interpret the rules "imaginatively" and record business transactions in ways that technically comply with GAAP but actually display an economic illusion to the world.

As long as investors—including supposedly sophisticated institutions—place fancy valuations on reported "earnings" that march steadily upward, you can be sure that some managers and promoters will exploit GAAP to produce such numbers, no matter what the truth may be. Over the years, Charlie and I have observed many accounting-based frauds of staggering size. Few of the perpetrators have been punished; many have not even been censured. It has been far safer to steal large sums with a pen than small sums with a gun.[58]

## A.   *The Purchase-Pooling Debate*[59]

[The application of accounting to acquisitions] is currently a very contentious topic and, before the dust settles, Congress may even intervene (a truly terrible idea).

When a company is acquired, generally accepted accounting principles ("GAAP") currently condone two very different ways of recording the transaction: "purchase" and "pooling." In a pooling, stock must be the currency; in a purchase, payment can be made in either cash or stock. Whatever the currency, managements usually detest purchase accounting because it almost always requires that a "goodwill" account be established and subsequently written off–a process that saddles earnings with a large annual charge that normally persists for decades. In contrast, pooling avoids a goodwill account, which is why managements love it.

Now, the Financial Accounting Standards Board ("FASB") has proposed an end to pooling, and many CEOs are girding for battle. It will be an important fight, so we'll venture some opinions. To begin with, we agree with the many managers who argue that goodwill amortization charges are usually spurious.[60]

For accounting rules to mandate amortization that will, in the usual case, conflict with reality is deeply troublesome: Most accounting charges *relate* to what's going on, even if they don't precisely measure it. As an example, depreciation charges can't with precision calibrate the decline in value that physical assets suffer, but these charges do at least describe something that is truly occurring: Physical assets invariably deteriorate. Correspondingly, obsolescence charges for inventories, bad debt charges for receivables and accruals for warranties are among the charges that reflect true costs. The annual charges for these expenses can't be exactly measured, but the necessity for estimating them is obvious.

---

[58] [Introductory essay, 1988.]

[59] [1999.]

[60] [*See* the essay Economic Goodwill Versus Accounting Goodwill in Part VI.C.]

In contrast, economic goodwill does not, in many cases, diminish. Indeed, in a great many instances–perhaps most–it actually grows in value over time. In character, economic goodwill is much like land: The value of both assets is sure to fluctuate, but the direction in which value is going to go is in no way ordained. At See's, for example, economic goodwill has grown, in an irregular but very substantial manner, for 78 years. And, if we run the business right, growth of that kind will probably continue for at least another 78 years.

To escape from the fiction of goodwill charges, managers embrace the fiction of pooling. This accounting convention is grounded in the poetic notion that when two rivers merge their streams become indistinguishable. Under this concept, a company that has been merged into a larger enterprise has not been "purchased" (even though it will often have received a large "sell-out" premium). Consequently, no goodwill is created, and those pesky subsequent charges to earnings are eliminated. Instead, the accounting for the ongoing entity is handled as if the businesses had forever been one unit.

So much for poetry. The reality of merging is usually far different: There is indisputably an acquirer and an acquiree, and the latter has been "purchased," no matter how the deal has been structured. If you think otherwise, just ask employees severed from their jobs which company was the conqueror and which was the conquered. You will find no confusion. So on this point the FASB is correct: In most mergers, a purchase has been made. Yes, there are some true "mergers of equals," but they are few and far between.

Charlie and I believe there's a reality-based approach that should both satisfy the FASB, which correctly wishes to record a purchase, and meet the objections of managements to nonsensical charges for diminution of goodwill. We would first have the acquiring company record its purchase price–whether paid in stock or cash–at fair value. In most cases, this procedure would create a large asset representing economic goodwill. We would then leave this asset on the books, not requiring its amortization. Later, if the economic goodwill became impaired, as it sometimes would, it would be written down just as would any other asset judged to be impaired.

If our proposed rule were to be adopted, it should be applied retroactively so that acquisition accounting would be consistent throughout America–a far cry from what exists today. One prediction: If this plan were to take effect, managements would structure acquisitions more sensibly, deciding whether to use cash or stock based on the real consequences for their shareholders rather than on the unreal consequences for their reported earnings.

## B. *Stock Options*[61]

The most egregious case of let's-not-face-up-to-reality behavior by executives and accountants has occurred in the world of stock options. In Berkshire's 1985 annual report, I laid out my opinions about the use and misuse of options.[62] But even when options are structured properly, they are accounted for in ways that make no sense. The lack of logic is not accidental: For decades, much of the business world has waged war against accounting rulemakers, trying to keep the costs of stock options from being reflected in the profits of the corporations that issue them.

Typically, executives have argued that options are hard to value and that therefore their costs should be ignored. At other times managers have said that assigning a cost to options would injure small start-up businesses. Sometimes they have even solemnly declared that "out-of-the-money" options (those with an exercise price equal to or above the current market price) have no value when they are issued.

Oddly, the Council of Institutional Investors has chimed in with a variation on that theme, opining that options should not be viewed as a cost because they "aren't dollars out of a company's coffers." I see this line of reasoning as offering exciting possibilities to American corporations for instantly improving their reported profits. For example, they could eliminate the cost of insurance by paying for it with options. So if you're a CEO and subscribe to this "no cash-no cost" theory of accounting, I'll make you an offer you can't refuse: Give us a call at Berkshire and we will happily sell you insurance in exchange for a bundle of long-term options on your company's stock.

Shareholders should understand that companies incur costs when they deliver something of value to another party and not just when cash changes hands. Moreover, it is both silly and cynical to say that an important item of cost should not be recognized simply because it can't be quantified with pinpoint precision. Right now, accounting abounds with imprecision. After all, no manager or au-

---

61 [Divided by hash lines: 1992; 1998.]
62 [*See* the essay A Principled Approach to Executive Pay in Part I.F.]

ditor knows how long a 747 is going to last, which means he also does not know what the yearly depreciation charge for the plane should be. No one knows with any certainty what a bank's annual loan loss charge ought to be. And the estimates of losses that property casualty companies make are notoriously inaccurate.

Does this mean that these important items of cost should be ignored simply because they can't be quantified with absolute accuracy? Of course not. Rather, these costs should be estimated by honest and experienced people and then recorded. When you get right down to it, what other item of major but hard-to-precisely-calculate cost—other, that is, than stock options—does the accounting profession say should be ignored in the calculation of earnings?

Moreover, options are just not that difficult to value. Admittedly, the difficulty is increased by the fact that the options given to executives are restricted in various ways. These restrictions affect value. They do not, however, eliminate it. In fact, since I'm in the mood for offers, I'll make one to any executive who is granted a restricted option, even though it may be out of the money: On the day of issue, Berkshire will pay him or her a substantial sum for the right to any future gain he or she realizes on the option. So if you find a CEO who says his newly-issued options have little or no value, tell him to try us out. In truth, we have far more confidence in our ability to determine an appropriate price to pay for an option than we have in our ability to determine the proper depreciation rate for [a] corporate jet.

The accounting profession and the SEC should be shamed by the fact that they have long let themselves be muscled by business executives on the option-accounting issue. Additionally, the lobbying that executives engage in may have an unfortunate by-product: In my opinion, the business elite risks losing its credibility on issues of significance to society—about which it may have much of value to say—when it advocates the incredible on issues of significance to itself.

———————————

Our General Re acquisition put a spotlight on an egregious flaw in accounting procedure. Sharp-eyed shareholders reading our proxy statement probably noticed an unusual item on page 60. In the pro-forma statement of income–which detailed how the combined 1997 earnings of the two entities would have been affected by the merger–there was an item stating that compensation expense would have been increased by $63 million.

This item, we hasten to add, does not signal that either Charlie or I have experienced a major personality change. (He still travels coach and quotes Ben Franklin.) Nor does it indicate any short-coming in General Re's accounting practices, which have followed GAAP to the letter. Instead, the pro-forma adjustment came about because we are replacing General Re's longstanding stock option plan with a cash plan that ties the incentive compensation of General Re managers to their operating achievements. Formerly what counted for these managers was General Re's stock price; now their payoff will come from the business performance they deliver.

The new plan and the terminated option arrangement have matching economics, which means that the rewards they deliver to employees should, for a given level of performance, be the same. But what these people could have formerly anticipated earning from new option grants will now be paid in cash. (Options granted in past years remain outstanding.)

Though the two plans are an economic wash, the cash plan we are putting in will produce a vastly different accounting result. This Alice-in-Wonderland outcome occurs because existing ac-counting principles ignore the cost of stock options when earnings are being calculated, even though options are a huge and increas-ing expense at a great many corporations. In effect, accounting principles offer management a choice: Pay employees in one form and count the cost, or pay them in another form and ignore the cost. Small wonder then that the use of options has mushroomed. This lop-sided choice has a big downside for owners, however: Though options, if properly structured, can be an appropriate, *and even ideal*, way to compensate and motivate top managers, they are more often wildly capricious in their distribution of rewards, ineffi-cient as motivators, and inordinately expensive for shareholders.

Whatever the merits of options may be, their accounting treat-ment is outrageous. Think for a moment of that $190 million we are going to spend for advertising at GEICO this year. Suppose that instead of paying cash for our ads, we paid the media in ten-year, at-the-market Berkshire options. Would anyone then care to argue that Berkshire had not borne a cost for advertising, or should not be charged this cost on its books?

Perhaps Bishop Berkeley–you may remember him as the phi-losopher who mused about trees falling in a forest when no one was around–would believe that an expense unseen by an account-ant does not exist. Charlie and I, however, have trouble being philosophical about unrecorded costs. When we consider investing in an option-issuing company, we make an appropriate downward adjustment to reported earnings, simply subtracting an amount equal to what the company could have realized by publicly selling options of like quantity and structure. Similarly, if we contemplate an acquisition, we include in our evaluation the cost of replacing any option plan. Then, if we make a deal, we promptly take that cost out of hiding.

Readers who disagree with me about options will by this time be mentally quarreling with my equating the cost of options issued to employees with those that might theoretically be sold and traded publicly. It is true, to state one of these arguments, that employee options are sometimes forfeited–that lessens the damage done to shareholders–whereas publicly-offered options would not be. It is true, also, that companies receive a tax deduction when employee options are exercised; publicly-traded options deliver no such benefit. But there's an offset to these points: Options issued to employees are often repriced, a transformation that makes them much more costly than the public variety.

It's sometimes argued that a non-transferable option given to an employee is less valuable to him than would be a publicly-traded option that he could freely sell. That fact, however, does not reduce the *cost* of the non-transferable option: Giving an employee a company car that can only be used for certain purposes diminishes its value to the employee, but does not in the least diminish its cost to the employer.

The earning revisions that Charlie and I have made for options in recent years have frequently cut the reported per-share figures by 5%, with 10% not all that uncommon. On occasion, the downward adjustment has been so great that it has affected our portfolio decisions, causing us either to make a sale or to pass on a stock purchase we might otherwise have made.

A few years ago we asked three questions to which we have not yet received an answer: "If options aren't a form of compensation, what are they? If compensation isn't an expense, what is it? And, if expenses shouldn't go into the calculation of earnings, where in the world should they go?"

### C.  *"Restructuring" Charges*[63]

The role that managements have played in stock-option accounting has hardly been benign: A distressing number of both CEOs and auditors have in recent years bitterly fought FASB's attempts to replace option fiction with truth and virtually none have spoken out in support of FASB.  Its opponents even enlisted Congress in the fight, pushing the case that inflated figures were in the national interest.

Still, I believe that the behavior of managements has been even worse when it comes to restructurings and merger accounting.  Here, many managements purposefully work at manipulating numbers and deceiving investors.  And, as Michael Kinsley has said about Washington: "The scandal isn't in what's done that's *illegal* but rather in what's *legal*."

It was once relatively easy to tell the good guys in accounting from the bad: The late 1960's, for example, brought on an orgy of what one charlatan dubbed "bold, imaginative accounting" (the practice of which, incidentally, made him loved for a time by Wall Street because he never missed expectations).  But most investors of that period knew who was playing games.  And, to their credit, virtually all of America's most-admired companies then shunned deception.

In recent years, probity has eroded.  Many major corporations still play things straight, but a significant and growing number of otherwise high-grade managers–CEOs you would be happy to have as spouses for your children or as trustees under your will–have come to the view that it's okay to manipulate earnings to satisfy what they believe are Wall Street's desires.  Indeed, many CEOs think this kind of manipulation is not only okay, but actually their *duty*.

These managers start with the assumption, all too common, that their job at all times is to encourage the highest stock price possible (a premise with which we adamantly disagree).  To pump the price, they strive, admirably, for operational excellence.  But when operations don't produce the result hoped for, these CEOs resort to unadmirable accounting stratagems.  These either manufacture the desired "earnings" or set the stage for them in the future.

Rationalizing this behavior, these managers often say that their shareholders will be hurt if their currency for doing deals–that

---

[63] [1998.]

is, their stock–is not fully-priced, and they also argue that in using accounting shenanigans to get the figures they want, they are only doing what everybody else does.  Once such an everybody's-doing-it attitude takes hold, ethical misgivings vanish.  Call this behavior Son of Gresham: Bad accounting drives out good.

The distortion *du jour* is the "restructuring charge," an accounting entry that can, of course, be legitimate but that too often is a device for manipulating earnings.  In this bit of legerdemain, a large chunk of costs that should properly be attributed to a number of years is dumped into a single quarter, typically one already fated to disappoint investors.  In some cases, the purpose of the charge is to clean up earnings misrepresentations of the past, and in others it is to prepare the ground for future misrepresentations.  In either case, the size and timing of these charges is dictated by the cynical proposition that Wall Street will not mind if earnings fall short by $5 per share in a given quarter, just as long as this deficiency ensures that quarterly earnings in the future will consistently exceed expectations by five cents per share.

This dump-everything-into-one-quarter behavior suggests a corresponding "bold, imaginative" approach to — golf scores.  In his first round of the season, a golfer should ignore his actual performance and simply fill his card with atrocious numbers–double, triple, quadruple bogeys–and then turn in a score of, say, 140.  Having established this "reserve," he should go to the golf shop and tell his pro that he wishes to "restructure" his imperfect swing.  Next, as he takes his new swing onto the course, he should count his good holes, but not the bad ones.  These remnants from his old swing should be charged instead to the reserve established earlier.  At the end of five rounds, then, his record will be 140, 80, 80, 80, 80 rather than 91, 94, 89, 94, 92.  On Wall Street, they will ignore the 140–which, after all, came from a "discontinued" swing–and will classify our hero as an 80 shooter (and one who *never* disappoints).

For those who prefer to cheat up front, there would be a variant of this strategy.  The golfer, playing alone with a cooperative caddy-auditor, should defer the recording of bad holes, take four 80s, accept the plaudits he gets for such athleticism and consistency, and then turn in a fifth card carrying a 140 score.  After rectifying his earlier scorekeeping sins with this "big bath," he may mumble a few apologies but will refrain from returning the sums he has previously collected from comparing scorecards in the clubhouse.  (The caddy, need we add, will have acquired a loyal patron.)

Unfortunately, CEOs who use variations of these scoring schemes in real life tend to become addicted to the games they're playing–after all, it's easier to fiddle with the scorecard than to spend hours on the practice tee–and never muster the will to give them up. Their behavior brings to mind Voltaire's comment on sexual experimentation: "Once a philosopher, twice a pervert."

In the acquisition arena, restructuring has been raised to an art form: Managements now frequently use mergers to dishonestly re-arrange the value of assets and liabilities in ways that will allow them to both smooth and swell future earnings. Indeed, at deal time, major auditing firms sometimes point out the possibilities for a little accounting magic (or for a lot). Getting this push from the pulpit, first-class people will frequently stoop to third-class tactics. CEOs understandably do not find it easy to reject auditor-blessed strategies that lead to increased future "earnings."

An example from the property-casualty insurance industry will illuminate the possibilities. When a p-c company is acquired, the buyer sometimes simultaneously increases its loss reserves, often substantially. This boost may merely reflect the previous inade-quacy of reserves–though it is uncanny how often an actuarial "rev-elation" of this kind coincides with the inking of a deal. In any case, the move sets up the possibility of "earnings" flowing into income at some later date, as reserves are released.

Berkshire has kept entirely clear of these practices: If we are to disappoint you, we would rather it be with our earnings than with our accounting. In all of our acquisitions, we have left the loss reserve figures exactly as we found them. After all, we have con-sistently joined with insurance managers knowledgeable about their business and honest in their financial reporting. When deals occur in which liabilities are increased immediately and substan-tially, simple logic says that at least one of those virtues must have been lacking–or, alternatively, that the acquirer is laying the groundwork for future infusions of "earnings."

Here's a true story that illustrates an all-too-common view in corporate America. The CEOs of two large banks, one of them a man who'd made many acquisitions, were involved not long ago in a friendly merger discussion (which in the end didn't produce a deal). The veteran acquirer was expounding on the merits of the possible combination, only to be skeptically interrupted by the other CEO: "But won't that mean a huge charge," he asked, "per-haps as much as $1 billion?" The "sophisticate" wasted no words: "We'll make it bigger than that–that's why we're doing the deal."

A preliminary tally by R.G. Associates, of Baltimore, of special charges taken or announced during 1998–that is, charges for restructuring, in-process R&D, merger-related items, and write-downs–identified no less than 1,369 of these, totaling $72.1 billion. That is a staggering amount as evidenced by this bit of perspective: The 1997 earnings of the 500 companies in *Fortune's* famous list totaled $324 billion.

Clearly the attitude of disrespect that many executives have today for accurate reporting is a business disgrace. And auditors, as we have already suggested, have done little on the positive side. Though auditors *should* regard the investing public as their client, they tend to kowtow instead to the managers who choose them and dole out their pay. ("Whose bread I eat, his song I sing.")

A big piece of news, however, is that the SEC, led by its chairman, Arthur Levitt, seems determined to get corporate America to clean up its act. In a landmark speech last September, Levitt called for an end to "earnings management." He correctly observed, "Too many corporate managers, auditors and analysts are participants in a game of nods and winks." And then he laid on a real indictment: "Managing may be giving way to manipulating; integrity may be losing out to illusion."

I urge you to read the Chairman's speech (you can find it on the Internet at www.sec.gov) and to support him in his efforts to get corporate America to deliver a straight story to its owners. Levitt's job will be Herculean, but it is hard to think of another more important for him to take on.

### D. *Segment Data and Consolidation*[64]

Under one major change mandated by GAAP for 1988, we have been required to fully consolidate all our subsidiaries in our balance sheet and earnings statement. In the past, Mutual Savings and Loan, and Scott Fetzer Financial (a credit company that primarily finances installment sales of World Book and Kirby products) were consolidated on a "one-line" basis. That meant we (1) showed our equity in their combined net worths as a single-entry asset on Berkshire's consolidated balance sheet and (2) included our equity in their combined annual earnings as a single-line income entry in our consolidated statement of earnings. Now the rules require that we consolidate each asset and liability of these

---

[64] [1988.]

companies in our balance sheet and each item of their income and expense in our earnings statement.

This change underscores the need for companies also to report segmented data: The greater the number of economically diverse business operations lumped together in conventional financial statements, the less useful those presentations are and the less able investors are to answer the three questions posed earlier. Indeed, the only reason we ever prepare consolidated figures at Berkshire is to meet outside requirements. On the other hand, Charlie and I constantly study our segment data.

Now that we are required to bundle more numbers in our GAAP statements, we have decided to publish additional supplementary information that we think will help you measure both business value and managerial performance. (Berkshire's ability to discharge its obligations to creditors—the third question we listed [in the introductory essay in this Part]—should be obvious, whatever statements you examine.) In these supplementary presentations, we will not necessarily follow GAAP procedures, or even corporate structure. Rather, we will attempt to lump major business activities in ways that aid analysis but do not swamp you with detail. Our goal is to give you important information in a form that we would wish to get it if our roles were reversed.

### E.  *Deferred Taxes*[65]

I referred earlier to a major change in GAAP that is expected in 1990. This change relates to the calculation of deferred taxes, and is both complicated and controversial—so much so that its imposition, originally scheduled for 1989, was postponed for a year.

When implemented, the new rule will affect us in various ways. Most important, we will be required to change the way we calculate our liability for deferred taxes on the unrealized appreciation of stocks held by our insurance companies.

Right now, our liability is layered. For the unrealized appreciation that dates back to 1986 and earlier years, $1.2 billion, we have booked a 28% tax liability. For the unrealized appreciation built up since, $600 million, the tax liability has been booked at 34%. The difference reflects the increase in tax rates that went into effect in 1987.

It now appears, however, that the new accounting rule will require us to establish the entire liability at 34% in 1990, taking the

---

[65] [Divided by hash lines: 1988; 1989; 1992.]

charge against our earnings. Assuming no change in tax rates by 1990, this step will reduce our earnings in that year (and thereby our reported net worth) by $71 million. The proposed rule will also affect other items on our balance sheet, but these changes will have only a minor impact on earnings and net worth.

We have no strong views about the desirability of this change in calculation of deferred taxes. We should point out, however, that neither a 28% nor a 34% tax liability precisely depicts economic reality at Berkshire since we have no plans to sell the stocks in which we have the great bulk of our gains.

---

A new accounting rule is likely to be adopted that will require companies to reserve against all gains at the current tax rate, whatever it may be. With the rate at 34%, such a rule would increase our deferred tax liability, and decrease our net worth, by about $71 million—the result of raising the reserve on our pre-1987 gain by six percentage points. Because the proposed rule has sparked widespread controversy and its final form is unclear, we have not yet made this change.

[W]e would owe taxes of more than $1.1 billion were we to sell all of our securities at year-end market values. Is this $1.1 billion liability equal, or even similar, to a $1.1 billion liability payable to a trade creditor 15 days after the end of the year? Obviously not—despite the fact that both items have exactly the same effect on audited net worth, reducing it by $1.1 billion.

On the other hand, is this liability for deferred taxes a meaningless accounting fiction because its payment can be triggered only by the sale of stocks that, in very large part, we have no intention of selling? Again, the answer is no.

In economic terms, the liability resembles an interest-free loan from the U.S. Treasury that comes due only at our election (unless, of course, Congress moves to tax gains before they are realized). This "loan" is peculiar in other respects as well: It can be used only to finance the ownership of the particular, appreciated stocks and it fluctuates in size—daily as market prices change and periodically if tax rates change. In effect, this deferred tax liability is equivalent to a very large transfer tax that is payable only if we elect to move from one asset to another. Indeed, we sold some relatively small holdings in 1989, incurring about $76 million of "transfer" tax on $224 million of gains.

Because of the way the tax law works, the Rip Van Winkle style of investing that we favor—if successful—has an important mathematical edge over a more frenzied approach. We have not, we should stress, adopted our strategy favoring long-term investment commitments because of these mathematics. Indeed, it is possible we could earn greater after-tax returns by moving rather frequently from one investment to another. Many years ago, that's exactly what Charlie and I did.

Now we would rather stay put, even if that means slightly lower returns. Our reason is simple: We have found splendid business relationships to be so rare and so enjoyable that we want to retain all we develop. This decision is particularly easy for us because we feel that these relationships will produce good—though perhaps not optimal—financial results. Considering that, we think it makes little sense for us to give up time with people we know to be interesting and admirable for time with others we do not know and who are likely to have human qualities far closer to average.

---

A new accounting rule having to do with deferred taxes becomes effective in 1993. It undoes a dichotomy in our books that I have described in previous annual reports and that relates to the accrued taxes carried against the unrealized appreciation in our investment portfolio. At yearend 1992, that appreciation amounted to $7.6 billion. Against $6.4 billion of that, we carried taxes at the current 34% rate. Against the remainder of $1.2 billion, we carried an accrual of 28%, the tax rate in effect when that portion of the appreciation occurred. The new accounting rule says we must henceforth accrue all deferred tax at the current rate, which to us seems sensible.

The new marching orders mean that in the first quarter of 1993 we will apply a 34% rate to all of our unrealized appreciation, thereby increasing the tax liability and reducing net worth by $70 million. The new rule also will cause us to make other minor changes in our calculation of deferred taxes.

Future changes in tax rates will be reflected immediately in the liability for deferred taxes and, correspondingly, in net worth. The impact could well be substantial. Nevertheless, what is important in the end is the tax rate at the time we sell securities, when unrealized appreciation becomes realized.

### F.  *Retiree Benefits*[66]

Another major accounting change, whose implementation is required by January 1, 1993, mandates that businesses recognize their present-value liability for post-retirement health benefits. Though GAAP has previously required recognition of pensions to be paid in the future, it has illogically ignored the costs that companies will then have to bear for health benefits. The new rule will force many companies to record a huge balance-sheet liability (and a consequent reduction in net worth) and also henceforth to recognize substantially higher costs when they are calculating annual profits.

In making acquisitions, Charlie and I have tended to avoid companies with significant post-retirement liabilities. As a result, Berkshire's present liability and future costs for post-retirement health benefits—though we now have [tens of thousands of] employees—are inconsequential. I need to admit, though, that we had a near miss: In 1982 I made a huge mistake in committing to buy a company burdened by extraordinary post-retirement health obligations. Luckily, though, the transaction fell through for reasons beyond our control. Reporting on this episode in the 1982 annual report, I said: "If we were to introduce graphics to this report, illustrating favorable business developments of the past year, two blank pages depicting this blown deal would be the appropriate centerfold." Even so, I wasn't expecting things to get as bad as they did. Another buyer appeared, the business soon went bankrupt and was shut down, and thousands of workers found those bountiful health-care promises to be largely worthless.

In recent decades, no CEO would have dreamed of going to his board with the proposition that his company become an insurer of uncapped post-retirement health benefits that other corporations chose to install. A CEO didn't need to be a medical expert to know that lengthening life expectancies and soaring health costs would guarantee an insurer a financial battering from such a business. Nevertheless, many a manager blithely committed his own company to a self-insurance plan embodying precisely the same promises—and thereby doomed his shareholders to suffer the inevitable consequences. In health-care, open-ended promises have created open-ended liabilities that in a few cases loom so large as to threaten the global competitiveness of major American industries.

---

[66] [1992.]

I believe part of the reason for this reckless behavior was that accounting rules did not, for so long, require the booking of post-retirement health costs as they were incurred. Instead, the rules allowed cash-basis accounting, which vastly understated the liabilities that were building up. In effect, the attitude of both managements and their accountants toward these liabilities was "out-of-sight, out-of-mind." Ironically, some of these same managers would be quick to criticize Congress for employing "cash-basis" thinking in respect to Social Security promises or other programs creating future liabilities of size.

Managers thinking about accounting issues should never forget one of Abraham Lincoln's favorite riddles: "How many legs does a dog have if you call his tail a leg?" The answer: "Four, because calling a tail a leg does not make it a leg." It behooves managers to remember that Abe's right even if an auditor is willing to certify that the tail is a leg.

### G.  *Distribution of the Corporate Tax Burden*[67]

The Tax Reform Act of 1986 affects our various businesses in important and divergent ways. Although we find much to praise in the Act, the net financial effect for Berkshire is negative: our rate of increase in business value is likely to be at least moderately slower under the new law than under the old. The net effect for our shareholders is even more negative: every dollar of increase in per-share business value, assuming the increase is accompanied by an equivalent dollar gain in the market value of Berkshire stock, will produce 72¢ of after-tax gain for our shareholders rather than the 80¢ produced under the old law. This result, of course, reflects the rise in the maximum tax rate on personal capital gains from 20% to 28%.

Here are the main tax changes that affect Berkshire:

• The tax rate on corporate ordinary income is scheduled to decrease from 46% in 1986 to 34% in 1988. This change obviously affects us positively—and it also has a significant positive effect on two of our three major investees, Capital Cities/ABC and The Washington Post Company.

I say this knowing that over the years there has been a lot of fuzzy and often partisan commentary about who really pays corporate taxes—businesses or their customers. The argument, of course, has usually turned around tax increases, not decreases.

---

[67] [Divided by has lines: 1986; 1998.]

Those people resisting increases in corporate rates frequently argue that corporations in reality pay none of the taxes levied on them but, instead, act as a sort of economic pipeline, passing all taxes through to consumers. According to these advocates, any corporate-tax increase will simply lead to higher prices that, for the corporation, offset the increase. Having taken this position, proponents of the "pipeline" theory must also conclude that a tax decrease for corporations will not help profits but will instead flow through, leading to correspondingly lower prices for consumers.

Conversely, others argue that corporations not only pay the taxes levied upon them, but absorb them also. Consumers, this school says, will be unaffected by changes in corporate rates.

What really happens? When the corporate rate is cut, do Berkshire, The Washington Post, Cap Cities, etc., themselves soak up the benefits, or do these companies pass the benefits along to their customers in the form of lower prices? This is an important question for investors and managers, as well as for policymakers.

Our conclusion is that in some cases the benefits of lower corporate taxes fall exclusively, or almost exclusively, upon the corporation and its shareholders, and that in other cases the benefits are entirely, or almost entirely, passed through to the customer. What determines the outcome is the strength of the corporation's business franchise and whether the profitability of the franchise is regulated.

For example, when the franchise is strong and after-tax profits are regulated in a relatively precise manner, as is the case with electric utilities, changes in corporate tax rates are largely reflected in prices, not in profits. When taxes are cut, prices will usually be reduced in short order. When taxes are increased, prices will rise, though often not as promptly.

A similar result occurs in a second arena—in the price-competitive industry, whose companies typically operate with very weak business franchises. In such industries, the free market "regulates" after-tax profits in a delayed and irregular, but generally effective, manner. The marketplace, in effect, performs much the same function in dealing with the price-competitive industry as the Public Utilities Commission does in dealing with electric utilities. In these industries, therefore, tax changes eventually affect prices more than profits.

In the case of unregulated businesses blessed with strong franchises, however, it's a different story: the corporation and its shareholders are then the major beneficiaries of tax cuts. These companies benefit from a tax cut much as the electric company would if it lacked a regulator to force down prices.

Many of our businesses, both those we own in whole and in part, possess such franchises. Consequently, reductions in their taxes largely end up in our pockets rather than the pockets of our customers. While this may be impolitic to state, it is impossible to deny. If you are tempted to believe otherwise, think for a moment of the most able brain surgeon or lawyer in your area. Do you really expect the fees of this expert (the local "franchise-holder" in his or her specialty) to be reduced now that the top personal tax rate is being cut from 50% to 28%?

Your joy at our conclusion that lower rates benefit a number of our operating businesses and investees should be severely tempered, however, by another of our convictions: scheduled 1988 tax rates, both individual and corporate, seem totally unrealistic to us. These rates will very likely bestow a fiscal problem on Washington that will prove incompatible with price stability. We believe, therefore, that ultimately—within, say, five years—either higher tax rates or higher inflation rates are almost certain to materialize. And it would not surprise us to see both.

• Corporate capital gains tax rates have been increased from 28% to 34%, effective in 1987. This change will have an important adverse effect on Berkshire because we expect much of our gain in business value in the future, as in the past, to arise from capital gains. For example, our three major investment holdings—Cap Cities, GEICO, and Washington Post—at yearend had a market value of over $1.7 billion, close to 75% of the total net worth of Berkshire, and yet they deliver us only about $9 million in annual income. Instead, all three retain a very high percentage of their earnings, which we expect to eventually deliver us capital gains.

The new law increases the rate for all gains realized in the future, including the unrealized gains that existed before the law was enacted. At yearend, we had $1.2 billion of such unrealized gains in our equity investments. The effect of the new law on our balance sheet will be delayed because a GAAP rule stipulates that the deferred tax liability applicable to unrealized gains should be stated at last year's 28% tax rate rather than the current 34% rate. This rule is expected to change soon. The moment it does, about $73 million will disappear from our GAAP net worth and be added to the deferred tax account.

• Dividend and interest income received by our insurance companies will be taxed far more heavily under the new law. First, all corporations will be taxed on 20% of the dividends they receive from other domestic corporations, up from 15% under the old law. Second, there is a change concerning the residual 80% that applies only to property/casualty companies: 15% of that residual will be taxed if the stocks paying the dividends were purchased after August 7, 1986. A third change, again applying only to property/casualty companies, concerns tax-exempt bonds: interest on bonds purchased by insurers after August 7, 1986 will only be 85% tax-exempt.

The last two changes are very important. They mean that our income from the investments we make in future years will be significantly lower than would have been the case under the old law. My best guess is that these changes alone will eventually reduce the earning power of our insurance operation by at least 10% from what we could previously have expected.

• The new tax law also materially changes the timing of tax payments by property/casualty insurance companies. One new rule requires us to discount our loss reserves in our tax returns, a change that will decrease deductions and increase taxable income. Another rule, to be phased in over six years, requires us to include 20% of our unearned premium reserve in taxable income.

Neither rule changes the amount of the annual tax accrual in our reports to you, but each materially accelerates the schedule of payments. That is, taxes formerly deferred will now be front-ended, a change that will significantly cut the profitability of our business. An analogy will suggest the toll: if, upon turning 21, you were required to immediately pay tax on all income you were due to receive throughout your life, both your lifetime wealth and your estate would be a small fraction of what they would be if all taxes on your income were payable only when you died.

Attentive readers may spot an inconsistency in what we say. Earlier, discussing companies in price-competitive industries, we suggested that tax increases or reductions affect these companies relatively little, but instead are largely passed along to their customers. But now we are saying that tax increases will affect profits of Berkshire's property/casualty companies even though they operate in an intensely price-competitive industry.

The reason this industry is likely to be an exception to our general rule is that not all major insurers will be working with identical tax equations. Important differences will exist for several reasons: a new alternative minimum tax will materially affect some companies but not others; certain major insurers have huge loss carry-forwards that will largely shield their income from significant taxes for at least a few years; and the results of some large insurers will be folded into the consolidated returns of companies with non-insurance businesses. These disparate conditions will produce widely-varying marginal tax rates in the property/casualty industry. That will not be the case, however, in most other price-competitive industries, such as aluminum, autos and department stores, in which the major players will generally contend with similar tax equations.

The absence of a common tax calculus for property/casualty companies means that the increased taxes falling on the industry will probably not be passed along to customers to the degree that they would in a typical price-competitive industry. Insurers, in other words, will themselves bear much of the new tax burdens.

• A partial offset to these burdens is a "fresh start" adjustment that occurred on January 1, 1987 when our December 31, 1986 loss reserve figures were converted for tax purposes to the newly-required discounted basis. (In our reports to you, however, reserves will remain on exactly the same basis as in the past—undiscounted except in special cases such as structured settlements.) The net effect of the "fresh start" is to give us a double deduction: we will get a tax deduction in 1987 and future years for a portion of our incurred-but-unpaid insurance losses that have already been fully deducted as costs in 1986 and earlier years.

The increase in net worth that is produced by this change is not yet reflected in our financial statements. Rather, under present GAAP rules (which may be changed), the benefit will flow into the earnings statement and, consequently, into net worth over the next few years by way of reduced tax charges. We expect the total benefit from the fresh-start adjustment to be in the $30-$40 million range. It should be noted, however, that this is a one-time benefit, whereas the negative impact of the other insurance-related tax changes is not only ongoing but, in important respects, will become more severe as time passes.

• The General Utilities Doctrine was repealed by the new tax law. This means that in 1987 and thereafter there will be a double tax on corporate liquidations, one at the corporate level and another at the shareholder level. In the past, the tax at the corporate level could be avoided. If Berkshire, for example, were to be liquidated—which it most certainly won't be—shareholders would, under the new law, receive far less from the sales of our properties than they would have if the properties had been sold in the past, assuming identical prices in each sale. Though this outcome is theoretical in our case, the change in the law will very materially affect many companies. Therefore, it also affects our evaluations of prospective investments. Take, for example, producing oil and gas businesses, selected media companies, real estate companies, etc. that might wish to sell out. The values that their shareholders can realize are likely to be significantly reduced simply because the General Utilities Doctrine has been repealed—though the companies' operating economics will not have changed adversely at all. My impression is that this important change in the law has not yet been fully comprehended by either investors or managers.

---

Berkshire's tax situation is sometimes misunderstood. First, capital gains have no special attraction for us: A corporation pays a 35% rate on taxable income, whether it comes from capital gains or from ordinary operations. This means that Berkshire's tax on a long-term capital gain is fully 75% higher than what an individual would pay on an identical gain.

Some people harbor another misconception, believing that we can exclude 70% of all dividends we receive from our taxable income. Indeed, the 70% rate applies to most corporations and also applies to Berkshire in cases where we hold stocks in non-insurance subsidiaries. However, almost all of our equity investments are owned by our insurance companies, and in that case the exclusion is 59.5%. That still means a dollar of dividends is considerably more valuable to us than a dollar of ordinary income, but not to the degree often assumed.

## H.  *Taxation and Investment Philosophy*[68]

Berkshire is a substantial payer of federal income taxes. In aggregate, we will pay 1993 federal income taxes of $390 million, about $200 million of that attributable to operating earnings and $190 million to realized capital gains.[69] Furthermore, our share of the 1993 federal and foreign income taxes paid by our investees is well over $400 million, a figure you don't see on our financial statements but that is nonetheless real. Directly and indirectly, Berkshire's 1993 federal income tax payments will be about ½ of 1% of the total paid last year by all American corporations.[70]

---

[68] [Divided by hash lines: 1993; 2000.]
[69] [For 1996, the aggregate figure was $860 million; for 1998, $2.7 billion.]
[70] [The 1998 letter includes the following:]

Speaking for our own shares, Charlie and I have absolutely no complaint about these taxes. We know we work in a market-based economy that rewards our efforts far more bountifully than it does the efforts of others whose output is of equal or greater benefit to society. Taxation should, and does, partially redress this inequity. But we still remain extraordinarily well-treated.

Berkshire and its shareholders, in combination, would pay a much smaller tax if Berkshire operated a partnership or "S" corporation, two structures often used for business activities. For a variety of reasons, that's not feasible for Berkshire to do. However, the penalty our corporate form imposes is mitigated—though far from eliminated—by our strategy of investing for the long term. Charlie and I would follow a buy-and-hold policy even if we ran a tax-exempt institution. We think it the soundest way to invest, and it also goes down the grain of our personalities. A third reason to favor this policy, however, is the fact that taxes are due only when gains are realized.

Through my favorite comic strip, Li'l Abner, I got a chance during my youth to see the benefits of delayed taxes, though I missed the lesson at the time. Making his readers feel superior, Li'l Abner bungled happily, but moronically, through life in Dogpatch. At one point he became infatuated with a New York temptress, Appassionatta Van Climax, but despaired of marrying her because he had only a single silver dollar and she was interested solely in millionaires. Dejected, Abner took his problem to Old Man Mose, the font of all knowledge in Dogpatch. Said the sage: Double your money 20 times and Appassionatta will be yours (1, 2, 4, 8 . . . . 1,048,576).

My last memory of the strip is Abner entering a roadhouse, dropping his dollar into a slot machine, and hitting a jackpot that spilled money all over the floor. Meticulously following Mose's advice, Abner picked up two dollars and went off to find his next double. Whereupon I dumped Abner and began reading Ben Graham.

---

One beneficiary of our increased size has been the U.S. Treasury. The federal income taxes that Berkshire and General Re have paid, or will soon pay, in respect to 1998 earnings total $2.7 billion. That means we shouldered *all* of the U.S. Government's expenses for more than a half-day.

Follow that thought a little further: If only 625 other U.S. taxpayers had paid the Treasury as much as we and General Re did last year, no one else–neither corporations nor 270 million citizens–would have had to pay federal income taxes or any other kind of federal tax (for example, social security or estate taxes). Our shareholders can truly say that they "gave at the office."

Mose clearly was overrated as a guru: Besides failing to anticipate Abner's slavish obedience to instructions, he also forgot about
taxes. Had Abner been subject, say, to the 35% federal tax rate
that Berkshire pays, and had he managed one double annually, he
would after 20 years only have accumulated $22,370. Indeed, had
he kept on both getting his annual doubles and paying a 35% tax
on each, he would have needed 7½ years more to reach the $1 mil-
lion required to win Appassionatta.

But what if Abner had instead put his dollar in a single investment and held it until it doubled the same 27½ times? In that case,
he would have realized about $200 million pre-tax or, after paying
a $70 million tax in the final year, about $130 million after-tax. For
that, Appassionatta would have crawled to Dogpatch. Of course,
with 27½ years having passed, how Appassionatta would have
looked to a fellow sitting on $130 million is another question.

What this little tale tells us is that tax-paying investors will realize a far, far greater sum from a single investment that com-
pounds internally at a given rate than from a succession of
investments compounding at the same rate. But I suspect many
Berkshire shareholders figured that out long ago.

---

There's a powerful financial reason behind Berkshire's preference [to acquire 100% of a business rather than a small fraction],
and that has to do with taxes. The tax code makes Berkshire's
owning 80% or more of a business far more profitable for us, proportionately, than our owning a smaller share. When a company
we own all of earns $1 million after tax, the entire amount inures to
our benefit. If the $1 million is upstreamed to Berkshire, we owe
no tax on the dividend. And, if the earnings are retained and we
were to sell the subsidiary—not likely at Berkshire!—for $1 million
more than we paid for it, we would owe no capital gains tax. That's
because our "tax cost" upon sale would include both what we paid
for the business and all earnings it subsequently retained.

Contrast that situation to what happens when we own an investment in a marketable security. There, if we own a 10% stake in
a business earning $10 million after tax, our $1 million share of the
earnings is subject to additional state and federal taxes of (1) about
$140,000 if it is distributed to us (our tax rate on most dividends is
14%); or (2) no less than $350,000 if the $1 million is retained and
subsequently captured by us in the form of a capital gain (on which
our tax rate is usually about 35%, though it sometimes approaches
40%). We may defer paying the $350,000 by not immediately real-

izing our gain, but eventually we must pay the tax. In effect, the government is our "partner" twice when we own part of a business through a stock investment, but only once when we own at least 80%.

# EPILOGUE[71]

We will keep most of our major holdings, regardless of how they are priced relative to intrinsic business value. This 'til-death-do-us-part attitude, combined with the full prices these holdings command, means that they cannot be expected to push up Berkshire's value in the future as sharply as in the past. In other words, our performance to date has benefited from a double-dip: (1) the exceptional gains in intrinsic value that our portfolio companies have achieved; (2) the additional bonus we realized as the market appropriately "corrected" the prices of these companies, raising their valuations in relation to those of the average business. We will continue to benefit from good gains in business value that we feel confident our portfolio companies will make. But our "catch-up" rewards have been realized, which means we'll have to settle for a single-dip in the future.

We face another obstacle: In a finite world, high growth rates must self-destruct. If the base from which the growth is taking place is tiny, this law may not operate for a time. But when the base balloons, the party ends: A high growth rate eventually forges its own anchor.

Carl Sagan has entertainingly described this phenomenon, musing about the destiny of bacteria that reproduce by dividing into two every 15 minutes. Says Sagan: "That means four doublings an hour, and 96 doublings a day. Although a bacterium weighs only about a trillionth of a gram, its descendants, after a day of wild asexual abandon, will collectively weigh as much as a mountain [ . . . ] in two days, more than the sun—and before very long, everything in the universe will be made of bacteria." Not to worry, says Sagan: Some obstacle always impedes this kind of exponential growth. "The bugs run out of food, or they poison each other, or they are shy about reproducing in public."

Even on bad days, Charlie Munger (Berkshire's Vice Chairman and my partner) and I do not think of Berkshire as a bacterium. Nor, to our unending sorrow, have we found a way to double its net worth every 15 minutes. Furthermore, we are not the least bit shy about reproducing—financially—in public. Nevertheless, Sagan's observations apply.

---

A fat wallet is the enemy of superior investment results. And Berkshire now has a net worth of $11.9 billion compared to about

---

[71] [Divided by hash lines: 1989; 1994; 1996 Owner's Manual, updated annually.]

$22 million when Charlie and I began to manage the company. Though there are as many good businesses as ever, it is useless for us to make purchases that are inconsequential in relation to Berkshire's capital. We now consider a security for purchase only if we believe we can deploy at least $100 million in it. Given that minimum, Berkshire's investment universe has shrunk dramatically.

Nevertheless, we will stick with the approach that got us here and try not to relax our standards. Ted Williams, in *The Story of My Life*, explains why: "My argument is, to be a good hitter, you've got to get a good ball to hit. It's the first rule in the book. If I have to bite at stuff that is out of my happy zone, I'm not a .344 hitter. I might only be a .250 hitter." Charlie and I agree and will try to wait for opportunities that are well within our own "happy zone."

We will continue to ignore political and economic forecasts, which are an expensive distraction for many investors and businessmen. Thirty years ago, no one could have foreseen the huge expansion of the Vietnam War, wage and price controls, two oil shocks, the resignation of a president, the dissolution of the Soviet Union, a one-day drop in the Dow of 508 points, or treasury bill yields fluctuating between 2.8% and 17.4%.

But, surprise—none of these blockbuster events made the slightest dent in Ben Graham's investment principles. Nor did they render unsound the negotiated purchases of fine businesses at sensible prices. Imagine the cost to us, then, if we had let a fear of unknowns cause us to defer or alter the deployment of capital. Indeed, we have usually made our best purchases when apprehensions about some macro event were at a peak. Fear is the foe of the faddist, but the friend of the fundamentalist.

A different set of major shocks is sure to occur in the next 30 years. We will neither try to predict these nor to profit from them. If we can identify businesses similar to those we have purchased in the past, external surprises will have little effect on our long-term results.

What we promise you—along with more modest gains—is that during your ownership of Berkshire, you will fare just as Charlie and I do. If you suffer, we will suffer; if we prosper, so will you. And we will not break this bond by introducing compensation arrangements that give us a greater participation in the upside than the downside.

We further promise you that our personal fortunes will remain overwhelmingly concentrated in Berkshire shares: We will not ask you to invest with us and then put our own money elsewhere. In addition, Berkshire dominates both the investment portfolios of most members of our families and of a great many friends who belonged to partnerships that Charlie and I ran in the 1960s. We could not be more motivated to do our best.

We achieved our gains through the efforts of a superb corps of operating managers who get extraordinary results from some ordinary-appearing businesses. Casey Stengel described managing a baseball team as "getting paid for home runs other fellows hit." That's my formula at Berkshire, also.

It's far better to own a significant portion of the Hope diamond than 100% of a rhinestone, and the companies just mentioned easily qualify as rare gems. Best of all, we aren't limited to simply a few of this breed, but instead possess a growing collection.

Stock prices will continue to fluctuate—sometimes sharply—and the economy will have its ups and downs. Over time, however, we believe it is highly probable that the sort of businesses we own will continue to increase in value at a satisfactory rate.

----

I think it's appropriate that I conclude with a discussion of Berkshire's management, today and in the future. As our first owner-related principle tells you, Charlie and I are the managing partners of Berkshire. But we subcontract all of the heavy lifting in this business to the managers of our subsidiaries.

Charlie and I mainly attend to capital allocation and the care and feeding of our key managers. Most of these managers are happiest when they are left alone to run their businesses, and that is customarily just how we leave them. That puts them in charge of all operating decisions and of dispatching the excess cash they generate to headquarters. By sending it to us, they don't get diverted by the various enticements that would come their way were they responsible for deploying the cash their businesses throw off. Furthermore, Charlie and I are exposed to a much wider range of possibilities for investing these funds than any of our managers could find in his or her own industry.

Most of our managers are independently wealthy, and it's therefore up to us to create a climate that encourages them to choose working with Berkshire over golfing or fishing. This leaves us needing to treat them fairly and in the manner that we would wish to be treated if our positions were reversed.

As for the allocation of capital, that's an activity both Charlie and I enjoy and in which we have acquired some useful experience.

In a general sense, grey hair doesn't hurt on this playing field: You don't need good hand-eye coordination or well-toned muscles to push money around (thank heavens). As long as our minds continue to function effectively, Charlie and I can keep on doing our jobs pretty much as we have in the past.

On my death, Berkshire's ownership picture will change but not in a disruptive way: First, only about 1% of my stock will have to be sold to take care of bequests and taxes; second, the balance of my stock will go to my wife, Susan, if she survives me, or to a family foundation if she doesn't. In either event, Berkshire will possess a controlling shareholder guided by the same philosophy and objectives that now set our course.

At that juncture, the Buffett family will not be involved in managing the business, only in picking and overseeing the managers who do. Just who those managers will be, of course, depends on the date of my death. But I can anticipate what the management structure will be: Essentially my job will be split into two parts, with one executive becoming responsible for investments and another for operations. If the acquisition of new businesses is in prospect, the two will cooperate in making the decisions needed. Both executives will report to a board of directors that will be responsive to the controlling shareholder, whose interests will in turn be aligned with yours.[72]

I will continue to keep my family posted on the succession issue. Since Berkshire stock will make up virtually my entire estate and will account for a similar portion of the assets of either my wife or the foundation for a considerable period after my death, you can be sure that I have thought through the succession question carefully. You can be equally sure that the principles we have employed to date in running Berkshire will continue to guide the managers who succeed me.

Lest we end on a morbid note, I also want to assure you that I have never felt better. I love running Berkshire, and if enjoying life promotes longevity, Methuselah's record is in jeopardy.[73]

---

[72] [Berkshire issued a press release in October 2000 indicating that Warren Buffett would be succeeded as director of investments by GEICO's Louis Simpson and as chief executive officer by either Berkshire's Ajit Jain, GEICO's Tony Nicely, or Executive Jet's Richard Santulli; and that, in addition, his eldest son Howard Buffett would assume the role of chairman.]

[73] [According to the Bible, Methuselah lived 969 years. *Genesis* 5:27.]

The original edition of *The Essays of Warren Buffett: Lessons for Corporate America* was the centerpiece of a symposium held in the Fall of 1996 at the Benjamin N. Cardozo School of Law under the auspices of its Samuel and Ronnie Heyman Center on Corporate Governance. This gathering brought hundreds of Cardozo students together for a two-day dissection of all the ideas in the collection, featuring a series of vibrant debates among some 30 distinguished law professors, judges, investors, managers, and other students, with Warren E. Buffett and Charles T. Munger participating throughout from their seats in the front row.

*The Essays* is the standard textbook for a specialized course at Cardozo in proper business practices and is adopted by dozens of professors at other law and business schools for classes such as investment, finance and accounting. Some investment firms have distributed copies to their professional employees and clients as part of training programs. I am grateful for the positive feedback from these students, teachers, and other users and delighted to know that the lessons are being taught and learned.

This first revised edition of *The Essays* retains the architecture and philosophy of the original edition but adds selections from Mr. Buffett's annual shareholder letters written since the time of the symposium. As with the other letters, these are woven together into a fabric that reads as a complete and coherent narrative of a sound business and investment philosophy. As an aid to all readers, and to enable readers of the original edition to see what is new in this one, a disposition table shows the various places in this collection where selections from each year's letter appear.

The new edition is called for not because anything has changed about the fundamentals of sound business and investment philosophy but because Mr. Buffett's articulation of that philosophy is always done in the context of contemporary events and business conditions. So periodic updating is warranted to maintain its currency.

In preparing the original edition I was aided by numerous people, to whom I expressed gratitude in the afterword to that edition, and I want to thank them again. Among those, I especially thank Mr. Buffett. His generosity not only made the symposium possible but his participation enriched it manifold; his willingness to entrust the rearrangement and republication of his letters to me is a great honor. His partner, Charlie Munger, deserves repeated thanks too, for not only did he participate in the symposium from the front row he also graciously chaired, on a moment's notice, one of the panels.

Continuing thanks also to Mr. Buffett's good friend and advisor, Robert Denham, whom I have had the pleasure of getting to know in the years following the symposium. Mr. Denham, a partner in the law firm Munger, Tolles & Olsen, introduced Mr. Buffett to Cardozo and me through another mutual friend, former Munger, Tolles colleague and now Cardozo professor Monroe Price, and I thank both of them for opening that wonderful door. Thanks also to Carol Loomis, a close friend of Mr. Buffett's and the person who annually edits each shareholder letter. For institutional support in countless ways, thanks as always to Sam and Ronnie Heyman, whom Cardozo Law School boasts among its best friends. Most personally, thanks to my wife JoAnna.

*Lawrence A. Cunningham*
*Boston College*
*885 Centre Street*
*Newton, MA  02459*
*Lawrence.Cunningham.1@bc.edu*

---

*To order copies of this collection, send $25.00 per copy to Prof. Cunningham at the address set forth above.*

# INDEX

**Cigar Butt Investing.** A foolish method of investing akin to taking the last puff on a cigar, it is the purchase of a stock at a sufficiently low price that there will be some short-term profit, though the business' long-term performance is terrible. *See* Part II.F.

**Circle of Competence.** The limits of one's ability to judge the economics of businesses, intelligent investors draw a thick boundary and stick with companies they can understand. *See* Part II.E.

**Dividend Test.** Retention of earnings is only justified if each dollar retained produces at least a one dollar increase in per share market value. *See* Part IV.C.

**Double-Barreled Acquisition Style.** A sensible acquisition policy of buying either 100% of businesses in negotiated acquisitions or less than 100% in stock market purchases. *See* Part I.A.

**Institutional Imperative.** A pervasive force in organizations that leads to irrational business decisions from resistance to change, absorption of corporate funds in suboptimal projects or acquisitions, indulgence of the cravings of senior executives, and mindless imitiation of peer companies. *See* Part II.F.

**Intrinsic Value.** A hard-to-calculate but crucial measure of business value, it is the discounted present value of the cash that can be taken out of a business during its remaining life. *See* Part VI.E.

**Look-through Earnings.** An alternative to GAAP rules governing investments in marketable securities of the investee less than 20%, this measures the investor's economic performance based on its percentage interest of the investee's undistributed earnings (after an incremental reduction for income taxes). *See* Part VI.B.

**Margin-of-Safety.** Probably the single most important principle of sound and successful investing, Ben Graham's principle says not to purchase a security unless the price being paid is substantially lower than the value being delivered. *See* Part II.D.

**Mr. Market.** Ben Graham's allegory for the overall stock market, a moody manic-depressive where price and value diverge, making superior intelligent investing possible. *See* Part II.A.

**Owner Earnings.** A better measure of economic performance than cash flow or GAAP earnings affected by purchase accounting adjustments, equal to *(a)* operating earnings *plus (b)* depreciation and other non-cash charges *minus (c)* required reinvestment in a business to maintain present competitive position and unit volume. *See* Part VI.D.

**DISPOSITION TABLE**

This table shows where in this collection you may find excerpts from various annual letters. The first column at left indicates the year of each letter, beginning with "79" for 1979 and going through "00" for the year 2000. Across the top of the table the rows divides this collection according to its Parts (I through VII) and its sub-headings (A through D, F, or H).
Letters excerpted in the opening paragraphs of a Part are reported in the table as being excerpted in Section A of that Part.

I. Corporate Governance — II. Corporate Finance and Investing — III. Alternatives to Common Stock — IV. Common Stock — V. Mergers and Acquisitions — VI. Accounting and Valuation — VII. Accounting Policy and Tax Matters

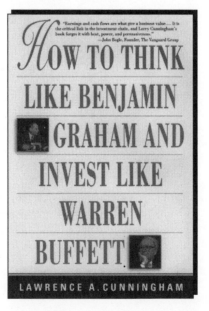